"*Born This Way?* is an important contrib⟨...⟩ in society at large, and especially in the ⟨Christian community⟩⟨...⟩ explicitly Christian, the vast majority of the text is the presentation and review of secular, scientifically-obtained data! The biblical perspective is gentle and respectful of the high emotion surrounding this issue, but consistent with an orthodox evangelical theology and a high view of Scripture. The chapter on the church's response to those caught in this sin should inform us and challenge us."

— **Andrew J. Holder,** professor of computational/organic chemistry,
University of Missouri, Kansas City

"I am delighted to recommend this timely and much needed new work by Alan Branch. I have gained much from it already and think it soon will be thought essential to anyone engaging today's culture on the most pressing issue of our time — that of resisting pressures to normalize same-sex attractions and behavior based on what science is alleged to have proven. Professor Branch deals at length and in detail with the best science to-date and demonstrates how the unchanging word of God is worth trusting now more than ever."

— **Daniel R. Heimbach,** Senior Professor of Christian Ethics;
Fellow, L. Rush Bush Center for Faith & Culture,
Southeastern Baptist Theological Seminary

"In this book Dr. Branch speaks to the subject of genetic determinism in regard to sexual orientation. While this topic can be quite complex, the content of this volume unfolds in such a way that it is accessible to those unfamiliar with the topic, yet it will be respected by experts in the field. Perhaps more importantly, the tone of this book is balanced and winsome, making it clear that Dr. Branch's aim is both the education of like-minded readers and ministry to those who would disagree."

— **David W. Jones,** professor of Christian ethics,
Southeastern Baptist Theological Seminary.

"Dr. Branch's interaction with the scientific community in *Born This Way?* indicates a willingness to treat this sensitive subject with as much fairness to all as the facts he reveals can possibly allow. The book is an informative and state-of-the debate examination of the matter that anyone concerned with the debate should read."

— **Steven H. Thompson,** assistant professor of pastoral ministry,
Midwestern Baptist Theological Seminary

Born This Way?

Homosexuality, Science, and the Scriptures

J. Alan Branch

WEAVER BOOK
COMPANY
WOOSTER, OHIO

Born This Way? Homosexuality, Science, and the Scriptures
© 2016 by J. Alan Branch

First edition published by
Weaver Book Company
1190 Summerset Dr.
Wooster, OH 44691
Visit us at weaverbookcompany.com

Cover: Frank Gutbrod
Interior design and layout: { In a Word }
Editing: Line for Line Publishing Services

Print: 978-1-941337-50-9
EPUB: 978-1-941337-51-6

Library of Congress Cataloging-in-Publication Data

Names: Branch, J. Alan, 1967- author.
Title: Born this way? : homosexuality, science, and the scriptures /
    J. Alan Branch.
Description: First edition. | Wooster : Weaver Book Company, 2016. |
    Includes bibliographical references and index.
Identifiers: LCCN 2015042579 | ISBN 9781941337509
Subjects: LCSH: Homosexuality—Genetic aspects. |
    Homosexuality—Religious aspects.
Classification: LCC HQ76.25 .B726 2016 | DDC 306.76/6—dc23
LC record available at http://lccn.loc.gov/2015042579

Printed in the United States of America
16 17 18 19 20 / 5 4 3 2 1

Contents

Acknowledgements

THIS WORK COULD NOT HAVE BEEN COMPLETED without the many words of insight, correction, and encouragement from many colleagues. I would like to thank Chris Cornine, Larry Cornine, Barrett Duke, Andy Holder, Jan Hudzicki, Thor Madsen, Robert Matz, Harry Michael, Alan Tomlinson, and Rustin Umstadtt for their patient help and willingness to answer my many questions. I am especially grateful to Steve Thompson for his invaluable help in editing and friendly encouragement. I am also very thankful for Midwestern Baptist Theological Seminary's wonderful reference librarian Mrs. Judy Howie, who patiently helped me acquire an untold number of articles not normally held in a seminary library. The final conclusions are my own, and none of these friends and colleagues should be criticized for weaknesses or flaws in the presentation.

J. Alan Branch (John 10:10)
Kansas City, Missouri
October 27, 2015

Introduction

IN 2011, POP MUSIC SENSATION LADY GAGA (Stefani Angelina Germanotta) released the song "Born This Way," a tune that has become the anthem for the homosexual community. The song's lyrics articulate a crude sort of biological-genetic justification for various forms of behavior, and in many ways reflects the shared values and practices of a society infatuated with a sexually libertine ethic. Lady Gaga asserts, "No matter gay, straight or bi/Lesbian, transgendered life/I'm on the right track, baby I was born to survive." She then parallels sexual practices to ethnicity, celebrating people who are "black, white, or beige, Chola or orient made." Her moral reflection reaches a crescendo when she says everyone is beautiful because "God makes no mistakes" and she is on the right track because "I was born this way!"[1]

Germanotta's lyrics reflect a moral reasoning common among many young people. She moves casually between the issues of sexual morality and ethnic heritage, asserting that the two are morally equivalent because each person is "born this way." To add greater strength to the argument, God Himself is credited with being the author of both racial distinctions and homosexuality. The obvious inference is that homosexuality, like race, is hard-wired into who we are from birth. Since these sexual preferences are innate, they must be from God. Therefore, no moral criticism should be leveled at people involved in the homosexual lifestyle. After all, homosexuals are "born this way." Signs emblazoned with the words "Born This Way" are now ubiquitous at rallies relating to homosexual rights.

The moral argumentation of Lady Gaga's "Born This Way" reflects the way scientific research about homosexuality is communicated on a street level.

---

1 Stefani Germanotta, *Born This Way*. A-Z Lyrics, accessed January 16, 2013, http://www .azlyrics.com/lyrics/ladygaga/bornthisway.html. The term "chola" is apparently used by Germanotta as a reference to people of Mexican or Mexican-American ethnic heritage.

In the last forty years, an intense effort has been underway to establish in the public mind that science confirms a biological-genetic causation for homosexual behavior, thus removing moral stigma associated with homosexual acts. Sadly, in our day of sound-bite moral reflection, most people have not thought deeply or seriously about the relationship between biology, genetics, and moral accountability. Instead of rigorously examining the topic, it is easier to engage in crude moral argumentation and say, "If there's a genetic component, then people must be born that way. It's not fair to judge people for the way they are born." The assumption is that if any biological or genetic aspect of homosexuality is discovered, then it is prejudicial to form a negative moral opinion about homosexual behavior.

How should Christians respond to the born-this-way moral argument? It is not enough for us to mourn the societal slide towards Sodom and Gomorrah. We must attempt to interact with, evaluate, and respond to the research associated with homosexuality. As we do so, several questions emerge: To what degree, if any, does biology or genetics contribute to homosexuality? If there is a biological-genetic aspect of homosexual behavior at any level, then should people be held morally accountable for homosexual acts? If a biological-genetic component exists, then how do we reconcile this with the clear denunciations of homosexual behavior in Scripture?

The urgent question for us to answer is, "Are homosexuals really *born this way*?" In this book, I hope to offer a plausible answer to these and other questions associated with the relationship between scientific research and the moral status of homosexuality. A review of the research will show that, while there are some genetic or biological factors that *correlate* with a higher incidence of same-sex attraction and homosexual behavior, as of yet there is no proof of genetic or biological *causation* for homosexuality. The vital distinction between correlation and causation is central to my argument.

Beginning with the work of Sigmund Freud and Alfred Kinsey, I will address the American Psychiatric Association's change in its stance regarding homosexuality in 1973 and 1974. Then, I will discuss research-related issues, focusing on some of the most significant findings in relation to homosexuality and brain plasticity, prenatal hormones, brain structure, twin studies, genetics, and attempts to change sexual orientation. I will conclude with a discussion concerning scientific research regarding homosexuality and Christian moral reflection. Of course, my summary of various research findings is only a snapshot in time of various arguments in 2015. More claims and counter-claims will continue to emerge in the years to come, requiring constant interaction with new assertions about homosexuality based on scientific reports.

The epithet "homophobe" is now casually tossed at any person disagreeing with the cultural acceptance of same-sex marriage or advocating traditional Christian sexual ethics. Calling someone a homophobe is intended to express contempt for anyone expressing moral objection to homosexual behavior, while simultaneously participating in socially acceptable abuse of the opponent. Based on two words "homo" (same) and "phobia" (fear), the word implies that anyone who disagrees with homosexual behavior is repressing a secret fear of homosexuals, giving the impression that the person critiquing pro-homosexual arguments may be ignorant or emotionally unbalanced. The term is used in much the same way as the words "racist" or "bigot" are used; calling your opponent a homophobe implies he or she is unfairly prejudiced against gays or lesbians and hates people who participate in same-sex behavior. As a result, we live in an environment of public intimidation and the erosion of free speech, leaving some Christians afraid to say anything considered remotely negative about homosexual behavior.

By calling anyone who disagrees with pro-homosexual arguments a homophobe, homosexual activists engage in a form of intellectual intimidation and coercion. By making the terms "homophobe" and "racist" morally equivalent, the homosexual activist is able to short-circuit any serious and open discussion about the roots of homosexuality. Labeling someone as a homophobe is frequently an attempt to get rid of an opponent whom a pro-homosexual activist cannot or does not want to answer.[2]

I do not hate people involved in same-sex behavior. Contrary to many homosexual activists, I firmly believe in an open marketplace of ideas. As I will demonstrate, I strongly believe some people who claim they have experienced same-sex attraction from youth are telling the truth. Yet our culture now says there is nothing inherently wrong with acting upon same-sex attraction, which is a moral stance in clear opposition to the Bible. My goal is to summarize some of the more important research regarding same-sex attraction in order to foster a more clear understanding of what science has and has not discovered about homosexuality. My hope is that pastors, parents, Christians confused by feelings of same-sex attraction, and people considering becoming a follower of Jesus Christ will have an accurate grasp of current debates concerning the origin of homosexuality. In doing so, I hope to bring some balance to serious debate that is often short-circuited by the vacuous claim, "I was born this way."

---

2   My language here is influenced by T. B. Maston. He used similar terminology in reference to the terms "liberal" and "conservative." See T. B. Maston, "Problems of Christian Life — Compromise," *Baptist Standard*, December 18, 1968, 13; found in William M. Tillman, Jr., Rodney S. Taylor, and Lauren C. Brewer, eds., *Both-And: A Maston Reader: Selected Readings from the Writings of T. B. Maston* (Dallas: T. B. Maston Foundation for Christian Ethics, 2011), 257.

CHAPTER 1

Sigmund Freud and Homosexuality

IN 1895, BRITISH POET OSCAR WILDE (1844–1900) was sentenced to two years in prison for having a homosexual affair with a young man named Alfred Douglas (1870–1945). Douglas himself wrote a poem about homosexual desire in 1894 titled *The Two Loves,* in which he famously referred to homosexuality as "the love that dare not speak its name."[1] For homosexuals, the idea that their love "dare not speak its name" is a common theme, claiming they are shamed into silence, guilty only of loving another person. During the early 1950s, homosexuals began to insist there is neither shame nor remorse in their lifestyle, strongly rejecting the near unanimous consensus of American culture at that time which saw homosexuality as morally repugnant. By the end of the century, homosexuality was widely celebrated and accepted.

How did the moral conscience of American culture shift in such a short period of time from rejection of homosexuality to modern approval and promotion of it? Part of the answer is found in the work of the famous psychiatrist Sigmund Freud. His ideas about sexual development were foundational in emerging research regarding homosexuality in the mid-twentieth century. A survey of Freud's thought shows he had varying ideas regarding the origin of homosexuality, explaining why he is cited both as favorable and opposed to born-this-way arguments.

THE FATHER OF PSYCHOANALYSIS

Sigmund Freud (1856–1939) was born to a Jewish family in the Austro-Hungarian Empire. Earning his M.D. in 1881 in Vienna, he lived in the city

---

1   Alfred Douglas, *The Two Loves,* "The Three Trials of Oscar Wilde," University of Missouri – Kansas City School of Law, accessed September 13, 2013. http://law2.umkc.edu/faculty/projects/ftrials/wilde/poemsofdouglas.htm.

until he had to move to London in 1938 to escape the virulent anti-Semitism when the Nazis took over Austria. Freud initially practiced general medicine, but in 1886 began to specialize in the treatment of psychological disorders. Though Freud was born to a Jewish family, as an adult he was an atheist who actively clashed with religion, which he considered an impediment to development of human intellect.[2]

Freud's early work in psychiatry focused on the use of hypnosis, but he soon began to develop an approach called *psychoanalysis*, a theory that assumes conscious thoughts and actions are directed by unconscious influences. Of particular interest to Freud was the triad-relationship between mother, father, and child, particularly in the very early years of childhood. In developing his theory of psychoanalysis, Freud drew various elements from literature, mythology, medicine, and philosophy. Terms and phrases common in daily conversation originate in Freud's thought, such as "neurotic," "Freudian slip," "anal retentive," "penis envy," and "Oedipus Complex."

FREUD, CHILDREN, AND PSYCHOSEXUAL DEVELOPMENT

Freud's most provocative concept relating to sexual development is his assertion that children are inherently sexual and passing through five stages of sexual development: oral, anal, phallic, latent, and genital stages. Freud claimed our pre-conscious childhood — the period of early life we can't remember — is composed of several stages, each requiring successful resolution of sexual tension in the mother-father-child triad if we hope to develop into sexually healthy adults. The important point to remember is Freud considered even small babies to be "sexual." For example, he believed small children derived sexual pleasure from sucking things during the "oral" stage. Freud's shocking proposal was the baby's entire body was a source of autoerotic pleasure, but it became focused during early development on three zones: oral, anal, and then genital.[3]

Some of Freud's suggestions concerning the sexual nature of small children seem implausible or quite odd. For example, he claims children who hold back their stool are doing so because they get sexual pleasure from their anus:

---

2   See Sigmund Freud, *Moses and Monotheism*, Katherine Jones, trans. (Letchworth, Hertfordshire: Hogarth Press and the Institute of Psychoanalysis, 1939).

3   Vernon A. Rosario, *Homosexuality and Science: A Guide to the Debates* (Santa Barbara, CA: ABC-CLIO, 2002), 51.

Children who are making use of the susceptibility to erotogenic stimulation of the anal zone betray themselves by holding back their stool till its accumulation brings about violent muscular contractions and, as it passes through the anus, is able to produce powerful stimulation to the mucous membrane. In so doing it must no doubt cause not only painful but also highly pleasurable sensations.[4]

Freud then goes further and uses child abuse as proof of children's sexual nature and says, "It is an instructive fact that under the influence of seduction children can become polymorphously perverse, and can be led into all possible kinds of sexual irregularities. This shows that an aptitude for them [various forms of sexual expression] is innately present in their disposition."[5] Freud assumes the children are *already sexual*, the predator simply brought out the latent element. Freud went so far as to suggest small boys' infatuation with trains is derived from the sexual pleasure, asserting a compulsive link between railway-travel and childhood sexuality because children derive pleasure from "the sensations of movement" while riding on a train.[6] Thus, for Freud, even a child's innocent pleasure of enjoying a train ride is intricately connected to their sexuality.

Freud believed everyone is born bisexual with a capacity for sexual fulfillment in either heterosexual or homosexual relationships. Operating from his atheistic worldview, Freud viewed childhood as a sort of "recapitulation" of the primeval history of man's evolution. He complained that too many scientists searched into the primeval history of mankind to find answers to sexual problems instead of the "other primeval period, which falls within the lifetime of the individual himself — that is, to childhood."[7] Freud argued prenatal development demonstrates that people begin as bisexual and then differentiate into male or female, except in cases of children born with indistinct genitalia. The practical implication of Freud's argument is to blur the lines of distinction concerning what is "normal" versus "abnormal" in sexuality.

FREUD AND HOMOSEXUALITY

Freud has been cited affirmatively by both opponents and supporters of born-this-way arguments for homosexual rights. This is because there is a

---

4 Sigmund Freud, "Infantile Sexuality," in *Three Essays on the Theory of Sexuality*, trans. James Strachey (New York: HarperCollins, 1975), 52.

5 Ibid., 57.

6 Ibid., 68.

7 Ibid., 39.

certain ambiguity in Freud's stance concerning homosexuality: On one hand, he considered homosexuality to be an inhibition of normal development, but at the same time he noted that some homosexuals have contributed important developments to culture and are capable of being quite happy and well adjusted. Yet Freud referred to homosexuality as "inversion" because attraction to the same sex represented an aberration of sexual object choice.[8] Freud admired homosexuals and seemed to have no particular animus towards them, yet described the development of homosexuality in ways that seem negative.

In his *Three Essays on the Theory of Sexuality,* Freud suggested there were three categories of homosexuality. "Absolute" homosexuals have a sexual desire exclusively for people of their own sex.[9] Freud's second category was "amphigenic" homosexuals, or what we might today call bisexuals. Freud describes these people as "psychosexual hermaphrodites" and says "their sexual objects may equally well be of their own or of the opposite sex."[10] His third category was "contingent" homosexuals, being people who normally choose the opposite sex, but in absence of the ability to have intercourse with someone of the opposite sex, they can derive sexual fulfillment from same-sex contact. But how did Freud think people become homosexual? Concerning males, Freud suggested at least four different pathways by which men become homosexual.[11]

HOMOSEXUALITY, OVERLY ATTENTIVE MOTHERS, AND NARCISSISM

In what is probably Freud's most well-known theory about homosexuality, the relationship between a young boy and his mother is complicated by the mother being overly attentive. Because of the mother's excessive affection, the boy refuses to surrender his relationship to her, the first object of his libido. In an effort to maintain an unconscious bond with his mother, the young boy identifies with her and chooses as his object of sexual desire boys who resemble himself. Freud said soon after puberty "the young man, who until this time

---

8   Vernon A. Rosario, *Homosexuality and Science: A Guide to the Debates,* 50.

9   Sigmund Freud, "The Sexual Aberrations," in *Three Essays on the Theory of Sexuality,* 2.

10   Sigmund Freud, "The Sexual Aberrations," in *Three Essays on the Theory of Sexuality,* 2. "Amphigenic" basically means "both sexes."

11   The following summary of Freud's four theories of homosexuality is primarily derived from Kenneth Lewes, *Psychoanalysis and Male Homosexuality: Twentieth Anniversary Edition* (Lanham, MD: Rowman & Littlefield, 2009), 24–31.

has been strongly fixated to his mother, turns in his course, identifies himself with his mother, and looks about for love-objects in whom he can re-discover himself, and whom he wishes to love as his mother loved him."[12] In loving these people who remind him of himself, the homosexual male can experience the erotic bond that once bound him to his mother. Thus, this theory implies a form of narcissism in male homosexuality because the selection of future love interests involves those individuals who most resemble himself.[13]

HOMOSEXUALITY AND UNSATISFACTORY RESOLUTION OF THE OEDIPUS COMPLEX

Freud's next theory of male homosexuality revolves around two ideas central to psychoanalysis: the Oedipus complex and castration anxiety.[14] The Oedipus complex refers to Freud's idea that the mother is the object of the young boy's libido, causing the boy then to see his father as a rival. Around the same time in childhood development, Freud's theory asserted that when boys discover girls do not have a penis, they assume the girls are boys who have been castrated. Ultimately, the boy even assumes his mother is a male who has been castrated and fears his father will now castrate him, possibly related to a fear of punishment for his erotic feelings towards his mother.[15]

If the boy navigates this crisis of the Oedipus complex and castration anxiety successfully, he will then identify with his father in a healthy way and mature into a heterosexual identity. But in some cases, the boy is now repulsed by his mother's lack of male genitalia, severs the erotic bond with her and women in general, and afterwards chooses a compromise figure for his sexual object choice: a feminine looking boy.[16] Thus, homosexuality is associ-

---

12   Sigmund Freud, "Certain Neurotic Mechanisms in Jealousy, Paranoia and Homosexuality," Joan Riviere, trans., in *Sexuality and the Psychology of Love* (New York: Collier Books, 1963), 167.

13   Gareth Mitchell, "The Development of Psychoanalytic Understandings of Male Homosexuality: Moving Beyond Pathology," *Psycho-Analytic Psychotherapy in South Africa* 20.1 (2012): 5.

14   This theory is discussed in Freud's case history of "Little Hans" and also in his discussion of Leonardo Da Vinci.

15   Gareth Mitchell, "The Development of Psychoanalytic Understandings of Male Homosexuality," 6.

16   In other words, the boy alters his sexual object from his mother to a female with a penis.

ated with a failure of successful navigation of the Oedipus complex/castration anxiety dilemma.

Homosexuality and an "Inverted" Oedipus Complex

In Freud's third theory, the purported Oedipus complex is inverted — the boy sexually desires his father instead of his mother.[17] In a complicated theory, Freud suggested the boy is this case resolves his Oedipus complex by rejecting his desire to have sex with his mother, and instead wants to have sex with his father. In this way, the boy takes on a feminine identity and reverts to the eroticism of his "anal" stage. The boy takes the feminine stance so that he can attract the attention of his father in order to be loved by him.[18] As a result, the boy becomes a homosexual and plays the feminine role with a fixation on erotic feelings associated with the anus.

Homosexuality and Jealousy of Siblings

Freud's fourth theory is similar to the other three in that it begins with a boy's intense love for his mother, but it is different because it does not involve fear of a female's lack of a penis, identification with the mother, or a choice of sexual desire driven by narcissism.[19] Instead, this last approach suggested a young boy's intense love for his mother leads to a vitriolic jealousy of his father and siblings. This jealousy leads to an intense hatred of one's rivals and thoughts of violence towards them. These thoughts are repressed and transformed at some point into feelings of homosexual love in a process Freud called "reaction formation," a defense mechanism wherein a person embraces an outward behavior that is opposite to how he or she actually feels.[20] Freud suggested this final form of homosexuality did not necessarily lead to exclusive homosexual attraction.

---

17   Freud's third pathway was actually a form of repressed homosexuality and was a theory derived from his experience with one patient known as "the Wolf Man," a moniker derived from a terrifying childhood dream the patient had of being devoured by wolves.

18   Gareth Mitchell, "The Development of Psychoanalytic Understandings of Male Homosexuality," 7.

19   Ibid.

20   Some people today argue opposition to homosexuality is really a form of reaction formation: People who subconsciously or secretly struggle with homosexual attractions display public disgust with homosexuality.

FREUD AND BORN-THIS-WAY ARGUMENTS

Did Freud believe homosexuals are "born this way"? As noted, his comments on the topic are complex and, at times, somewhat contradictory. But there is also evidence Freud believed in a strong innate component for at least some forms of homosexuality. In a 1922 article, Freud said that "recognition of the organic factor in homosexuality does not relieve us of the obligation of studying the psychical processes of its origin."[21] By "organic" factor, Freud means what we would call either biological or genetic causes, thus indicating he affirmed an innate component to homosexuality.

Freud was likely trying to find a middle ground between positions stating homosexuality is an innate characteristic versus others who asserted homosexuality is the result of environmental factors. Perhaps his clearest statement of opinion on the debate came in his 1922 article, "The Psychogenesis of a Case of Homosexuality in a Woman," where he discussed the family background of a homosexual, female patient. Freud commented that "a part even of this acquired disposition (if it *was* really acquired) has to be ascribed to inborn constitution. So we see in practice a continual mingling and blending of what in theory we should try to separate into a pair of opposites — namely, inherited and acquired characters."[22] Freud at least seemed quite open to the idea that some homosexuals are indeed "born this way."

Did Freud believe a homosexual could change his or her sexual desires through psychoanalysis? Again, while Freud made somewhat contradictory statements on this topic, it appears that he viewed attempts to change homosexuals in a negative light. Freud indicated the potential for change rested a great deal on whether the patient came of his or her own free will or came at the coercion of concerned family members. Freud expressed strong doubt that homosexuality could be changed to a heterosexual orientation:

> Such an achievement — the removal of genital inversion or homosexuality — is in my experience never an easy matter. . . . In general, to undertake to convert a fully developed homosexual into a heterosexual does not offer

---

21 Sigmund Freud, "Certain Neurotic Mechanisms in Jealousy, Paranoia and Homosexuality," 167.

22 Sigmund Freud, "The Psychogenesis of a Case of Homosexuality in a Woman," in *Freud on Women: A Reader*, ed. Elizabeth Young-Brueh (New York: W. W. Norton & Company, 1990), 264.

much more prospect of success than the reverse, except that for good practical reason the latter is never attempted.[23]

Freud says that trying to change someone from "homosexual" to "heterosexual" is as odd as changing someone from "heterosexual" to "homosexual." In this way, Freud is often cited in favor of born-this-way arguments.

Perhaps the most oft-repeated statement from Freud about homosexuality is found in a letter he wrote to an unknown American mother in 1935.[24] Freud famously commented on homosexuality in a positive way: "Homosexuality is assuredly no advantage, but it is nothing to be ashamed of, no vice, no degradation, it cannot be classified as an illness; we consider it to be a variation of the sexual function produced by certain arrest of sexual development."[25] As we will see, Freud's assertion that homosexuality was "no illness" became important in later years for the nascent homosexual rights movement. Freud also expressed concern that homosexuality was often considered a crime. He then told the mother that her son's chance of "change" was somewhat slim: "By asking me if I can help, you mean, I suppose, if I can abolish homosexuality and make normal heterosexuality take its place. The answer is, in a general way, we cannot promise to achieve it."[26] Freud did suggest psychoanalysis could help men achieve a level of heterosexual functionality, but "in the majority of cases it is no more possible."[27] Freud concluded by saying psychoanalysis can definitely help one improve a low quality of life, regardless of whether or not they change their sexual desires.

SUMMARY AND CRITIQUE

Freud had somewhat conflicting views about homosexuality and this can lead to confusion concerning his stance on the topic.[28] Andrew Kirby, a psychotherapist in New Zealand, says, "Taken out of context, Freud can be portrayed

---

23 Sigmund Freud, "The Psychogenesis of a Case of Homosexuality in a Woman," 246.

24 The letter itself was not published until 1951 in *The American Journal of Psychiatry.*

25 Sigmund Freud, "Letter to the Mother of a Homosexual," *American Journal of Psychiatry* 107 (1951): 787; Paul Halsall, ed., Internet History Sourcebooks Project, accessed February 19, 2014, http://www.fordham.edu/halsall/pwh/freud1.asp.

26 Sigmund Freud, "Letter to the Mother of a Homosexual," 787.

27 Ibid.

28 Freud's vacillation concerning the etiology of homosexuality reflects both contradictions within his own thought as well as refinements of his theory throughout his life.

as either virulently anti-homosexual . . . or as a closeted friend of gays; this contradiction has been used to promote both sides of a polarized debate on the theory and treatment of homosexuality."[29]

The contradictions noted, Freud developed four important ideas related to homosexuality. First, homosexuality usually results from some form of inhibition in a child's sexual development. Second, he agreed that at least in some cases homosexuality is an innate characteristic. Third, he seemed somewhat pessimistic about the chance of someone changing their sexual orientation. Finally, Freud's idea of "sexualized children" influences some modern people who talk about helping very small boys and girls discover their sexual orientation. Taken as a whole, Freud's thought substantiates certain aspects of born-this-way arguments.

From a Christian perspective, some of Freud's ideas are at least partially helpful. It is certainly true that Christians are aware of the manner in which an early sexual debut can distort someone's sexual development. Because Christians believe sex is a gift designed by God to be enjoyed by adults (a husband and a wife) in marriage, Christians insist an unusually premature sexual debut is quite detrimental to future sexual fulfillment within marriage. Christians are particularly concerned about cases of child abuse in which an adult exploits a child for his or her own twisted sexual pleasure. If the abuser is the same sex of the child, this seems to produce particular difficulties and can negatively affect the abused child's ability to experience a healthy sexual life as an adult. Freud himself seemed to acknowledge the manner in which homosexual child abuse could influence a child's future sexual orientation. In addition to his proposed variables of the Oedipus complex and castration anxiety, Freud suggested these factors are further complicated when "on them is superimposed the effect *of any seduction* bringing about a premature fixation of the libido."[30]

Furthermore, Christians affirm the importance of the father-mother-child triad. In fact, it is no coincidence that our society has seen an expansion of homosexual rights during an era — 1970 to present — when more and more children are raised in homes without their biological mother and father. As fewer and fewer children are exposed to a healthy nuclear family, one should indeed expect more sexual confusion to ensue. For Christians, an essential

---

29   Andrew Kirby, "Freud on Homosexuality," *Psychotherapy Papers,* accessed March 28, 2014, http://psychotherapypapers.wordpress.com/2008/11/12/kirby1/.

30   Sigmund Freud, "Certain Neurotic Mechanisms in Jealousy, Paranoia and Homosexuality," 168. Emphasis added.

aspect of parenting is for children to see parents who genuinely love each other and embrace appropriate gender roles.

But Freud's system as a whole seems quite flawed on three levels: (1) as a worldview founded on atheistic assumptions, (2) data based on Freud's subjective interpretations of his patient's experiences, and (3) Freud's distorted view of children's sexuality.

Freud was an atheist and his theory of sexual development is itself intricately related to his atheism. For Freud, humans are the result of a mindless evolutionary process and each person's purportedly innate bisexuality is a residual trait from our distant mammalian past. Just as animals may exhibit same-sex behavior, humans can as well. Yet Scripture teaches our gender is not an accident of evolution but is a part of the goodness of God's creation.[31] Furthermore, sex is not an evolutionary instinct, but is a gift from God to be celebrated in heterosexual and monogamous marriage (Gen. 2:24–25). There is no way to reconcile Freud's meta-analysis of human sexuality with Scripture.

Freud's subjective interpretations of various experiences recounted during psychoanalysis lead him to some suspect conclusions. His views of childhood sexuality seem to emanate from his own thoughts projected on children. Certainly children are prone to exploration and curiosity about their bodies as they mature, but are children really driven by sexual urges at every stage of development? Does a stubborn child who refuses to go to the bathroom really do so because it brings sexual pleasure?

Freud embraced some of the early advocates of sexual freedom and he assumed repressed sexual freedom at young ages leads to sexual difficulty later in life. But one of the most dangerous places for a child to be is in a home with parents who practice no sexual discretion. Usually, such homes have callous and indifferent adults who prematurely force sexual ideas on small boys and girls to the harm of the children. In contrast, Christians see children as a heritage from the Lord (Ps. 127:3) and understand we have a responsibility to nurture them in a loving environment with appropriate boundaries. Our responsibility is to provide a safe environment to teach age-appropriate material and ideas about sex with the goal of them becoming a well-rounded adult who finds joy in following God's guidelines.

We have noted Freud's somewhat conflicting statements concerning homosexuality and concluded that Freud wanted to navigate a middle path between genetic/biological causes for homosexuality and environmental factors. Freud's view of sexuality as a whole is flawed and inconsistent with Christian ethics.

---

31   I'm taking this phrase directly from *The Baptist Faith and Message, 2000.*

Still, it is not uncommon for Christians to assert ideas about homosexuality rooted in Freud's theories, especially emphasizing a distorted mother-father-child triad as an important component for homosexuality. While these dynamics may be true in some cases, it is certainly not a universal paradigm for homosexuality.

Taken as a whole, Freud's comments are helpful to born-this-way arguments. Perhaps more importantly, Freud set the stage for the opening salvo of the sexual revolution soon to come. In the decade after Freud's death, a somewhat obscure zoology professor from the University of Indiana became a determined crusader to liberate America from its perceived inhibitions about sex in general and homosexuality in particular — Alfred Kinsey.

CHAPTER 2

Alfred Kinsey and Homosexuality

THE MACY'S THANKSGIVING DAY PARADE has been an American tradition since 1924 and is a spectacle filled with the famous balloons shaped like Snoopy and Woodstock, Yogi Bear, or Bugs Bunny. The parade always concludes with Santa in his sleigh, a part of the parade made even more famous by the charming Christmas film from 1947, *Miracle on 34th Street*. Viewed on television by over forty million people, the parade always occurs on Thanksgiving morning and many families watch it with their children prior to Thanksgiving dinner.

On November 28, 2013, the Macy's Parade — an event known for delighting children — included a song and dance performance by transvestite men. For several years, the parade has included performances from Broadway musicals, and in 2013 the parade included some cast members from the Tony award-winning *Kinky Boots*, a musical about a straight-laced young man who inherits a shoe factory from his father and begins producing fetish footwear for transvestite men. The performance in the 2013 Macy's Parade included several men wearing seductive women's apparel plus one man (the factory owner) wearing a coat and tie, his underwear, and thigh-length stiletto boots. Harvey Fierstein, the writer for *Kinky Boots*, was pleased with the Thanksgiving Day performance and released a statement saying, "I'm so proud that the cast of *Kinky Boots* brought their message of tolerance and acceptance to America's parade."[1]

Transvestites dancing in the Macy's Thanksgiving Day Parade demonstrate the degree to which American culture has become desensitized to moral clarity regarding sexual ethics. All of this would have delighted Alfred Kinsey (1894–1956), the father of the American Sexual Revolution. He would have been especially glad that alternative sexualities are being presented to young children as

---

1   Josh Haskell, "Men Dancing in Drag Angers Some Thanksgiving Day Parade Watchers," *ABC News*, November 29, 2013, accessed December 4, 2013, http://abcnews.go.com/US/kinky-boots-performance-yorks-thanksgiving-parade-sparks-outrage/story?id=21050776.

normal and appropriate, because Kinsey was convinced that Christian sexual morals are detrimental to children, inhibiting their ability to experiment in any number of sexual behaviors.

Kinsey's research about American sexual practices during the 1940s and 1950s is still cited by those advocating born-this-way arguments. Nonetheless, a rigorous examination of Kinsey's data demonstrates his findings were seriously flawed in many ways. This claim will be substantiated by briefly reviewing Kinsey's life, summarizing the claims he made about sexual practices in America during his era, and then reviewing several flaws in his research.

THE FATHER OF THE SEXUAL REVOLUTION

Alfred Charles Kinsey was born to devoutly Christian parents in 1894 in Hoboken, New Jersey. His father was very active in church and enforced a strict moral upbringing. When Kinsey was 10, his family moved to South Orange, NJ where Kinsey taught Sunday school at the First Methodist Church, was an Eagle Scout, and the valedictorian of Columbia High School class of 1912. As a teenager, Kinsey had a reputation as a pious Christian, but he eventually abandoned the Christian worldview, especially Christian sexual ethics. He graduated from Bowdoin College in 1916 and went on to earn a doctorate in biology at Harvard where he graduated in 1919. While at Harvard, he studied under William Morton Wheeler (1865–1937), a scientist noted for his advocacy of eugenics and evolutionary ethics. But by the time Kinsey graduated from Harvard, his worldview shifted to evolutionary atheism. Kinsey then began teaching biology at Indiana University in 1920 and married graduate student Clara Bracken McMillen 1921. The two would go on to have four children together, one of whom died at age five.

Kinsey was a world-renowned specialist concerning wasps and spent the early years of his career collecting thousands of specimens of gall wasps. Kinsey's career took a startling change in direction in 1938 when he started teaching Indiana University's new "marriage class." Kinsey began asking students in these classes detailed questions about their sexual experiences and soon decided to study human sexual practices. Kinsey officially began sexual research in 1941 with the help of funds from the Rockefeller Foundation and the assistance of the National Research Council. In 1947, Kinsey founded the Institute for Sex Research at Indiana University, now simply known as The Kinsey Institute.

Kinsey transferred his obsessive and taxonomic approach of research on wasps to the study of human sexuality. Much like the gall wasps he collected, Kinsey and his colleagues gathered thousands of "interviews" in which he or his researchers asked detailed questions about the sexual backgrounds of research participants. Kinsey compiled the findings from these interviews into two books: *Sexual Behavior in the Human Male* (1948) and *Sexual Behavior in the Human Female* (1953). Both works contain many sweeping assertions and often move quickly from tables full of data to moral speculation about the repressed sexual ethics of America.

What has become clearer in the years since the publication of the Kinsey reports is that Kinsey was not merely gathering information about other people's sexual experiences, but he was also engaging in assorted sexual practices with various members of the research team. Instead of the staid atmosphere most people associate with academia, the Institute for Sex Research became a kind of sexual utopia for the gratification of the appetites of Kinsey and his team. Kinsey himself engaged in various forms of heterosexual and homosexual intercourse, including filming sexual acts in the attic of his home. [2]

As Kinsey and his colleagues tabulated the data, they used a novel approach and employed a graded scale to define a person's sexuality. Prior to Kinsey, people were generally considered to be either heterosexual or homosexual. Instead of this binary approach, Kinsey saw sexual behavior on a continuum of experiences in which only rarely are individuals either strictly homosexual or heterosexual. The Kinsey Scale is as follows:

0 - Exclusively heterosexual with no homosexual
1 - Predominantly heterosexual, only incidentally homosexual
2 - Predominantly heterosexual, but more than incidentally homosexual
3 - Equally heterosexual and homosexual
4 - Predominantly homosexual, but more than incidentally heterosexual
5 - Predominantly homosexual, but incidentally heterosexual
6 - Exclusively homosexual[3]

On this scale, six out of the possible seven scores could be interpreted as indicating some level of homosexual attraction. In this way, the Kinsey Scale

---

2   James. H. Jones, *Alfred C. Kinsey: A Life* (New York: W. W. Norton & Company, 1997), 603.

3   The Kinsey scale is found at Alfred Kinsey, Wardell Pomeroy, and Clyde Martin, *Sexual Behavior in the Human Male* (Philadelphia: W. B. Saunders Company, 1948), 638. Notice that while a score of "0" is defined as "heterosexual with no homosexual," a score of 6 simply says "homosexual," without a corresponding "with no heterosexual."
Kinsey, *Sexual Behavior in the Human Male*, 597.

normalizes homosexuality and helped contribute to inflated percentages of homosexuals in some of his findings. The Kinsey scale has since been widely used in numerous research projects. In some ways, the Kinsey scale expands on Freud's idea that we are born bisexual and are, thus, capable of a variety of sexual experiences. In so doing, the Kinsey scale reinforces born-this-way arguments by assuming few people will have sexual experiences limited exclusively to heterosexual intercourse.

KINSEY'S CLAIMS

When *Sexual Behavior in the Human Male* was released in 1948, it sold thousands of copies and created an immediate sensation. The report asserted that nearly 69% of white males in the United States had sex with prostitutes[4] and also said "it is probably safe to suggest that about half of all married males have intercourse with women other than their wives, at some time while they are married."[5] Most surprisingly, Kinsey claimed 37% of males had homosexual physical contact to the point of orgasm at least once.[6] Furthermore, he claimed 10% of all males are exclusively homosexual for at least three years between the ages of 16–55, and 4% of males are exclusively homosexual throughout the entirety of their lives.[7] In *Sexual Behavior in the Human Female* (1953), Kinsey further asserted between 2–6% of unmarried females are exclusively homosexual between the ages of twenty and thirty-five.[8]

Reflecting on the public morality of the day, Kinsey suggested American society's moral revulsion concerning many of the sexual acts he described originated in "ignorance and superstition" and not in "scientific examinations of objectively gathered data."[9] After dismissing traditional faith-based morality as superstition, Kinsey then argued traditional moral categories are irrelevant and bemoaned "the futility of classifying individuals as normal or abnormal, or well-adjusted or poorly adjusted, when in reality they may be nothing more than frequent or rare, or conformists or non-conformists with the socially

---

4 Kinsey, *Sexual Behavior in the Human Male*, 597.

5 Ibid., 585.

6 Ibid., 650.

7 Ibid., 651.

8 Alfred Kinsey, Wardell Pomeroy, Clyde E. Martin, and Paul H. Gebhard, *Sexual Behavior in the Human Female* (Philadelphia: W. B. Saunders Company, 1953), 473–74. See also the statistical chart on page 488.

9 Kinsey, *Sexual Behavior in the Human Male*, 203.

pretended custom."[10] Kinsey supports the born-this-way argument by saying homosexual behavior is not immoral, but is merely a sexual act practiced by a fewer number of people.

The collective influence of the two Kinsey reports on American sexual ethics is difficult to overstate. Presenting himself as a staid, emotionally detached scientist merely gathering data, Kinsey's claims of rampant infidelity within marriage and the widespread prevalence of bizarre sexual practices shocked post-WWII America. A closer look at Kinsey's research reveals many problems with his findings. We will explore six major problems in Kinsey's research: Sample distortion, the presentation of data, volunteer bias, disturbing data about childhood sexuality, the claim that pre-marital sex is beneficial, and Kinsey's atheistic worldview.

SAMPLE DISTORTION

The most glaring problem with Kinsey's data is the composition of his sample. The sample for *Sexual Behavior in the Human Male* numbered over 5,000, a figure intended to impress the average reader. But a massive sample does not guarantee an accurate sample. For example, a disproportionate number of his interviews came from prison inmates, many of whom were sex offenders. A frustrating aspect and major flaw in *Sexual Behavior in the Human Male* is that Kinsey never provides the reader with a precise description of his overall sample.[11] Specifically, he never says precisely how many men in his sample were garnered from prisons, but he does reference "many hundreds of histories which we have from men who have been confined to penal institutions."[12] Some have suggested as much as 25% of Kinsey's male sample came from prison inmates,[13] though the exact number is difficult to identify because of Kinsey's vagueness. Regardless, it is clear people incarcerated for sex offenses were overrepresented in Kinsey's sample, skewing his findings towards people embracing a sexually libertine ethic.

---

10   Ibid., 203.

11   Clyde V. Kiser, "A Statistician Looks at the Report," in *Problems of Sexual Behavior: Proceedings of a Symposium Held by the American Social Hygiene Association March 30–April 1, 1948* (New York: American Social Hygiene Association, 1948), 33. Kiser was favorable to Kinsey's overall research.

12   Kinsey, *Sexual Behavior in the Human Male*, 210.

13   Judith A. Reisman and Edward W. Eichel, *Kinsey, Sex, and Fraud: The Indoctrination of a People* (Lafayette, LA: Huntington House Publishers, 1990), 9.

Not only were prison inmates over-sampled, but the Kinsey sample did not accurately reflect the makeup of the United States in the late 1940s. The Kinsey team interviewed some African Americans, but their data was not included in the tabulations, thus all the data is from white males and white females only. College students as well as people from the Midwestern United States also represented a disproportionate number of his sample.[14] More problematic is the fact Kinsey over-sampled people recruited via homosexual-friendly organizations or magazines. In many ways, Kinsey's sample in which prison inmates and people recruited from homosexual groups were over-represented assured he found what he was hoping to find: statistical confirmation of sexually adventurous and immoral behavior.

PRESENTATION OF DATA

The manner in which Kinsey presents his data is also quite problematic. Both the male and female reports contain numerous charts with tabulations of data, but this data is interspersed with the Kinsey team's own opinions on sexual morality, thus blurring the important distinction between hard data and personal reflection. *Sexual Behavior in the Human Male* in particular often blurs the distinction between the statistical data gathered by the Kinsey researchers about sexual behavior with "supplementary data." By supplementary data, Kinsey meant correspondences in which research participants shared day-to-day records of their sexual activities along with their thinking on the various aspects of sex. Apparently, this supplementary data became the source for most of Kinsey's conclusions concerning sexual ethics and public policy in the mid-twentieth century. Writing in 1949, W. Allen Wallis of the University of Chicago criticized Kinsey's failure clearly to distinguish between hard statistical data and the more broad category of supplementary data and said, "Conclusions based on the sociological interpretations or the supplementary data are frequently stated along with those based on the statistical data, and it is frequently difficult to judge what the basis is for a given conclusion."[15]

Much of what Kinsey called "data" was actually vulgar, pornographic material with no morally redeeming value. He went so far as to include graffiti from bathroom walls in his research. Attempting to dignify the unwholesome filth

---

14   *See* Alfred Kinsey, *Sexual Behavior in the Human Female*, 31

15   W. Allen Wallis, "Statistics of the Kinsey Report," *Journal of the American Statistical Association* 44.248 (December 1949): 466.

often scrawled in public bathrooms, Kinsey noted, "From the days of ancient Greece and Rome, it has been realized that uninhibited expressions of sexual desires may be found in the anonymous inscriptions scratched in out-of-the-way places by authors who may freely express themselves because they never expect to be identified."[16] So, some of Kinsey's conclusions were influenced by bathroom graffiti.

Volunteer Bias

Another glaring problem in Kinsey's report is the phenomenon of volunteer bias: Survey participants who volunteered to be questioned about their sexual experience were also more likely to be sexually adventurous and out of the mainstream.[17] Volunteer bias may have been especially prominent considering that most of Kinsey's research was done prior to 1950, an era of much more conservative ethics. Many people in that era simply would not have discussed the intimate details of their sexual life, and those who were willing to do so were more prone to have a sexually libertine ethic. Writing in 1952, Abraham Maslow and James M. Sakoda, both professors at Brooklyn College, noted the problem of volunteer bias in Kinsey's research and invited Kinsey to interview Brooklyn College students about their sexual practices. Maslow and Sakoda then compared self-esteem scores for students from Brooklyn College who agreed to volunteer for Kinsey's sex research versus those who chose not to volunteer for his research and found that students who volunteered had a higher mean self-esteem score. Maslow and Sakoda concluded that "bias introduced into a sex study by the use of volunteers is, in general, in the direction of inflating the percentage reporting unconventional or disapproved sexual behavior."[18] Because of his work with Maslow and Sakoda, we know Kinsey was aware of the volunteer-bias problem. He even acknowledged that the people who answered his questions may have been "less inhibited sexually."[19] Just as was seen in the problems with his sample, the problem of volunteer bias skewed Kinsey's data toward the conclusions he wanted.

---

16   *Sexual Behavior in the Human Female*, 87.

17   Bruce Westfall, "Kinsey Report," in *Encyclopedia of Biblical and Christian Ethics*, R. K. Harrison, ed., rev. ed. (Nashville: Thomas Nelson, 1992), 221.

18   Abraham H. Maslow and James M. Sakoda, "Volunteer-Error In the Kinsey Study," *Journal of Abnormal Psychology* 47.2 (April 1952): 261. Maslow and Sakoda approved of Kinsey's basic procedures, but wanted to refine the techniques used.

19   Kinsey, *Sexual Behavior in the Human Male*, 99.

People with a more restrained sexual ethic are less likely, even today, to discuss intimate matters of sexual history with a stranger, even in the name of scientific research. People eager to respond to such questions are often less restrained in their sexual ethics and more prone to engage in promiscuous sexual behavior.

Disturbing Data about Childhood Sexuality

The most disturbing and hotly debated part of Kinsey's research is chapter 5 of *Sexual Behavior in the Human Male* titled, "Early Sexual Growth and Activity." Kinsey gathered data from people who can only rightly be called *child molesters*. Describing the source of some of his data on small children he said, "Better data on pre-adolescent climax come from the histories of adult males who have had sexual contacts with younger boys and who, with their adult backgrounds, are able to recognize and interpret the boys' experiences."[20] Kinsey then goes on to say that "9 of our adult male subjects have observed such [pre-adolescent] orgasm. Some of these adults are technically trained persons who have kept diaries or other records which have been put at our disposal; and from them we have secured information on 317 pre-adolescents who were either observed in self masturbation, or who were observed in contacts with other boys or older adults."[21] This disturbing description of child molestation is accompanied by a statistical chart that documents the observation of pre-adolescent experiences in orgasm for children between the ages of *2 months and 15 years old*. In this way, Kinsey analytically describes what can only be called child molestation as a mere scientific observation, dignifying a horrendous crime.

Later on in *Sexual Behavior in the Human Male*, Kinsey discusses masturbation and says, "Of course, there are cases of infants under a year of age who have learned the advantage of specific manipulation, sometimes as a result of being so manipulated by older persons; and there are some boys who masturbate quite specifically and with some frequency from the age of two or three."[22] Another chart in the male report titled "Speed of Adolescent Orgasm" records the length of time it took for children to reach climax and includes the notation, "Duration of stimulation before climax; observations

---

20 Alfred Kinsey, *Sexual Behavior in the Human Male*, 176–77.

21 Ibid., 177.

22 Ibid., 501.

timed with a second hand or stop watch. Ages range from five months of age to adolescence."[23] Perhaps the most painful reading in the male report is the description of children who supposedly orgasm, a description supplied from adults who had sex with children, describing the children "groaning, sobbing, or more violent cries, sometimes with an abundance of tears (especially among younger children)" and also children who "will fight away from the partner."[24] This final description sounds like a terrified child being raped. Notice as well that Kinsey refers to the offending adult as the child's "partner," as if a young child could voluntarily choose such behavior.

Judith Reisman has strongly suggested Kinsey's researchers were the ones guilty of perpetrating the violence on the children.[25] Reisman's claims have been quite controversial and The Kinsey Institute itself categorically denies that Kinsey or his researchers participated in experiments on children. John Bancroft, director of the Kinsey Institute from 1995–2004, contends all the data in Kinsey's statistical tables regarding pre-adolescent orgasm in *Sexual Behavior in the Human Male* came from one man who had sex with many adults and children beginning in 1917 until the time Kinsey interviewed him in the mid-1940s. Since Kinsey mentions gathering data from nine people who molested children, Bancroft says he does not know why Kinsey did not want to admit all the data came from one person, but suggests Kinsey "did not want to draw attention to this one man, or alternatively because he was particularly interested in this evidence and did not want to diminish its possible scientific credibility by revealing its single source."[26] Bancroft further argues that Kinsey did not promote child molestation, did not train people to molest children, and was not in any sense a pedophile.

What do we make of the data on children in *Sexual Behavior in the Human Male?* John Bancroft contends all of Kinsey's data concerning adolescents came from one man. If Bancroft is correct, then Kinsey is *at least* guilty of lying in his research by asserting the data came from several people when in actuality it came from one man, a man who can only be described as a serial child molester. The debate is heated, but there seem to be only three options concerning the childhood data in *Sexual Behavior in the Human Male*:

---

23   Ibid., 178.

24   Ibid., 161.

25   Judith A. Reisman and Edward W. Eichel, *Kinsey, Sex and Fraud: The Indoctrination of a People*, see especially pages 46–47.

26   John Bancroft, "Alfred C. Kinsey and the Politics of Sex Research," *Annual Review of Sex Research* 1.15 (2004): 16–17.

Option 1: Kinsey gathered data from nine different adults not directly affiliated with his institute who had sexual contact with children. In this case, Kinsey is guilty of failing to report nine different child molesters.

Option 2: Kinsey claimed to gather data from nine different adults who had sexual contact with children, but actually all of the data came from one person, a man not directly affiliated with his institute. In this case, Kinsey is guilty of lying and his report is dishonest in addition to failing to report a serial child molester.

Option 3: The data on childhood sexuality was gathered by researchers directly connected with Kinsey's institute. In this case, the Kinsey Institute staff were child molesters.

Which option is correct? Bancroft protests that Kinsey did not encourage child molestation, but this seems to be a weak defense. In 2011, Joe Paterno was fired as the Penn State football coach because he did not report a child molester to the police, which is *at least* the same thing Kinsey failed to do. In contrast, Judith Reisman argues the childhood molestation data in the Kinsey reports is the result of prospective, directed research performed by employees of the Kinsey Institute or under their supervision.[27] It seems likely to me that the Kinsey Institute staff themselves were not the ones actually molesting children. This leaves us with either option one or two, both of which would entail Kinsey and his staff enabling child molesters to continue harming children. I reject Bancroft's notion that Kinsey did not encourage child molestation since Kinsey reflected an eagerness to find data on childhood sexuality without regard to the source. At a bare minimum one would expect Bancroft to concede the lack of informed consent on the part of the children, but he does not do so.

In *Sexual Behavior in the Human Female* Kinsey made more claims about childhood sexuality: "On the basis of adult recall and the observations which we have just recorded, we can report 4 cases of females under one year of age coming to orgasm, and a total of 23 cases of small girls three years of age or younger reaching orgasm."[28] He also claimed 659 of the females in his sample experienced pre-adolescent orgasm, of whom he claimed 2%

---

27   Judith A. Reisman and Edward W. Eichel, *Kinsey, Sex, and Fraud,* 47.
28   Alfred Kinsey, *Sexual Behavior in the Human Female,* 105.

had "their first orgasm in physical contacts with dogs or cats."[29] Further-more, Kinsey claimed 1,075 of the females had experienced sexual advances by adult male while the females were still preadolescents. But Kinsey then shockingly claimed young girls could actually learn to enjoy such encounters: "Repetition [of sexual contact with preadolescent girls] had most frequently occurred when the children were having their contacts with relatives who lived in the same household. In many instances, the experiences were re-peated because the children had become interested in the sexual activity and had more or less actively sought repetitions of their experience."[30] Kinsey is clearly describing what a rational observer would call child abuse, but Kinsey mimics the twisted claim of many sex offenders: "The victim really enjoyed the experience."

What is most disturbing is Kinsey's refusal to make any moral judgment concerning the "data" he obtained about children. Notice the terms he uses for child molestation: the observers were "technically trained," the molesters are called "adult observers," and the molesters are actually called the child's sexual "partner." Perhaps Kinsey's own distorted view of child sexuality is best found in *Sexual Behavior in the Human Female* in which he says, "It is diffi-cult to understand why a child, except for its cultural conditioning, should be disturbed at having its genitalia touched, or disturbed at seeing the genitalia of other persons, or disturbed at even more specific sexual contacts."[31] Kinsey could not sympathize with the reaction of the children to being molested. The inability to sympathize with victims is a character trait associated with a person whose conscience is seared and non-functional.

In Kinsey's own thinking, his approach to childhood sexuality intersects with Freud's theories concerning the sexual nature of small children, with Kinsey trumpeting his own research as "an important substantiation of the Freudian view of sexuality as a component that is present in the human an-imal from earliest infancy."[32] In this way, Freud's theories and Kinsey's data are joined in support of the born-this-way argument. Kinsey insisted some small children actually enjoyed homosexual sexual molestation. Since small children are capable of such "pleasure," perhaps more people would actually embrace the homosexual lifestyle if it were not for antiquated and repressive Judeo-Christian sexual ethics.

---

29 Ibid., 106.

30 Ibid., 118.

31 Ibid., 121.

32 Kinsey, *Sexual Behavior in the Human Male*, 180.

Pre-Marital Sex Is Good for Marriages

One of Kinsey's claims which was most upsetting to his first generation of readers was that individuals who have extensive pre-marital sexual experiences are more sexually successful with their spouse once married. This claim is most clearly seen in *Sexual Behavior in the Human Female* where Kinsey claims women with extensive pre-marital sexual activity find it much easier to achieve orgasm with their husbands once married.[33] Kinsey completely ignores various negative consequences associated with pre-marital sexual intercourse, such as sexually transmitted diseases, unplanned pregnancies, and emotional exploitation of young people by older, more aggressive sexual predators. Furthermore, 1 Corinthians 6:16 teaches that sex joins two people in a deep and profound way. This is why pre-marital sex is actually destructive to future marriages. When people are joined to multiple sexual partners, all of those previous sexual experiences are brought into a marriage, thus making it more — not less — difficult for a husband and wife to join to each other and experience the deep oneness God intends.

Kinsey's Atheistic Worldview

Kinsey rejected Christianity and embraced the atheistic worldview along with its corresponding ethical implications. Benjamin Wiker summarizes Kinsey's moral stance and says, "The sexual deviation from present moral codes by certain members of society represented not moral deviation, but rather a return to the expression of the original, natural, amoral sexual passions."[34] Building on his atheistic worldview and the ethical convictions of moral Darwinism, Kinsey hoped to eliminate "taboos" against various forms of vulgar behavior. He said, "Most of the complications which are observable in sexual histories are the result of society's reactions when it obtains knowledge of an individual's behavior, or the individual's fear of how society would react if he were discovered."[35] In context, one must remember that the "sexual histories" to which Kinsey is referring include bestiality, pedophilia, homosexuality and adultery. Reflecting his naturalistic roots, he follows this by saying, "Whatever the moral

---

33   *Sexual Behavior in the Human Female*, 384–86.

34   Benjamin Wiker, *Moral Darwinism: How We Became Hedonists* (Downers Grove, IL: InterVarsity Press, 2002), 279.

35   *Sexual Behavior in the Human Male*, 202.

interpretation, there is no scientific reason for considering particular types of sexual activity as intrinsically, in their biologic origins, normal or abnormal."[36]

For Kinsey, sex is simply an animal instinct developed via natural selection over eons of time. He comments, "In any case, at any social level, the human animal is more hampered in its pursuit of sexual contacts than the primitive anthropoid in the wild; and, at any level, the restrictions would appear to be most severe for males who are not married."[37] Since man is only an animal and not made in God's image, it is also impossible for sex to have any sacred dimension in Kinsey's world. Sex is simply response to stimulus. Furthermore, Kinsey contended the moral codes against promiscuous behavior are irrational and said, "The sociologist and anthropologist find the origins of such customs in ignorance and superstition, and in the attempt of each group to set itself apart from its neighbors.[38] Thus, for Kinsey, moral ideas prohibiting incest, molestation of children, adultery, and rampant promiscuity are based on ignorance that needs to be eliminated by sexually enlightened people such as himself.

KINSEY'S ENDURING LEGACY AND BORN-THIS-WAY ARGUMENTS

Two aspects of Kinsey's research have had the most enduring impact in relation to homosexuality and born-this-way arguments: The Kinsey Scale and the "10%" myth. As noted above, the Kinsey Scale is weighted to find any level of homosexual attraction and it is still used in research today. By using the Kinsey Scale, some assessments have a built-in bias. Giving exclusive heterosexual attraction a score of "0" can possibly skew the conclusions about the prevalence of homosexuality.[39] But perhaps the most enduring influence of Kinsey's report is the 10% myth — the idea that 10% of people are homosexual. However, the claim that "10% of all people are gay" is a misstatement of Kinsey's claim. As was noted earlier, Kinsey claimed 10% of males are exclu-

---

36 Ibid.

37 Ibid., 268.

38 Kinsey, *Sexual Behavior in the Human Female*, 203.

39 Pro-homosexual author Fausto-Sterling comments, "In studies that search for a genetic link to homosexuality . . . the middle of the Kinsey scale disappears; researchers seek to compare the extreme ends of the spectrum in hopes of maximizing the chance that they will find something of interest." Anne Fausto-Sterling, *Sexing the Body: Gender Politics and the Construction of Sexuality* (New York: Basic Books, 2000), 10.

sively homosexual between the ages of 16–55 and 4% of males are exclusively homosexual throughout their life.

The true number of people who are homosexual is much lower than Kinsey suggests. The pro-homosexual Williams Institute at UCLA's School of Law reported in 2011 that about 3.5% of American adults self-identify as lesbian, gay, or bisexual and that a further .03% identify as transgender. Among the 3.5% who identify as gay, lesbian, or bisexual, bisexuals comprise a slight majority of 1.8% as opposed to 1.7% who identify as gay or lesbian. About 1.1% of women and 2.2% of men self-identify as exclusively homosexual.[40] This is consistent with findings from a 1993 study of sexual behavior of men in the United States which claimed only 2% of men aged 20–39 had any same-gender sexual activity in the previous ten years, and only 1% reported being exclusively homosexual during this interval.[41]

Kinsey's data supports born-this-way arguments by insisting homosexual behavior is a normal and frequent part of human sexuality. By insisting homosexuality is common, many people contend it is an inherent component of human behavior, arguing, "If that many people engage in homosexual acts, there must be some innate biological reason why." But the frequency or infrequency of a particular act is not determinative for the act's morality. Any number of destructive behaviors — for example, heterosexual promiscuity, substance abuse, marital infidelity, stealing — have a high statistical occurrence among the human population, but that does not mean we suspend moral judgment about those behaviors.

Despite many flaws in Kinsey's research, he successfully brought the topic of sex into the marketplace of ideas in mid-twentieth century America. But more than just researching the topic of sex, Kinsey was a crusader against Christian sexual ethics, a man driven to change the way society thought about sex and sexual ethics. Kinsey's vision was of a nation that eschewed biblical

---

40   Gary J. Gates, "How Many People are Lesbian, Gay, Bisexual, and Transgender?," The Williams Institute, April, 2011, accessed January 3, 2013, http://williamsinstitute.law.ucla.edu/wp-content/uploads/Gates-How-Many-People-LGBT-Apr-2011.pdf. Pro-homosexual authors Wilson and Rahman use a "feelings-based criteria" to claim 2 – 3.5% of men and 0.5 – 1.5% of women are exclusively homosexual. Glenn Wilson and Qazi Rahman, *Born Gay: The Psychobiology of Sex Orientation* (London: Peter Owen Publishers, 2005, 2008), 22. One is left to wonder why the Kinsey Institute can claim, "Interestingly, most statistics, such as homosexual behavior, did not change significantly from the original reports." This statement is plainly inaccurate and sounds self-serving. The Kinsey Institute, "Facts About *Kinsey,* The Film," accessed December 21, 2012, www.kinseyinstitute.org/about/Movie-facts.html.

41   J. O. Billy, K. Tanfer, W. R. Grady, and D. H. Klepinger, "The Sexual Behavior of Men in the United States," *Family Planning Perspectives* 25.2 (March-April 1993): 52–60.

morality for an atheistic, materialistic sexual ethic without the constraints of God, marriage vows, or caution and concern for overtly sexualizing young children. Though he died in 1956, Kinsey was the father of the Sexual Revolution. His work opened the door for public discussion of homosexuality and helped set the stage for one of the most defining moments in the Gay Rights movement — the removal of homosexuality as a mental disorder from DSM-II in 1973.

CHAPTER 3

The American Psychiatric Association and Homosexuality

THE DEFINING MOMENT IN THE GAY RIGHTS MOVEMENT began early on the morning of June 28, 1969, in the streets of New York. New York Police raided a homosexual bar named The Stonewall Inn in Greenwich Village, long noted as a hang-out for transvestite prostitutes. Police had already made arrests at several gay bars in the area that summer, but on this night, the patrons of the Stonewall Inn resisted law enforcement and rioted. As police hustled some of their arrests into a van to take them to jail, a crowd of angry homosexuals gathered outside the bar and began throwing coins, bottles, and cans at the police. The police then retreated into the Stonewall Inn itself, only to have the building pelted with bricks, cobblestones, and even makeshift bombs.[1] Eventually, the police were able to leave the building, but the brawl between law enforcement and homosexual patrons sparked more riots over the next several days. This event is now generally considered the start of the Gay Rights movement in the United States.

President Obama ennobled the Stonewall Riots in his second inaugural address and said, "We, the people, declare today that the most evident of truths — that all of us are created equal — is the star that guides us still; just as it guided our forebears through Seneca Falls, and Selma, and Stonewall."[2] President Obama connected women's rights (Seneca Falls, 1848), racial equality (Selma, 1965), and gay rights (Stonewall, 1969). In this way, even the President makes a born-this-way argument — one's involvement in the homosexual life-

---

1   Description of the Stonewall riot from Betsy Kuhn, *Gay Power! The Stonewall Riots and the Gay Rights Movement, 1969* (Minneapolis: Twenty-First Century Books, 2011), 5.

2   The White House, Office the Press Secretary, "Inaugural Address of President Barack Obama," January 21, 2013, accessed December 16, 2013, http://www.whitehouse.gov/the-press-office/2013/01/21/inaugural-address-president-barack-obama.

style is no different from being born a woman or being born with a particular skin color.

Soon after the Stonewall riots, homosexuals in New York organized themselves into the Gay Liberation Front (GLF), a group that quickly expanded to include chapters in other major US cities and England. The GLF was a radical group with a decentralized leadership structure, an inherent organizational weakness which meant many of the various chapters ceased to exist within a few years. During its short existence, the GLF joined its demand for sexual liberation with a hatred of capitalism and the traditional family. The GLF borrowed some of these ideas from Marxism since Marx and Engels saw the traditional family as central to maintaining a capitalist system of economics.[3] In a similar way, the GLF saw the traditional family as an obstacle to gay rights since the traditional family reinforces heterosexual and monogamous marriage, the traditional roles of mother, father, and the importance of raising children in a home with both a mother and father present.

In 1971, the GLF in England released a manifesto announcing their presuppositions and goals and the manifesto begins by listing ways homosexuals are oppressed. The first item on their list was the traditional family, saying, "At some point nearly all gay people have found it difficult to cope with having the restricting images of man or woman pushed on them by their parents."[4] The manifesto asserts it is unfair for someone to be raised in an environment where traditional sex roles are modeled by the parents. The document also argues against monogamy and expresses a willingness to use violence to achieve the goal of homosexual liberation.

Emboldened by the Stonewall Riots, radical homosexual activists quickly adopted the tactics used by student protestors and anti-war rioters in the 1960s to attack what they perceived to be their most hated enemy: The American Psychiatric Association (APA). In a few short years, homosexuals were able to achieve a major victory by forcing the nation's leading organization for mental health professionals to adopt a drastic change in its stance towards homosexuality. As a result, born-this-way arguments received a major push forward.

---

3   *See* Karl Marx and Friedrich Engels, *The German Ideology,* At Chapter 1. A, "Private, Property and Communism," accessed April 29, 2011, http://www.marxists.org/archive/marx/works/1845/german-ideology.

4   Gay Liberation Front: *Manifesto*, London, 1971, revised 1978; Paul Halsall, ed., Internet History Sourcebooks Project, accessed December 16, 2013, http://www.fordham.edu/halsall/pwh/glf-london.asp.

THE APA AND HOMOSEXUALITY PRE-STONEWALL

Founded in 1844, the APA is the world's largest professional organization for psychiatrists. It publishes the *Diagnostic and Statistical Manual of Mental Disorders* (DSM), the standard professional reference work used by psychiatrists and mental health professionals for determining a diagnosis. The DSM's first edition was published in 1952 with subsequent revisions following in 1968 (DSM II), 1980 (DSM III), 1994 (DSM IV), and in 2013 (DSM V).

The stance of the APA towards homosexuality prior to Stonewall was fairly uniform and reflected a position influenced by Freud's theories. As noted earlier, Freud was somewhat conciliatory towards homosexuality and believed there were low chances of reversing a homosexual orientation. But in the 1940s and 1950s, American psychiatry considered homosexuality to be a disease in need a cure, a stance somewhat divergent from Freud. At the same time, male homosexuality was considered to be caused by pathological parent-child relationships, particularly the relationship between a boy and his mother, a theory with its origins in Freud's thought.

Irving Bieber (1911–1991) represented the "orthodox" view of homosexuality in psychiatry prior to 1973. A distinguished psychoanalyst and professor, having taught at Yale Medical College, New York University, and New York Medical College, he argued unimpeded normal development leads to heterosexuality in adulthood. In contrast, homosexuality is caused by severe early developmental disturbances. Referring to homosexual males in particular, Bieber believed a dysfunctional mother, father, child triad strongly influenced one towards homosexuality: "Typically, mothers of homosexuals are inappropriately close, binding, often seductive, and tend to inhibit boyish aggressiveness. The fathers are overtly or covertly hostile: this is expressed in detachment, streaks of cruelty, or frank brutality."[5] Overbearing mothers responded to their son's heterosexual drives with hostility, expressing demasculinizing and feminine attitudes towards their sons. Subsequently, these over-bearing mothers interfered with the father-son relationship, often favoring their sons over their husbands. These conflicts also inhibited the development of normal peer relationships with other boys. Likewise, the fathers of homosexual boys were depicted as detached, hostile, and openly rejecting. When all of these factors were taken together, the predominant psychiatric theory said the result was a young man who

---

5   Irving Bieber, "Homosexuality — An Adaptive Consequence of Disorder in Psychosexual Development," *American Journal of Psychiatry* 130.11 (November 1973): 1,210.

was looking for male validation and thus became homosexual.[6] This "orthodox" consensus was challenged and overturned by homosexual activists, a process that began in 1969.

THE NATIONAL INSTITUTE FOR MENTAL HEALTH'S 1969 REPORT ON HOMOSEXUALITY

In October 1969 The National Institutes of Mental Health Task Force on Homosexuality submitted a report that urged the end to anti-sodomy laws and discrimination against homosexuals. The committee had been appointed by Stanley F. Yolles, the Director of the Nation Institutes of Health from 1964–1970, and was chaired by Evelyn Hooker (1907–1996), a psychologist at UCLA. Paul Gebbard, then serving as the director of The Kinsey Institute, was also a committee member. While the Nixon administration stalled official publication of the report until 1972, the report itself was circulated within the homosexual community prior to its release.[7]

The Committee acknowledged the Sexual Revolution in progress and said, "Many people believe that we are currently [1969] undergoing a revolution in sexual mores and behaviors."[8] Picking up on the idea of a right to privacy, the report strongly urged that consensual homosexual behavior between adults be decriminalized: "Discreet homosexuality, together with many other aspects of human sexual behavior, is being recognized more and more as the private business of the individual rather than a subject for public regulation through statute."[9] The report also urged a major change in employment practices and policies and urged an end to discrimination in employment for homosexuals.

Evelyn Hooker's choice as committee chairman was a fortunate one for homosexuals. In 1958, she published a landmark research article titled "The Adjustment of the Male Overt Homosexual." Hooker observed that many of the theories about homosexuality current in the 1950s were based on inter-

---

6   This is a summary of Ronald Bayer, *Homosexuality and American Psychiatry: The Politics of Diagnosis* (Princeton, NJ: Princeton University Press, 1987), 31.

7   Vern L. Bullough, *Science in the Bedroom: A History of Sex Research* (New York: HarperCollins / Basic Books, 1994), 355, n. 107.

8   "Final Report of the Task Force on Homosexuality," in *National Institute of Mental Health Task Force on Homosexuality: Final Report and Background Papers*, John Livingood, ed. (Washington DC, GPO, 1972), 6.

9   Ibid.

actions with people seeking psychological help, hospitalized in mental health facilities, or in prison populations. She decided to study the mental health of men who claimed to be happy as homosexuals and find out if they met the criteria for mental illness.

Hooker worked with the homosexual-friendly Mattachine Society of Los Angeles to locate homosexuals for her research and eventually found thirty homosexual men to be compared with a control group of thirty heterosexual men. The participants were matched for factors such as education and social status. Of special importance, none of them were in therapy at the time of the experiment. Hooker administered three different psychological tests to the two groups of men: The Rorschach "ink blot" test, the Thematic Apperception Test (TAT), and Make-A-Picture-Story (MAPS) Test. Hooker then had two experts evaluate the responses to the Rorschach test while a third expert evaluated the responses to the TAT and MAPS tests.

Hooker's small group of three mental health professionals were not told which participants were homosexual or heterosexual, but were asked to score each participant on a five-point scale of mental health. When they finished scoring the participants tests, an equal number of homosexuals and heterosexuals were scored as being psychologically "well adjusted" or better. Furthermore, when Hooker asked the researchers if they could identify the homosexuals and heterosexuals, they were able to do so at a rate only slightly better than "50/50." Hooker concluded that "clearly there is no inherent connection between pathology and homosexuality."[10] She went so far as to say, "Homosexuality as a clinical entity does not exist."[11] What Hooker was saying is that homosexual behavior in and of itself is not indicative of mental illness or psychological impairment. With this in mind, it is not surprising that The National Institutes of Mental Health Task Force on Homosexuality, which she chaired, released a report with a positive view of homosexuality. Hooker's findings were groundbreaking and became the basis for a fundamental change in the way psychology and psychiatry viewed homosexuality.

---

10 Evelyn Hooker, "The Adjustment of the Male Overt Homosexual," *Journal of Projective Techniques* 21.1 (1957): 23.

11 Ibid., 30.

Change in the DSM II

Both DSM I[12] and II[13] listed homosexuality as a mental disorder, but soon after the publication of DSM II in 1968, homosexual activists began exerting strong pressure to remove homosexuality as a mental illness. At a 1970 meeting of the APA held in San Francisco, homosexual activists used tactics similar to student anti-war protests of the era and interrupted the meetings, yelling at psychiatrists and shouting down different program speakers. For example, Irving Bieber was presenting a paper on homosexuality and transsexualism when he was interrupted by protesters, one of whom shouted, "I've read your book, Dr. Bieber, and if that book talked about black people the way it talks about homosexuals, you'd be drawn and quartered and you'd deserve it."[14] Homosexual activists were even more animated during a panel discussion addressing issues in sexuality and asked one speaker, "Where did you take your residency, Auschwitz?"[15]

The APA was caught off guard by the fierce protests. Responding to the pressure, the APA's 1971 annual meeting held in Washington, DC, hosted a special panel discussion composed of homosexuals themselves. Not satisfied with merely having a slot on the agenda, protestors associated with the Gay Liberation Front stormed into the building and interrupted the professional meeting, demanding the APA change its stance on homosexuality. The riots outside of the Stonewall Inn had now moved into the usually calm meeting rooms of professional psychiatrists.

Having successfully intimidated the APA into reconsidering its stance on homosexuality, some psychiatrists began to argue in favor of homosexuals. One of the most vocal was Judd Marmor (1910–2003), then the director of the Divisions of Psychiatry at Cedars-Sinai Medical Center. Marmor had collaborated with Evelyn Hooker, having also served on The National Institutes of Mental Health Task Force on Homosexuality. In 1972, Marmor wrote an

---

12   DSM I referred to homosexuality as "sexual deviation," a form of "sociopathic personality disturbance." The Committee on Nomenclature and Statistics of the American Psychiatric Association, *Diagnostic and Statistical Manual of Mental Disorders* (Washington, DC: American Psychiatric Association Mental Hospital Service, 1952), 38–39.

13   DSM II also listed homosexuality as a "sexual deviation." The Committee on Nomenclature and Statistics of the American Psychiatric Association, *DSM II / Diagnostic and Statistical Manual of Mental Disorders* (Washington, DC: The American Psychiatric Association, 1968), 44.

14   Ronald Bayer, *Homosexuality and American Psychiatry: The Politics of Diagnosis*, 103.

15   Ibid. The question was directed at Australian Psychiatrist Nathaniel McConaghy.

article in *The International Journal of Psychiatry* in which he strongly argued for a change in the APA's stance on homosexuality. Marmor insisted there is no more justification for labeling homosexuality a mental illness than for labeling heterosexuality a mental illness: Both are commonly occurring patterns of human behavior. Marmor argued for a born-this-way stance and said "there may be a hidden genetic predisposition as the basis for [homosexual] preferences."[16] At the same time, Marmor acknowledged some cases of homosexuality may "be the exclusive resultant of postnatal programming, due to disturbed family relationships and identifications during certain critical developmental periods."[17] He also insisted, much like Evelyn Hooker, that homosexuals "are perfectly capable of making a successful adaptation in society."[18] Marmor compared psychiatric attempts to change a person's sexual orientation to attempts to change a person from left-handed to right-handed. Reflecting concerns about overpopulation of the Earth, Marmor even suggested homosexuality may be an evolutionary beneficial trait because "the existence of a group of men and women who do not propagate serves an adaptive, rather than maladaptive, function in terms of species survival."[19] In a later article, Marmor argued many homosexuals experience emotional and psychological struggles not because of their homosexuality, but as "a consequence of the prejudice and discrimination that they encounter in our society."[20]

Psychiatrists in agreement with Marmor were persuasive and change in policy quickly followed the homosexual protests. On December 15, 1973, the board of trustees of the APA voted to remove homosexuality as a mental disorder from DSM II. In 1974, the membership at large of the APA was asked to vote to sustain or deny the change to the DSM II. Ten thousand psychiatrists participated in the referendum and approved the change by a 58% margin. Thus, via political pressure and protests, homosexual activists were able to force a change in the DSM. The revised seventh printing of the DSM II now only mentioned "sexual orientation disturbance," and added, "This diagnostic category is distinguished from homosexuality, which by itself does not constitute a psychiatric disorder."[21] "Sexual orientation disturbance" was intended as

---

16   Judd Marmor, "Homosexuality: Mental Illness or Moral Dilemma?" *International Journal of Psychiatry* 10.1 (March 1972): 114.

17   Ibid., 115.

18   Ibid.

19   Ibid.

20   Judd Marmor, "Homosexuality and Cultural Value Systems," *American Journal of Psychiatry* 130.11 (November 1973): 1208.

21   The Committee on Nomenclature and Statistics of the American Psychiatric Asso-

a diagnosis only for people who were bothered by their desires for same-sex intercourse.

When the DSM III was released in 1980, "sexual orientation disturbance" was changed to "ego-dystonic homosexuality," again, a classification that was reserved only for homosexuals who were distressed about their orientation.[22] The revised language essentially allowed psychiatrists to treat homosexuals who were uncomfortable with their lifestyle. But the language of "ego-dystonic homosexuality" was removed from the DSM-III in 1987. The APA went further in 1998 and rejected any attempt to help people change their sexual orientation, saying, "The American Psychiatric Association opposes any psychiatric treatment, such as "reparative" or "conversion" therapy, which is based upon the assumption that homosexuality *per se* is a mental disorder, or based upon a prior assumption that the patient should change his/ her homosexual orientation."[23] DSM V was released in May, 2013, and further embraced a pro-homosexual stance. In this edition, gender identity disorder was changed to gender dysphoria, a change viewed as a victory for transsexual individuals. Under the new paradigm, a person intensely uncomfortable with his or her biological gender and who strongly identifies with and wants to be the opposite gender, may or may not be pathological. The DSM V states gender dysphoria is not meant to describe nonconformity to stereotypical gender role behavior such as "occasional cross-dressing in adult men."[24] Gender dysphoria is only for those who feel distressed about their desire to be the opposite gender.

THE APA AND BORN-THIS-WAY ARGUMENTS

The change in the APA's stance towards homosexuality has been one of the most significant strengths in born-this-way arguments. Prior to the APA's de-

---

ciation, *DSM II / Diagnostic and Statistical Manual of Mental Disorders*, 7th printing (Washington, DC: The American Psychiatric Association, 1974), 44. The American Psychological Association followed the American Psychiatric Association's lead and changed its stance on homosexuality in 1975.

22 Tyger Latham, "Scientific Homophobia: When It Comes to Homosexuality, We Have Not Always Practiced What We Preach," *Psychology Today*, April 19, 2011, accessed December 28, 2012, http://www.psychologytoday.com/blog/therapy-matters/201104/scientific-homophobia.

23 The American Psychiatric Association, "LGBT-Sexual Orientation," accessed December 28, 2012, http://www.psychiatry.org/mental-health/people/lgbt-sexual-orientation.

24 American Psychiatric Association, *DSM V/American Psychiatric Association: Diagnostic and Statistical Manual of Mental Disorders*, 5th ed. (Arlington, VA: American Psychiatric Association, 2013), 458.

cision, researchers tried to find the causes for homosexuality in environmental factors with special emphasis on the mother-father-child triad. Since the APA's change, research on the origins of homosexuality almost exclusively focuses on genetic or biological causes. Instead of focusing on family dynamics and the age and type of a person's sexual debut, psychiatry now assumes homosexuality is innate, and rooted either in the genetic code itself, variations in prenatal exposure to exposure to hormones, or some combination. In this way, psychiatry as a profession affirms the born-this-way argument.

Psychiatry also supports the born-this-way argument by asserting homosexuality is not bad or less desirable than heterosexuality, but instead is a naturally occurring variation in human behavior, a stance very similar to Kinsey's. From an evolutionary perspective, it is viewed as neither moral nor immoral, it is just one of way sexuality expresses itself. For modern psychiatry, homosexuality is not *wrong*, it is merely a less frequent form of human behavior.

But what about people who claim they *want* to change their sexuality? Modern psychiatry generally says such people are actually succumbing to coercion to conform to the cultural norm. The current belief is that a psychiatrist is not actually "helping" when he or she provides assistance to someone trying to leave the gay lifestyle. Richard Isay (1934–2012), a noted homosexual psychiatrist, said efforts to helps someone overcome homosexuality and embrace heterosexuality "are psychologically harmful if a gay man cannot gain pleasure from his sexual activity, for the failure to do so adds to his perception that he is impaired because of his sexual orientation."[25] The vast majority of modern psychiatrists insist trying to help homosexuals change only accentuates needless guilt and self-loathing; the mental health professional should help the client embrace his or her own sexual identity in healthy and constructive ways. In fact, celebrating being born-this-way is liberating and leads to healthy integration of one's own self-image. For modern psychiatry, homosexuality is innate, immutable, and praiseworthy.

Christian Evaluation

Christians must think clearly about our reaction to the APA's change in stance about homosexuality. Some Christians have automatically assumed that we should affirm the psychoanalytical model since it viewed homosexuality nega-

---

25   Richard Isay, *Being Homosexual: Gay Men and Their Development*, rev. ed. (New York: Vintage Books, 2009), 8.

tively. Yet, we should remember that Freud's model of childhood development is open to many criticisms from a Christian perspective. But the deeper issue with the APA's stance, and the point which bothers most Christians, is that if homosexuality is no longer considered a psychological "disease," then it no longer needs to be treated. No cure is necessary if nothing is wrong. Furthermore (and this is where the APA's change can become oppressive) if nothing is wrong, *then we shouldn't try to help people stop engaging in homosexual behavior.* Christians understand the implications of such arguments means that some mental health professionals think Christians are wrong to call people to repent of homosexual behavior. This is one reason why Christians have reacted so strongly to the APA's change in stance over forty years ago.

How do we respond to the claims that many homosexuals are mentally healthy and well adjusted? We should not be surprised that this is so. Many people grow quite comfortable with any number of lifestyles plainly rejected in Scripture. As such, they can function normally in a day-to-day basis and even excel at specific tasks or careers. But in their morals they have what Paul described as a "seared" conscience (1 Tim. 4:2). The conscience is only as good as its reference point, and if the reference point for a person's conscience is his or her own desires and lusts, then any number of sinful behaviors seem morally plausible. God holds us morally accountable for the condition of our conscience, thus people engaging in sexual immorality are without excuse (Rom. 1:18 –32). Choices we make affect the way we think, and how we reflect on the morality of our decisions. Processes in the brain itself can be affected by repetitive choices. As we will see in the next chapter, it is the brain itself that is the focus of many born-this-way arguments.

CHAPTER 4

Brain Plasticity and Homosexuality

BRAIN PLASTICITY REFERS TO THE MANNER in which the human brain builds new pathways between neurons and discards old connections. Research in brain plasticity is helping us learn how the brain adapts and changes in response to our experiences. For example, in 2009 a group of researchers working in the Boston area identified positive effects of musical lessons on children's brains. After only fifteen months of musical training in early childhood, healthy, structural brain changes in children were identified which were strongly correlated with improvements in musically relevant motor and auditory skills. A comparison of MRIs before and after musical training showed an increase in size in the areas of the children's brains associated with motor control and auditory functioning. What was surprising to the researchers was that other areas of the brain not directly associated with motor or auditory functions also showed an increase in growth and development, suggesting these other regions might help integrate the different skills needed for learning a musical instrument. The scientists concluded by saying, "These results provide new evidence for training-induced brain plasticity in early childhood."[1]

While developing research in brain plasticity holds great hope for potential therapies related to traumatic brain injury, when discussing born-this-way arguments the important point is certain parts of the brain itself change in response to choices, experiences, and activities we undertake. In the research on children and musical training, brain plasticity was associated with a positive outcome. But is it possible for our choices, experiences, and activities to have negative effects on our brain? Can these changes be associated with sexual behavior? And from a Christian perspective, how does the concept

---

1 Krista L. Hyde, Jason Lerch, Andrea Norton, Marie Forgeard, Ellen Winner, Alan C. Evans, and Gottfried Schlaug, "The Effects of Musical Training on Structural Brain Development," *Annals of the New York Academy of Sciences* 1169 (July 2009): 185.

of brain plasticity inform our response to born-this-way arguments? This chapter will briefly address these ideas. Beginning with a concise description of basic components important in building neural pathways, brain plasticity will be summarized. Next, pornography will serve as a case study for the ways sexual choices affect the brain. These findings will then be followed with some observations relevant to born-this-way arguments and homosexuality. We will see that brain plasticity does not completely answer our questions concerning the origin of homosexuality. However, evidence indicates our choices and environment clearly affect the way our brain processes sexually laden messages.

The Amazing Neuron

The basic building block of the brain and the central nervous system is the neuron, a highly specialized cell that communicates information throughout the body via electrochemical processes. Neurons are different from other cells because they have specialized parts called axons and dendrites. Dendrites bring signals to the neuron and axons send messages out from the neuron. The connections between neurons are called synapses and chemicals known as neurotransmitters are released into these synapses to communicate with other neurons.[2] The synapses between neurons organize the brain by forming pathways that connect the different parts of the brain governing everything we do – including breathing, sleeping, thinking, and feeling. [3]

What we call "learning" involves creating, strengthening, and discarding connections among neurons. When we are born, we have about all the neurons we will ever have, close to one hundred billion. Unlike most other cells, neurons generally do not grow or repair after damage. Neurons are not replaced when they die, but new connections between neurons form throughout life and there are an estimated one hundred trillion synapses in our brain.[4] These connections are so intricate, it is possible for one neuron to be connected to

---

2   Robert Stufflebeam, "Neurons, Synapses, Action Potentials, and Neurotransmission," Consortium on Cognitive Science Instruction, accessed June 25, 2014, http://www.mind.ilstu.edu/curriculum/neurons_intro/neurons_intro.php.

3   U.S. Department for Health and Human Services, *Understanding the Effects of Maltreatment on Brain Development*, accessed January 7, 2013, https://www.childwelfare.gov/pubs/issue_briefs/brain_development/how.cfm.

4   Bryan Kolb and Robbin Gibb, "Brain Plasticity and Behavior in the Developing Brain," *Journal of the Canadian Academy of Child and Adolescent Psychiatry* 20.4 (November 2011): 266.

over 10,000 other neurons.[5] Forming new connections between neurons is an intricate process which allows for brain plasticity.

Brain Plasticity

Brain plasticity can be defined as the brain's ability to change structure and function.[6] But brain plasticity does not mean the brain changes its shape in the way a moldable material can. Nor are all parts of the brain equally plastic, with the cerebral cortex — the place where our cognitive thinking occurs — showing much greater plasticity than other regions. Brain plasticity does not mean the brain is infinitely malleable or that completely new brain structures can grow, but the brain can change the way it functions and how its cells are "wired" to each other.[7] In this light, brain plasticity refers to the ways in which the functional pathways in our brain can be strengthened by use over time. Likewise, other pathways can be discarded or severely weakened. Thus, the way we process information and the parts of the brain we use are central to the concept of brain plasticity.

The human brain has much greater plasticity at younger ages and less plasticity when older, with synapse development reaching its peak between ages one and two.[8] Our genetic code provides the general outlines of the connections between neurons in the brain, but the vast network of synapses is guided into place by various environmental cues and signals. Some theorize the brain overproduces both neurons and synapses in order for the young child to adapt to environmental changes. Bryan Kolb and Robbin Gibb of the University of Lethbridge compare the process of neuron and synapse formation in early childhood to a sculptor making a statue: "Just like a sculptor who creates a statue with a block of stone and a chisel to remove the unwanted pieces, the brain has a parallel system in which unneeded cells and connections are

---

5   W. B. Rouse, K. R. Boff, P. Sanderson, and David F. Batten, "Plasticity and Causal History in Complex Adaptive Systems: The Case of the Human Brain," *Information Knowledge Systems Management* 10 (2011): 331.

6   Bryan Kolb and Ian Q. Whishaw, "Brain Plasticity and Behavior," *Annual Review of Psychology* 49:1 (1998): 43.

7   Aage R. Moller, *The Malleable Brain: Benefits and Harms from Plasticity of the Brain* (New York: Nova Biomedical Books, 2009), 28.

8   Bryan Kolb and Robbin Gibb, "Brain Plasticity and Behavior in the Developing Brain," 266.

removed by cell death and synaptic pruning."[9] Scientists once believed brain plasticity was restricted to critical times in childhood development, but new research confirms the adult brain can also change its structure by function and activity.[10]

Since brain plasticity is much more pronounced at young ages, a child's early environment can have dramatic effects on development of the brain, a truth painfully made clear by recent research on orphans in Romania. During the reign of Nicolae Ceaușescu (ruled 1965–1989), Romania instituted a policy of compulsory fertility in which contraception was illegal and families had to pay a punitive tax if they had less than five children. These policies precipitated an orphan crisis in which unwanted children were raised by the state in facilities where one caregiver usually had charge over numerous small infants. In such an environment, children do not receive the normal amount of personal love and attention. In 2012, research published in the prestigious *Proceedings of the National Academy of Science* compared Romanian children raised in an institutionalized environment to those raised by a family or in foster care. The institutionalized children showed significantly less brain development as compared to the other children. However, institutionalized children moved to foster care did show significant improvement in brain development, suggesting the possibility for children to "catch up" to a certain degree even following extremely difficult circumstances.[11] The experience of the Romanian orphans demonstrates both the greater degree of brain plasticity at a young age and the detrimental effects of negative childhood experiences on brain development.

Research clearly indicates experience dependent changes in brain organization can continue throughout life. In other words, certain changes in the way the brain is structured are clearly related to our interaction with the world in which we live. While many details of brain plasticity are not yet understood, certain accepted principles are part of an emerging consensus about the topic. First, experience dependent changes in the brain tend to be focused in one particular area related to the specific stimulus and are not widespread across the brain. For example, psychoactive drugs may produce a wide range of be-

---

9 Ibid.

10 David F. Batten, "Plasticity and Causal History in Complex Adaptive Systems: The Case of the Human Brain," 331.

11 Margaret A. Sheridan, Nathan A. Fox, Charles H. Zeanah, Katie A. McLaughlin, and Charles A. Nelson, III, "Variation in Neural Development As A Result of Exposure To Institutionalization Early in Childhood," *Proceedings of the National Academy of Sciences of the United States of America* 109.32 (July 23, 2012), accessed January 14, 2014, http://www.pnas.org/content/early/2012/07/17/1200041109.full.pdf+html?sid=dbeea634-db89-4bbc-9336-7903edf61fdd.

havior, but their effects on the brain seem to be focused in particular areas.[12] Next, experiences earlier in life can influence the way we interpret later experiences, meaning various experiences interact with each other to affect neural pathways. Third, as noted above, age greatly influences brain plasticity. Even more interestingly, research in animals indicates similar stimuli elicit different responses based on age.[13] Finally, not all brain plasticity is good. For example, maladaptive behavior of drug addicts could be the result of changes in the brain due to the influence of drugs.[14] But how does the burgeoning science of brain plasticity inform our view of the way we handle sexual temptation? Research into pornographic addiction offers us some insight in this area.

Brain Plasticity and Pornography

Addiction to pornography leads to negative consequences in the male brain as a result of extended use of sexually explicit material. Extended exposure to pornography not only damages a man spiritually, but recent findings indicate the male brain itself is seriously affected by exposure to pornography. In *Wired for Intimacy: How Pornography Hijacks the Male Brain,* William Struthers of Wheaton College details the manner in which use of pornography has destructive effects on the male brain, effects closely associated with brain plasticity. When a man views pornography, a complex cascade of neurological, hormonal, and neurochemical events are set into motion. Memories about how to respond to pornography are set off and psychological, emotional, and behavioral responses begin. As the pattern of arousal and response to pornography continues, it deepens the neurological pathway associated with sexual desire.[15]

To explain the way pornography affects neural pathways, Struthers uses the analogy of a trail in the forest. Continuous use of a path in the woods by hikers eventually creates a visible trail. Each successive hiker makes the trail wider, deeper, and easier to follow. In a similar way, each successive viewing of pornography creates neural paths setting the course for the next time an erotic image is viewed. Struthers says, "Over time these neural paths become

---

12   Bryan Kolb and Robbin Gibb, "Brain Plasticity and Behavior in the Developing Brain," 268.

13   Ibid, 269.

14   Ibid. The authors list eight general principles of brain plasticity, but I have listed the four most relevant for my topic.

15   William M. Struthers, *Wired for Intimacy: How Pornography Hijacks the Male Brain* (Downers Grove, IL: InterVarsity Press, 2009), 106.

wider as they are repeatedly traveled with each exposure to pornography. They become the automatic pathway through which interactions with women are routed. The neural circuitry anchors the process solidly in the brain."[16] He goes on to say that the path can become more like a neural-Grand Canyon through which images of all women are destined to flow and concludes this tragic description of the destructive effects of pornography by saying, "[Men viewing porn] have unknowingly created a neurological circuit that imprisons their ability to see women rightly as created in God's image."[17]

Consistent and repetitive viewing of pornography results in the construction of strong neural pathways in the brain. In this way, pornography becomes addictive, with stronger and more extreme forms needed to achieve the erotic "high" associated with a person's first porn use. As with any addiction, the earlier the exposure the more quickly a person will become addicted. For example, a twelve-year-old will become addicted after one or two viewings and a twenty-year-old may take three or four viewings.[18] Unlike the positive benefits of brain plasticity associated with children mastering a musical instrument, brain plasticity is also connected to becoming a compulsive slave to erotic images. The effects of pornography teach us a person's sexual activities actually affect the very wiring of the brain.

Brain Plasticity and Born-This-Way Arguments

How does the concept of brain plasticity inform a Christian response to born-this-way arguments regarding homosexuality? While brain plasticity in and of itself does not explain all same-sex attraction, it can help us understand our own moral accountability based on our response to temptations we face. Furthermore, the negative effects of childhood maltreatment on brain plasticity reinforce the importance of healthy childhood nurture for many areas of development, including sexual identity. Brain plasticity helps us begin to grasp the serious nature of sexual temptation in general and same-sex attraction in particular.

Many born-this-way arguments assume a person experiencing same-sex attraction is not responsible in any way for the desires he or she experiences. But

---

16 Ibid., 85.

17 Ibid.

18 Fern Sutton, licensed sexual therapist, personal email correspondence, February 12, 2013.

regardless of the origins of our sexual appetites, we are morally accountable for the manner in which we respond to temptation. Desires and lusts we feed will certainly grow in intensity, and we are answerable for our management of the moral messages we allow into our lives. This is no less true for homosexual temptations than for any other type of temptation: What we feed will grow. This growth in a temptation's strength includes construction of stronger neural pathways with each subsequent indulgence of impure messages.

I realize some may take offense that I am moving from a discussion of pornography's effects on the brain to homosexuality. Some may protest that pornography is exploitive while the goal of the gay rights movement is to allow two loving people the right to marry or live as a same-sex couple in a free and open way. But my emphasis is on the analogy between two sexual habits. While some gay romances may in fact be free of exploitation or abuse, both pornography and homosexuality are forms of sexual expression inconsistent with biblical ethics. In this way, the manner in which pornography affects the brain informs our understanding of how other sexual choices, both good and bad, affect the brain as well.

While it is tempting for Christians to explain away all homosexual desires as a result of indulgence in impure thoughts or relationships and the subsequent reinforcement of neural pathways, brain plasticity does not explain all same-sex attraction. Yet the thoughts we indulge and the sexual practices we embrace can become habit-forming and compulsive, a compulsivity linked to changes in neural pathways in the brain brought about by the habits themselves. Perhaps Jesus himself had this very dynamic in mind when he said, "Everyone who commits sin is a slave of sin" (John 8:34). Sin can become compulsive and addictive, so much so that indulging in a particular sin itself feels natural and good.

The emerging science of brain plasticity also reinforces Christian concern for healthy family dynamics in early childhood. Christians insist children should be treasured by parents in a wholesome way. The tragic example of the stunted brain development in institutionalized children deprived of consistent affection reinforces the long standing Christian assertion that a family with a loving father and mother is the best place for a child to be raised, with the dynamic of a loving home being positively associated with healthy brain development during the stages of greater brain plasticity during early childhood.

As was noted in the discussion of Freud, Christians insist an unusually premature sexual debut is quite detrimental to future sexual development. In fact, several studies have found a positive association between physical and sexual abuse, neglect, and witnessing violence in childhood with same-sex sexuality in adulthood. Lesbians and gay men report 1.6 to 4 times greater prevalence of sexual and physical abuse than heterosexuals.[19] Recent research related to males indicates both brother-to-brother incest and childhood sexual abuse by a male increases the likelihood of engaging in homosexual behavior or adopting an identity defined by same-sex attraction as an adult.[20] Several explanations have been proposed for this phenomenon of childhood abuse and higher rates of homosexuality, but it is possible that maltreatment itself increases the likelihood of homosexuality in adulthood. The relationship between abuse and homosexuality may be different for each child, with differences in the type of abuse and the gender of the child being important factors.[21] It is not clear the degree to which such abuse may affect a child's brain development, but the damage to brain development associated with other childhood trauma at least gives cause for concern. Experiences earlier in life shape and form the way we interpret later experiences. An early sexual experience and the context in which it occurred may become the lens through which subsequent sexual desires are viewed. A person's first sexual encounter can have a powerful organizing effect on the manner in which future sexual encounters are interpreted.

Again, for Christians it may be tempting to assume all homosexuality is associated with childhood sexual trauma which then fixed a same-sex attraction. Such an explanation is appealing to some because it would mean homosexuals are not "born this way," but instead become homosexual because of sexual abuse. The "answer" to homosexuality could then be found in building strong homes and protecting children. While the evidence points to a greater prevalence of childhood abuse among homosexuals, not all or nor even the majority of homosexuals experienced such abuse. But the higher incidence of childhood abuse among homosexuals should lead to compassion for people who underwent childhood trauma, trauma that may have greatly confused their understanding of God's purposes for sex. Furthermore, since the brain is much more malleable at a young age, perhaps neural pathways for understanding or interpreting sex were initiated which become much stronger with age. Conclusions at this point are merely speculative and future research may

---

19   Andrea L. Roberts, M. Maria Glymour, and Kareston C. Koenen, "Does Maltreatment in Childhood Affect Sexual Orientation in Adulthood?" *Archives of Sexual Behavior* 42.2 (February 2013): 161.

20   Beard, Keith W., Stephen L. O'Keefe, Sam Swindell, Sandra S. Stroebel, Karen Griffee, Debra H. Young, and Thomas D. Linz, "Brother-Brother Incest: Data From an Anonymous Computerized Survey," *Sexual Addiction and Compulsivity* 20.3 (July–September, 2013): 217– 53.

21   Ibid., 170.

reveal unexpected connections to abuse and childhood brain plasticity or no connection at all.

When discussing the way our brain processes information, we must be careful not to become biological reductionists, seeing humans as merely highly complex chemical machines interacting with a changing environment. At the same time, the brain is part of the human body created and designed by God for a purpose. Christians do not believe the body is evil, but we confess that humans are "fearfully and wonderfully made" (Ps. 139:14). The greatest affirmation that the human body is good is the Christian hope of the resurrection, wherein believers will receive a new and glorified body (Rom. 6:5; 1 Cor. 15:42–44). Furthermore, humans are made in the image of God (Gen. 1:26–28) and humans alone have the responsibility as God's image bearers to exercise stewardship over creation. At the same time, Christians also believe humans have a soul, the immaterial aspect of a human that transcends nature.[22] We are not *just* a body; we are a body-soul unity, the body and soul being connected at all points.[23] While the condition of our body certainly affects the way we feel about ourselves, we are more than a complex biochemical machine. Because humans have a soul, we can exercise volitional control over our response to appetites, desires and temptations. In this light, we can see how brain plasticity is affected by our volitional choices and at the same time affects the way we perceive what is pleasurable and good as opposed to what is both unpleasant and morally wrong. But some suggest it is not so much brain plasticity which accounts for same-sex desire, but instead assert changes in the brain prior to birth account for homosexuality. We will turn to these theories in the next chapter.

---

22   There are basically two ideas about the origin of the soul that have been advocated by orthodox Christians. The first is *creationist,* which believes God creates each individual soul at the moment He gives it a body. The second is *traducianist,* which holds that each soul is derived, along with the body, from the parents.

23   The view I am advocating for the relationship of the soul to the body is perhaps best described by Millard Erickson as "conditional unity." Consistent with this view is rejection of ideas claiming the human body is inherently evil. See Millard Erickson, *Christian Theology,* 2nd ed. (Grand Rapids: Baker, 1998), 554–57.

CHAPTER 5

Homosexuality and Prenatal Hormones

THE UNIVERSAL FELLOWSHIP of Metropolitan Community Churches (MCC) is a denomination specifically for homosexuals. Founded in Los Angeles in 1968 by Troy Perry, the church claims to be a Christian fellowship for lesbians, gays, bisexual, and transgendered people. As a young man, Perry preached and served in various Pentecostal churches, but eventually he divorced his wife, embraced the homosexual lifestyle, and began the MCC in his living room. Perry describes his own journey in *The Lord is My Shepherd and He Knows I'm Gay*. In a bizarre passage, he reflects on his own purported pre-conception existence and says:

> One thing is certain about me: I feel I have a total sense memory that predates my birth by a good long time. It's like being a seedling soul in two parts, your mother's and your father's genes. I have an awareness of having been a seedling — a physical presence in my father's sperm and in my mother's ovum before they were united.[1]

While Perry's statement is strange, it apparently reflects his belief that he has both male and female aspects to his gender, thus partly accounting for his homosexual identity. What is of interest is the way he connects this back to his identity in the womb (and even before!). Much like Troy Perry's odd recounting of prenatal memories, many born-this-way arguments regarding homosexuality point back to prenatal factors as the source of a person's adult sexual orientation. Specifically, many pro-homosexual writers claim prenatal hormones "feminized" the brains of embryonic boys or "masculinized" the brains of embryonic girls, thus accounting for same sex attraction as adults.

---

1 Troy Perry, *The Lord Is My Shepherd and He Knows I'm Gay* (Los Angeles: Nash Publishing, 1972), 10.

Born-this-way arguments often assert that particular patterns of exposure to prenatal hormones can cause children to be born with a homosexual orientation. In other words, the hypothesis is that gender and sexual orientation are prenatally determined by hormonal influences. A seminal article advocating this theory was published in 1987 by Lee Ellis and Ashley Ames. Ellis and Ames claimed "sexual orientation in all mammals is primarily determined by the degree to which the nervous system is exposed to testosterone, its metabolite estradiol, and to certain other sex hormones while neuro-organization is taking place."[2] They were basically claiming that if a person gets a low dose of testosterone prenatally, she or he will be attracted to males. At the same time, high levels of prenatal testosterone create attraction to females. In particular, they claimed these inordinate testosterone levels affect the development of the hypothalamic brain structures. Furthermore, they asserted sexual orientation is determined between the middle of the second and the end of the fifth month of prenatal development.[3] One of the major factors they believed influenced the level of testosterone one receives is the amount of stress a mother encounters during pregnancy. The Ames-Ellis hypothesis has been often repeated in the years since and is embraced by many born-this-way advocates.[4] The theory has an explanatory force which many find appealing.

Does over-exposure or under-exposure to certain prenatal hormones really predispose someone to homosexuality as an adult? In this chapter, we will see that while prenatal hormones are essential for gender development in the womb and that some real problems can develop when the process does not proceed correctly, the born-this-way argument that prenatal hormones unalterably fix same-sex attraction has not been proven. To explore this subject, we will first explain the basics of how boys and girls develop in gender typical ways in the womb. Then, we will examine three specific instances when embryonic gender development does not progress correctly: Congenital Adrenal Hyperplasia, Androgen Insensitivity Syndrome, and 5-Alpha Reductase Deficiency. We will then conclude with a summary of born-this-way arguments regarding prenatal hormones along with a Christian evaluation and response.

---

2   Lee Ellis and M. Ashley Ames, "Neurohormonal Functioning and Sexual Orientation: A Theory of Homosexuality-Heterosexuality," *Psychological Bulletin* 101.2 (March 1, 1987): 248.

3   Ibid.

4   Wilson and Rahman define the prenatal androgen theory by saying "homosexuality in males is owing to under-masculinization (the partial absence of androgenizing effects) and lesbianism in women is because of over-masculinization (excess androgenizing effects) during early brain development." Glenn Wilson and Qazi Rahman, *Born Gay: The Psychobiology of Sex Orientation* (London: Peter Owen Publishers, 2008), 70.

Boys, Girls, Hormones, and Sexual Differentiation

What differentiates boys from girls? This question is central to many born-this-way arguments and requires a brief summary of prenatal gender-specific development.[5] As we will see, the prenatal process of gender differentiation follows a particular order: (1) the presence or absence of a Y chromosome, followed by (2) the development of ovaries or testes, which then leads to (3) the differentiation of internal male or female reproductive systems, and concludes with (4) the growth of external gender-appropriate genitalia.

The sex chromosomes a child inherits from his or her parents are the most vital and crucial aspect of gender differentiation. Genetically, girls have two X chromosomes while boys have one X and one Y chromosome, thus determining a child's sex and accounting for the physical differences we recognize as male and female. Of critical importance at this point in this process of prenatal gender development is the presence or absence of the SRY gene on the Y chromosome.[6] The main job of the SRY gene is to initiate a cascade of events which will promote development of the testes, and the testes will in turn produce hormones necessary for male genital development. If a functional SRY gene is absent or is present but does not function, an XY child will not develop in a male-typical way.[7]

Testes or ovaries develop first in prenatal development and then release hormones which drive the maturation of both the internal reproductive system and external genitalia.[8] At the very earliest stages of prenatal development, both male and female embryos have an identical nascent structure called the "gonadal ridge" (aka "genital ridge") which will develop into ovaries in girls and testes in boys, a differentiation which begins between weeks five and eight of pregnancy. After the gonads and the internal reproductive system have de-

---

5   Scientists generally do not like to use the word "gender" as a synonym for "sex," but I will do so.

6   Serge Nef and Luis F. Parada, "Hormones in Male Sexual Development," *Genes and Development* 14 (2000): 3075. The SRY gene was not isolated and sequenced until 1990.

7   Sometimes the SRY gene gets transferred to the X chromosome resulting in XX males. *See* Emmanuèle C Délot and Eric J. Vilain, "Nonsyndromic 46, XX Testicular Disorder of Sex Development," *Gene Reviews* last updated May 7, 2015, accessed May 19, 2015, http://www.ncbi.nlm.nih.gov/books/NBK1416/.

8   Liisa A. M. Galea, Kristian A. Uban, Jonathan R. Epp, Susanne Brummelte, Cindy K. Barha, Wendy L. Wilson, Stephanie E. Lieblich, and Jodi L. Pawluski, "Endocrine Regulation Of Cognition and Neuroplasticity: Our Pursuit to Unveil The Complex Interaction Between Hormones, the Brain, and Behavior," *Canadian Journal of Experimental Psychology* 62.4 (December 2008): 247.

veloped, gender-specific external genitalia begin to form and are identifiable between weeks thirteen and sixteen.

The entire process of prenatal gender-specific development is moved along by the release of hormones at specific junctures. Hormones can be thought of as chemical messengers and the proper amounts must be released at the right time for normal sexual development. Male hormones are called "androgens" and the correct ones must be released at the right time and in the proper amounts for male development to take place unhindered. The most well-known androgen is testosterone and it peaks in male babies at around sixteen weeks development, but after this declines to around the same level as in prenatal females. Sexual development in females is also driven by hormones, or more specifically the absence of male hormones. Since females do not have the SRY gene, the primitive gonads become ovaries and not testes. Since there are no testes, not enough testosterone is produced to masculinize genitalia and, thus, the external genitalia develop in a female manner.

Significant debate surrounds the degree to which hormones masculinize or feminize the brain in prenatal development with corresponding arguments about the purported differences between the brains of adult males and females. What does seem clear is hormones affect the human brain later in prenatal development than they do the external genitalia. Gillies and McArthur stress the key factor in the process is "the masculinizing/defeminizing effect of testosterone," meaning the increased testosterone surge in males masculinizes the male brain.[9] What is counter-intuitive is that the testosterone's role in shaping the male brain occurs because it is converted into estradiol (an estrogen) in the male brain.[10] The purported differences between male and female brains will be explored in more detail in the next chapter. To understand born-this-way arguments relating to prenatal hormones, the important point to remember is the scientific consensus is that during prenatal development male and female brains normally have different patterns of hormone exposure.

Sometimes the normal gender typical prenatal development of a baby does not move forward in the expected way. On rare occasions, children with XX chromosomes develop male-typical genitalia and in other cases children with XY chromosomes develop female-typical genitalia. Other children may have ambiguous genitalia, presenting both male and female characteristics. Such

---

9   Glenda E. Gillies and Simon McArthur, "Estrogen Actions in the Brain and the Basis for Differential Action in Men and Women," *Pharmacological Reviews* 62.2 (2010): 158.

10   See Melody V. Wu, Devanand S. Manoli, Eleanor J Fraser, Jennifer K. Coats, Jessica Tollkuhn, Shin-Ichiro Honda, Nobuhiro Harada, and Nirao M Shah, "Estrogen masculinizes neural pathways and sex-specific behaviors," *Cell* 139.1 (October 2, 2009): 61–72.

instances of irregular sexual development are called Disorders of Sexual Development (DSD), a broad term describing situations when the reproductive organs or genitalia do not develop normally. Among the many DSDs, three specific ones are often referenced in born-this-way arguments: Congenital Adrenal Hyperplasia, Androgen Insensitivity Syndrome, and 5-Alpha Reductase Deficiency.[11] Each of these disorders are important because they give us insight into the way in which abnormal prenatal hormone exposure affects a person's sexual identity as an adult. Since ethics protocols do not allow scientists to perform experiments on humans to see what happens when a child is exposed to abnormal levels of sex hormones, DSDs provide a form of a "natural experiment" giving us some idea of how atypical patterns of hormone exposure affect one's sexual development and sexual identity as an adult.

Congenital Adrenal Hyperplasia

Congenital Adrenal Hyperplasia (CAH) is a family of inherited conditions. The most common form of CAH, and our focus here, is 21-hydroxlase deficiency, a disorder caused by mutations in a gene on chromosome 6.[12] There are two basic kinds of CAH: Non-classical and classical, with the classical form being more serious. Non-classic CAH, also called "late onset" CAH, is not life-threatening and does not result in ambiguous genitalia. But classical CAH is of special interest to born-this-way arguments because it causes the body to produce too much androgen resulting in females born with genitalia more characteristic of males.[13] Boys born with CAH may have an enlarged

---

11   Ames and Ellis mentioned these three specifically.

12   CAH is an autosomal recessive trait. The carrier frequency for the defective gene is 1:50 to 1:60 in Western countries. Florbela Ferreira, Joao Martin Martins, Sónia do Vale, Rui Esteves, Garção Nunes and Isabel do Carmo, "Rare and Severe Complications of Congenital Adrenal Hyperplasia due to 21-hydroxylase deficiency: A Case Report," *Journal of Medical Case Reports* 7.39 (2013): 2. CAH affects the production of steroids in the adrenal glands. People with CAH do not have an enzyme required to make either or both of two important hormones: cortisol and aldosterone. The absence of either hormone affects a person's health because cortisol helps maintain blood sugar levels and is needed when we are sick or injured while aldosterone enables our bodies to retain salt in order to balance fluids and electrolytes.

13   Lawrence Baskin, Hillary Copp, Michael DiSandro, Ann Arnhym, Angelique Champeau, Christine Kennedy, "Disorders of Sexual Development," University of California, San Francisco, Pediatric Urology, March 18, 2013, accessed July 28, 2014, https://urology.ucsf.edu/sites/urology.ucsf.edu/files/uploaded-files/basic-page/disorders_of_sex_development_o.pdf.

penis, but they otherwise do not have ambiguous genitalia. Estimates vary, but perhaps 1:15,000 children are born with some form of classical CAH while perhaps as many as 1:1,000 children are born with the non-classical form.[14]

Classic CAH is usually detected in infancy or early childhood, and occurs in two different forms: salt-wasting and simple virilizing (non-salt-wasting). Both forms of classic CAH can result in ambiguous genitalia in girls. In salt-wasting classical CAH, the child has a dangerously low level of sodium in the blood because of the inability to synthesize aldosterone. In addition to ambiguous genitalia, the child can experience dehydration, low blood pressure, shock, and even death if untreated. In simple virilizing classical CAH, the child has a partial enzyme deficiency in which the adrenal glands produce some aldosterone and cortisol, but not enough. As a result, girls with this form of classical CAH have ambiguous genitalia without the other life-threatening elements associated with Salt Wasting CAH. The level of ambiguity in the genitalia of a girl with CAH varies greatly depending on the severity of her particular case.[15] In milder forms, there may be no great difficulty for the child, while other cases may be so dramatic that the girl is initially assigned the wrong gender at birth.

Research indicates a higher than average rate of homosexual activity among women with CAH than controls. In 1992, researchers from Germany studied 34 women with CAH and 14 sisters without CAH who served as controls. They found 20% of the CAH women wished for and/or had homosexual relationships. Furthermore, women with the salt-wasting variant of classical CAH differed in their sexual orientation more markedly than girls with the simple-virilizing form of CAH.[16]

In 1996, a Canadian study evaluated 34 women with CAH and compared them to 18 controls drawn from their sisters and cousins. Compared to the controls, the CAH women recalled more cross-gender role behavior and less comfort with their sense of "identity" during childhood, but the two

---

14   The incidence of classical 21-hydroxlase deficiency varies between 1:11,800 and 1:21,800, according to population background. Karen Lin-Su, Saroj Nimkarn, and Maria I. New, "Diagnosis and Management of Congenital Adrenal Hyperplasia," *Pediatric, Adolescent, and Young Adult Gynecology*, Albert Altchek and Liane Deligdisch, eds. (West Sussex, UK: Wiley-Blackwell, 2009), 25 suggest 1:14,000 have classical CAH while the University of Michigan Health System suggests 1:15,000. See Kyla Rose, Talyah Sands, and David E. Sandberg, "Congenital Adrenal Hyperplasia," University of Michigan Health System, last updated May 2011, accessed December 9, 2014, http://www.med.umich.edu/yourchild/topics/cah.htm.

15   The severity varies with the level of mutation in the CYP21A2 Gene.

16   R. W. Dittman, M. E. Kappes, M. H. Kappes, "Sexual Behavior in Adolescent and Adult Females With Congenital Adrenal Hyperplasia," *Psychoneuroendocrinology* 17 (May–July, 1992): 153–70.

groups did not differ in degree of gender dysphoria in adulthood.[17] These trends noted, the vast majority of CAH women in this study self-identified as heterosexual females. The researchers concluded "the results of our study are consistent with the hypothesis that excessive exposure to prenatal androgens in women with CAH shifts psychosexual differentiation to a point somewhere between a female-typical pattern and a male-typical pattern."[18] Yet, they then qualified their conclusion by admitting "the effects were found for only some aspects of psychosexual differentiation" and that "the majority of the CAH women were classified as exclusively heterosexual in their sexual orientation, despite the clear evidence that such women were exposed to prenatal levels of androgen that are in the range of normal males."[19] Research from 2008 also indicates more women with CAH are homosexual than the general population.[20] However, in this recent research the data must be read carefully as the authors use a Kinsey score of two or higher to place someone in the category of homosexual attraction, which is a very broad definition of homosexual.

Other findings regarding CAH women, especially in its classic form, indicates they exhibit more male typical behavior than other girls. They have more male-typical play in childhood than unaffected girls, are more likely to use physical aggression in conflict situations, have less interest in infants and nurturing activities, have spatial and mathematical abilities similar to men, and have more interest in male activities and careers.[21]

CAH is often cited favorably in born-this-way arguments. The findings that CAH women are more likely than average to self-identify as homosexual are significant because an average of around 1.1% of women in the general popu-

---

17   Kenneth J. Zucker et al., "Psychosexual Development of Women with Congenital Adrenal Hyperplasia," *Hormones and Behavior* 30 (1996): 300.

18   Ibid., 314.

19   Ibid.

20   Heino F. L. Meyer-Bahlburg, Curtis Dolezal, Susan W. Baker, and Maria I. New, "Sexual orientation in women with classical or non-classical congenital adrenal hyperplasia as a function of degree of prenatal androgen excess," *Archives of Sexual Behavior* 37.1 (2008): 85–99. See also Meyer-Bahlburg's research from 2001 in which he surveyed older CAH people raised as girls. Thirty-seven percent rated themselves as homosexual, bisexual, or had fewer heterosexual experiences than a control group, a finding which seems high compared to other research. *See* Heino F. L. Meyer-Bahlburg, "Gender and Sexuality in Classic Congenital Adrenal Hyperplasia," *Endocrinology and Metabolism Clinics of North America* 30.1 (March 2001): 155–71.

21   Deborah P. Merke and Stefan R. Bornstein, "Congenital Adrenal Hyperplasia," *Lancet* 365 (June 18, 2005): 2131.

lation self-identify as exclusively homosexual. Thus, some argue the inordinate exposure to male typical hormones during gestation predisposed these women towards homosexual attraction.

While it is clear exposure to too much prenatal androgen affects girls' genitalia, born-this-way advocates go further and claim the brains of at least some CAH girls are also masculinized. Commenting on the higher incidence of male-typical behavior in CAH girls, Merke and Bornstein suggest "exposure to excess androgens during prenatal development influences brain development."[22] Wilson and Rahman also believe prenatal hormones play a major factor in establishing a homosexual identity and say CAH "provides an interesting case because it allows us to examine the role of prenatal or sex hormones on sexual preferences while holding gender socialization reasonably constant."[23]

Born-this-way arguments assert that just as excess male hormones virilize a CAH girl's genitalia, these same hormones affect their brains as well and cause them to have a higher incidence of same-sex attraction and male-typical behavior. Born- this-way advocates then argue the same thing has happened to homosexuals, claiming they were also exposed to abnormal amounts of hormones prenatally and this subsequently affects the way their brains operate and is the source of their same sex attraction.

Born-this-way arguments based on CAH face at least three objections. First, intrinsic difficulties are related to the long period between when the child is exposed to prenatal hormones and the overt manifestation of homosexuality in adulthood.[24] Directly connecting a behavior with as many variables as homosexuality to a prenatal event is challenging indeed.

Second, CAH girls with masculinized genitalia have experienced a profoundly challenging childhood which is completely different from the childhood experiences of the vast majority of self-identified homosexuals. Many CAH girls underwent surgery to modify highly masculinized genitalia. Some encountered significant embarrassment or confusion when they discovered their bodies were different from other children. In some cases, children became aware that their own parents may have had doubts over the child's gender. As adults, many CAH women claim the disease affects their sex life and

---

22   Ibid.

23   Glenn Wilson and Qazi Rahman, *Born Gay: The Psychobiology of Sex Orientation* (London: Peter Owen Publishers, 2005), 74.

24   This insight is from Jacques Balthazart, "Minireview: Hormones and Human Sexual Orientation," *Endocrinology* 152.8 (August 2011): 2,940. Balthazart views the prenatal theory positively.

that they are dissatisfied with their genital appearance.[25] While homosexuality occurs more frequently in girls with CAH, it is difficult to separate the effects of excessive prenatal androgen exposure from these various sociological difficulties faced by people with CAH. As one group of researchers says, "Women with CAH have been subjected to major developmental interference and it is well to bear this in mind when interpreting psychological reports."[26]

The third objection to born-this-way arguments based on CAH is that the vast majority of women with CAH do not self-identify as homosexual. Thus, prenatal androgen exposure does not seem necessary or sufficient for a female to self-identify as a homosexual. Born-this-way arguments based on CAH begin with the fact that prenatal hormones have *some* influence on the sexual identity of CAH females and then wrongly infer homosexual behavior in people without DSDs is thus predetermined by an abnormal pattern of prenatal hormone exposure. This is certainly imprudent reasoning. A more restrained view of the data acknowledges the higher incidence of homosexuality among CAH women, but also notes the robust finding that the vast majority of CAH women self-identify as heterosexual. Therefore, CAH indicates prenatal hormones may have an undetermined level of influence on sexual identity, but such influences are neither necessary nor sufficient for the development of a homosexual identity.

Androgen Insensitivity Syndrome

Androgen Insensitivity Syndrome (AIS) is an X-chromosome linked genetic DSD. Children born with AIS are genetically male (1 X and 1 Y chromosome), but because they are unable to respond to androgens (male hormones), their genitalia either develop as females or are under-masculinized to various degrees. AIS actually represents a spectrum of defects which are divided into three different types: Complete Androgen Insensitivity (CAIS) in which XY children have completely female external genitalia; Partial Androgen Insensitivity (PAIS) in which XY children may have predominantly female, pre-

---

25   A. Nordenskjöld, G. Holmdahl, L Frisén, H. Falhammar, H. Filipsson, M. Thorén, P. O. Janson, K. Hagenfeldt, "Type of Mutation and Surgical Procedure Affect Long-Term Quality of Life for Women With Congenital Adrenal Hyperplasia," *Journal of Clinical Endocrinology and Metabolism* 93.2 (February 2008): 380–86.

26   Cara Megan Ogilvie, Naomi S. Crouch, Gill Rumsby, Sarah M. Creightont, Lih-Mei Liao, and Gerard S. Conway, "Congenital Adrenal Hyperplasia in Adults: A Review of Medical, Surgical, and Psychological Issues," *Clinical Endocrinology* 64 (2006): 7.

dominantly male, or ambiguous genitalia; and Mild Androgen Insensitivity (MAIS) in which XY children have typical male genitalia.[27] Estimates of the frequency of CAIS vary widely from 1:20,000 to 1:64,000 live male births. [28] CAIS children are almost always raised as females.

In CAIS, XY children appear to be females externally, but they do not have a uterus or ovaries and, thus, do not menstruate and cannot have children. At puberty, female sex characteristics such as breasts develop but pubic hair usually does not develop or develops only lightly. CAIS children usually have undescended testes which can become cancerous if they are not removed (usually after puberty).

The vast majority of CAIS girls have a heterosexual female identity. In 2003, Melissa Hines of the University of London along with colleagues from Cambridge compared 22 women with CAIS to 22 women without CAIS who were matched for age, race, and sex-of-rearing. The researchers found the women with CAIS were just as likely to be heterosexual and living with a male partner as the non-CAIS women.[29] In. 2009, Migeon and Pappas interviewed 15 CAIS women and 14 of them self-identified as heterosexual.[30] To summarize, CAIS women are genetically XY, but the vast majority are attracted to men.

In many ways, PAIS is more frustrating for both parents and the affected children. While CAIS results in a child that looks completely female from all external appearances, this is not so with PAIS. In PAIS, presentation of the external genitalia is highly variable and can range from a urethral opening on the underside of the penis along with a vagina-like pouch to micopenis and a scrotum that has not fused. Often, PAIS children have undescended testes. Usually, infants with PAIS are assigned to either the male or female gender

---

27   Bruce Gottlieb, Lenore K. Beitel, and Mark A. Trifiro, "Androgen Insensitivity Syndrome," *Gene Reviews,* last updated July 10, 2014, accessed August 6, 2014, http://www.ncbi .nlm.nih.gov/books/NBK1429/.

28   Angeliki Galani, Sophia Kitsiou-Tzeli, Christalena Sofokleous, Emmanuel Kanavakis, and Ariadni Kalpini-Mavrou, "Androgen Insensitivity Syndrome: Clinical Features and Molecular Defects," *Hormones* 7.3 (2008): 219. See also Angelo Poletti, Paola Negri-Cesi, Luciano Martini, "Reflections on the Diseases Linked to Mutations of the Androgen Receptor," *Endocrine* 28.3 (December 2005): 243–62. These authors actually suggest 1:20,400 births, but it is difficult to know if they mean AIS in general or CAIS in particular.

29   Melissa Hines, S. Faisal Ahmed, Leuan A. Hughes, "Psychological outcomes and gender-related development in complete androgen insensitivity syndrome," *Archives of Sexual Behavior* 32.2 (April 2003): 93–101.

30   Claude Migeon and Kara Pappas, "Androgen Insensitivity and Gonadal Dysgenesis," in *Pediatric, Adolescent, and Young Adult Gynecology,* Albert Altchek and Liane Deligdisch, eds. (West Sussex, UK: Wiley-Blackwell, 2009), 47.

at or soon after birth, depending to some extent on the feminine appearance of the genitalia.[31] In an exhaustive survey of research on PAIS children, Tom Mazur found that while PAIS children do have higher incidences of gender dysphoria, they usually have stable gender identities and do not desire to change genders when they are older, with the best predictor of gender identity outcome in adulthood being the initial gender assignment.[32]

Do AIS children provide substantive evidence for born-this-way arguments? Again, pro-homosexual authors emphasize the fact CAIS adults are XY genetically, but generally self-identify as heterosexual women. They argue that an atypical pattern of exposure to prenatal hormones pushed CAIS children (XY) towards a sexual attraction to someone of the same genetic sex (XY). Born-this-way advocates assert something similar occurs in homosexuals, claiming they experienced a different pattern of exposure to prenatal hormones. This atypical pattern then "hard-wired" them to experience same-sex attraction.

But the born-this-way argument regarding AIS, and CAIS children in particular, is seriously flawed in a very significant way: CAIS children have bodies that *look female* and their self-identity as female is closely related to the fact they have female genitalia. It is natural for these children to look at themselves and conclude, "I am a girl." Furthermore, their parents raise the children as girls. They are socially brought into relationships as females; thus when they reach sexual maturity it is natural for them to feel attraction to males. Homosexuals do not have this shared experience. Generally speaking, homosexuals do not have genitalia which are discordant for their genetic sex. Pro-homosexual researcher Simon LeVay contends CAIS children offer evidence for the influence of prenatal hormones on sexual orientation, but even he admits research cannot "distinguish between biological and social factors, given that these individuals look like females and are raised as such."[33]

CAIS children provide a wonderful example of resiliency in spite of a DSD. Most live happy and satisfied lives. While their inability to respond to androgens provides fascinating insight into the prenatal development of genitalia, CAIS children do not necessarily prove a born-this-way argument for homosexuality. Raised and socially accepted as females, their experience of sexual

---

31 This summary of PAIS is from Tom Mazur, "Gender Dysphoria and Gender Change in Androgen Insensitivity or Micropenis," *Archives of Sexual Behavior* 34 (2005): 411–21; in *Sex and the Brain,* Gillian Einstein, ed. (Cambridge, MA: MIT Press, 2007), 669.

32 Ibid., 675.

33 Simon LeVay, *Gay, Straight, and the Reason Why: The Science of Sexual Orientation* (New York: Oxford University Press, 2010), 137.

development and maturity is radically different from the average homosexual male or lesbian.

In a similar way PAIS children do not demonstrate concrete proof of the born-this-way argument. The strongest factor for their gender identity is the gender they are assigned in childhood, and for most PAIS children this remains stable throughout their life. Generally speaking, they do not blend gender identities or imitate the opposite gender in the way in which transsexuals do.

5-ALPHA REDUCTASE DEFICIENCY

One of the most intriguing DSDs is 5-Alpha Reductase Deficiency. This DSD first gained attention in a 1974 article in *Science* which detailed the unique experience of a group of children in the Dominican Republic. These XY children were born with ambiguous genitalia, often including a vaginal pouch, and were raised as girls. But at puberty, their voice deepened, muscle mass increased, they did not develop breasts, and (most amazingly) the children's phallus enlarged and became a functional penis. As the drastic changes took place at puberty, the children often ceased identifying as females and began identifying as heterosexual males. The change was so dramatic that local townspeople referred to these children as "guevedoces," a term which means "penis at 12."[34]

The affected children in the Dominican Republic were diagnosed with 5-Alpha Reductase Deficiency, a recessive genetic disorder caused by a mutation of a gene on chromosome 2. The disorder is common in communities characterized by consanguineous marriages and isolated groups with the genetic defect have also been found in New Guinea and Turkey. People with the disorder are genetically XY but do not produce enough of the androgen dihydrotestosterone (DHT) which has a critical role in male prenatal sexual development. The shortage of this hormone disrupts the formation of the external sex organs before birth and results in the ambiguous genitalia. Sometimes the children are born with genitalia which are clearly male, but the penis is extremely small and urethra opening is located on the underside of the penis. In many cases the testes are undescended at birth, but later descend at puberty.[35] The surge of hormones at puberty causes substantial growth of

---

34   Julianne Imperato-McGinley, Luis Guerrero, Teofilo Gautier, Ralph E. Peterson, "Steroid 5-Alpha Reductase Deficiency in Man: An Inherited Form of Male Pseudohermaphroditism," *Science* 186 (December 27, 1974): 1213.

35   This paragraph summarized from "5 Alpha Reductase Deficiency," Genet-

the phallus. As adults, libido is intact and it is possible to achieve an erection. They are usually infertile, but there have been reported cases in which affected people were able to father children.[36]

Born-this-way arguments appeal to 5-Alpha Reductase Deficiency children for support in three primary ways. First, they claim these children prove gender is a vague concept which can change and vary throughout life. Again, many of these children are raised as girls but adopt a male identity at puberty. Many homosexual or transgender activists claim this supports their desire to move in and out of various gender roles at different stages of life.

Second, born-this-way advocates claim 5-alpha reductase deficiency supports their claim that environmental and sociological influences in sexual identity are trumped by genetic and biological factors. In spite of the fact these children were treated as girls, most of them adopt a male identity at puberty. In this way it is claimed the genetic and biological forces have a stronger affect than the expectations forced on them by others. Likewise, homosexuals often claim something similar is happening within themselves: regardless of expectations placed on them by their families, churches, or culture, they have an overriding genetic and biological drive towards same-sex attraction.

Finally, since 5-alpha reductase deficiency children are *born* with this condition, born-this-way advocates suggest they too have been born with an innate condition based on similar genetic or biological factors.

While 5-alpha reductase deficiency presents us with profound questions about the degree to which hormones affect sexual orientation, the condition does not necessarily prove the born-this-way argument. First, the condition is a diagnosable genetic defect which is clearly *caused* by a specific mutation. As we will see, no such causal relationship between a particular gene and same-sex attraction has been found, but only a weak correlation between some areas of interest in the human genome and an increased propensity for same-sex attraction.

Second, a strong case can be made that the children are male and should, in most cases, be raised as such. At the same time, there may be cases where the feminization is so profound that a female identity may be the best choice for

---

ics Home Reference, April 2008, accessed May 19, 2015, http://ghr.nlm.nih.gov/condition/5-alpha-reductase-deficiency.

36   Yuan-Shan Zhu and Julianne Imperato-McGinley, "Male Sexual Differentiation Disorder and 5-Alpha Reductase-2 Deficiency," *The Global Library of Women's Medicine,* last updated November 2008, accessed April 23, 2015, http://www.glowm.com/section_view/heading/Male%20Sexual%20Differentiation%20Disorder%20and%205%CE%B1-Reductase-2%20Deficiency/item/349.

the child. In either case, the children have a unique situation not shared by the vast majority of homosexuals. To say that many 5-alpha reductase deficiency children "change" their gender at puberty is imprecise: It is more accurate to say they discover the gender which was already latent at birth.

PRENATAL HORMONES AND BORN-THIS-WAY ARGUMENTS

Central born-this-way arguments regarding prenatal hormones are the experiences of children born with DSDs. CAH girls are sometimes born with masculinized genitalia. Though the vast majority of CAH girls are heterosexual, more of them than average identify as homosexual. In CAIS, a child is born with an XY genetic identity, but develops feminine genitalia and secondary sex characteristics. The vast majority of these children are raised as girls and adopt a heterosexual female identity. While both instances demonstrate the way in which the normal development of genitalia can diverge in different directions due to prenatal hormones along with expected challenges in sexual development, neither case proves the born-this-way claim that homosexuals are exposed to prenatal hormones which hardwire their brains towards same-sex attraction. 5-Alpha Reductase Deficiency children face unique challenges, but their experience of genital transformation at puberty is not similar to the average homosexual.

CAH, CAIS, and 5-Alpha Reductase Deficiency do demonstrate prenatal hormones can possibly play a modest role in the sexual identity of homosexual adults. The increased incidence of homosexuality among CAH women demonstrates prenatal hormones may push one's own sexual feelings in different ways. Likewise, the experience of the 5-alpha reductase boys demonstrates that they indeed do *feel* male even though they are often raised as female. But influence of hormones in children with these DSDs hardly *proves* a homosexual orientation is predetermined prior to birth. [37]

Born-this-way arguments also utilize DSD children in a deeper form of argumentation and claim the DSDs prove both sexual expression and gender

---

37 William Reiner of the University of Oklahoma extensively evaluated patients born with various extreme forms of DSDs, including 45 with cloacal exstrophy (exposed intra-abdominal structures) or aphallia (no penis). Of 73 patients with a DSD and a Y chromosome (genetic males), 60 were reared as female. But as adults 32 of the 60 (53%) declared a male identity. Reiner concluded that active prenatal androgen effects appeared to increase dramatically the likelihood of recognition of male sexual identity independent of sex-of-rearing. William G. Reiner, "Gender Identity and Sex-of-Rearing in Children with Disorders of Sexual Differentiation," *Journal of Pediatric Endocrinology and Metabolism* 18.6 (June 2005): 549–53.

are ambiguous ideas, claims often based on a strong appeal to the experience of 5-alpha reductase children. The existence of DSD children is used as evidence *against* the Christian claim that sex was designed by God to be enjoyed in marriage by a husband and a wife. Instead, pro-homosexual activists claim the existence of children with DSDs confirms the entire idea of appropriate roles for each sex is misguided, since some of these children do not easily fit into the category of male or female. But the existence of DSD children does not prove that sexuality as a whole is ambiguous and thus any form of sexual expression should be embraced. Instead, DSD children are evidence that we, in fact, live in a fallen world where things sometimes go awry in the normal process of development. A Christian anthropology insists on the goodness of the two genders of male and female while acknowledging the rare cases of children with DSDs and the wisdom needed to navigate their difficult circumstances.

Christians should show mercy, compassion and deep sensitivity for children who face unusual and rare challenges associated with DSDs. But do these cases mean we should suspend all judgment about the myriad of sexual choices adults make? No, they do not. Instead, these children and their challenges call for greater sensitivity and pastoral care for the families involved along with a patient evaluation of the best medical choices for the children involved. In John 9, Jesus showed mercy to a man born blind. In the same way, as his followers we should show mercy to children born with DSDs. That means we walk with their families through the many difficult questions of childhood and puberty, showing great patience with the children as they move into adulthood. But unlike homosexual activists, our message is *not* that the existence of DSDs means no sexual or gender boundaries exist, instead we help DSD children embrace the gender which best fits their own unique situation and encourage them to live in accordance with biblical sexual ethics.

Children with DSDs live at the tragic intersection of Genesis 1:26–28 and Genesis 3. On one hand, the Bible affirms the gift of gender as part of the goodness of creation when we are told God made males and females in the image of God (Gen. 1:27), a pattern which is repeated and affirmed in the New Testament (Matt. 19:4). At the same time, a real and historic space-time Fall has occurred and creation itself groans under the weight of sin's effects on nature (Gen. 3). This does not mean DSD children are somehow "more fallen" than other people, but it simply means they must deal earlier and more forthrightly with the fact we live in a radically disordered world. But the existence of DSDs does not mean gender is merely a social construction or that each person is free to choose whichever gender one prefers.

In short, DSDs are the exception and not the rule. In contrast, born-this-way arguments attempt to make these rare exceptions the rule. The existence of DSDs as rare exceptions actually *proves the standard* that there are only two genders. For example, if I tell my students, "Over fall break, you will not be required to submit your weekly homework," then I am asserting the rule that usually their homework is due every week. Likewise, when we encounter DSDs in which a child's genitalia do not appear clearly to be male or female, we are asserting that normally the genders of male and female are easily identifiable.

Born-this-way arguments regarding prenatal hormones very often reference experiments on rodents to substantiate their claims. Numerous experiments have been performed over recent decades in which rodents were over-exposed or under-exposed to male and female hormones in utero. In some cases, males in such experiments have demonstrated a propensity to mount other males or submit themselves to mounting. Likewise, female rodents in these experiments mimic male sexual behavior. But animals act instinctually and comparing their behavior to humans is problematic. Humans are *volitional*: we make choices based on many factors which are often difficult to interconnect. Comparing human behavior to rodents who have been exposed to discordant levels of hormones hardly proves homosexuality is morally neutral or praiseworthy. Furthermore, the level of hormones to which these rodents are exposed in experiments is typically quite high and it is very unlikely that homosexuals received such discordant levels of prenatal hormones.

Certainly prenatal hormones can have a profound influence, but it has not been proven that homosexuals experience abnormal levels of hormone exposure like those in children with DSDs. Christians *do not* claim prenatal hormones have no influence or effect on one's desires or inclinations. What we do insist upon is that we are not merely sexual automatons mercilessly unable to resist any desire whatsoever. Clearly, inordinate patterns of exposure to prenatal hormones can have adverse and multifaceted effects on normal development. The higher incidence of homosexuality in some DSD groups indicates a possible low to modest level of influence by prenatal hormones on adult sexual identity. But the experience of individuals with DSDs does not prove the pro-homosexual claim that homosexual males are born with female brains or that homosexual females are born with male brains. In the next chapter we will explore specific claims regarding various regions of the brain and born-this-way arguments and precisely what differences, if any, seem to exist between the brains of heterosexuals and homosexuals.

CHAPTER 6

Heterosexual and Homosexual Brain Differences

MANY CHRISTIANS HAVE EXPERIENCED a family member who has "come out of the closet" and announced he or she is a homosexual. One such friend of mine was quite surprised when his older brother announced to the family he was embracing the gay lifestyle. Eventually, my friend's brother claimed, "I have a male body, but I have a female brain. That's why I'm attracted to men." Apparently, his brother had encountered pro-homosexual arguments asserting homosexual men have a brain structure similar to heterosexual women. For my friend's brother, being "born this way" meant he was born with a woman's brain, was attracted to men, and thus was morally free to embrace the gay lifestyle.

But is this claim accurate? Are there substantial differences between the brains of heterosexuals and homosexuals? Do homosexual men have brains more like heterosexual women and do homosexual women have brains more like heterosexual men? In this chapter we will see that while there have been some intriguing findings regarding brain differences of heterosexuals and homosexuals, no definitive link has yet been discovered between a particular brain structure or pattern of organization which necessarily causes homosexuality. To grasp the issues related with these "gay brain" arguments, we will begin by summarizing gender-specific brain differences in animal research, then move to gender differences in the human brain, and conclude with a Christian evaluation of born-this-way arguments based on purported brain differences.

GENDER DIFFERENCES, BORN-THIS-WAY ARGUMENTS, AND RODENT BRAINS

Born-this-way arguments about sex-related brain differences find their origin in research on rodent brains.[1] One of the most interesting discoveries oc-

---

1   For example see Geoffrey Raisman and Pauline Field, "Sexual Dimorphism in the

curred in 1978 when a team of neurobiologists led by Roger Gorski of UCLA identified differences between the hypothalamus in male and female rats. They observed a small cluster of cells (or a "nucleus") in the hypothalamus that was five times larger in male rats than in female rats. The difference in this particular area was so pronounced, Gorski found he could determine the animal's sex with near 100% accuracy using only the naked eye to examine their brains.[2] This observable area of in rat brains was named the "sexually dimorphic[3] nucleus of the preoptic area" (SDN-POA). While we now know humans do not have a SDN-POA like rats do, this type of research on rodent brains set the trajectory for the following decades concerning scientific inquiry into gender-specific differences in the human brain and corresponding research concerning brain structure and homosexuality.[4] If the hypothalamus in rat brains was so very different, many researchers wondered if there were corresponding differences in the human hypothalamus which could explain sexual identity and desire.

At this point, some may wonder why research on rat brains is brought up in debates about homosexuality. From an evolutionary view, all mammals share a common ancestor. Dates for this common ancestor vary widely from between

---

Preoptic Area of the Rat," *Science* 173 (August 20, 1971): 731–33; Geoffrey Raisman and Pauline Field, "Sexual Dimorphism in the Neuropil of the Preoptic Area of the Rat and Its Dependence on Neonatal Androgen," *Brain Research* 54 (1973): 1–29.

2   Roger Gorski, J. H. Gordon, J. E. Shryne, and A. M. Southam, "Evidence for a Morphological Sex Difference Within the Medial Preoptic Area of the Rat," *Brain Research* 148 (1978): 333–46.

3   Dimorphic means "having two forms," and in this context refers to the observable differences between males and females.

4   A 1985 study by Dutch scientists Swaab and Fliers purportedly found an area of the human hypothalamus which corresponded to the SDN-POA in rats, being larger in males than in females. D. F. Swaab and E. Fliers, "A Sexually Dimorphic Nucleus in the Human Brain," *Science* 228 #4703 (May 1985): 1112–15. Subsequent studies have found these claims to be overstated. Most significantly, in 1989, a team led by Laura Allen, a postdoctoral assistant in Gorski's lab at UCLA, was not able to verify Swaab and Flier's claim that humans have a SDN-POA similar to rats. Swaab continues to defend his claim while often side-stepping those who reject his assertions. For example, see his discussion in his 2008 article in which he mentions Allen's research in which her team identified INAH 1–4. Swaab claims the INAH 1 is equivalent to his SDN-POA without mentioning that Allen et al. rejected his claim. See Alicia Garcia-Galgueras and Dick F. Swaab, "A Sex Difference in the Hypothalamic Uncinate Nucleus: Relationship to Gender Identity," *Brain* 131 (November 2008): 3143. Allen et al. plainly say, "Since there appears to be more than one sexually dimorphic nucleus in this region, and there is presently no indication that INAH 1 is homologous to the SDN-POA of the rat, we do not believe that it is appropriate for INAH 1 to be called the SDN-POA, regardless of its potential dimorphism." Laura S. Allen, M. Hines, J. E. Shryne, and R. A. Gorski, "Two Sexually Dimorphic Cell Groups in the Human Brain," *Journal of Neuroscience* 9.2 (February 1989): 497–503.

65 to 200 million years ago, but the implication is rats and humans are long-lost relatives. Born-this-way advocates suspect parts of the hypothalamus in humans and rats are homologous, meaning they share the same evolutionary origins. Based on the premise that rats and humans share a common ancestor and combined with the fact the hypothalamus is connected with our sexual drive, scientific observations of rodent sexual behavior is considered informative for research into human sexual behavior.

GENDER DIFFERENCES IN THE HUMAN BRAIN

Born-this-way arguments presume a substantial difference exists between male and female brains. But to what degree are male and female brains actually different? Trying to discover consensus about the exact gender differences in our brains can be confusing. Competing and contradictory assertions abound, but several claims are commonly accepted within the scientific community.[5] The most consistently proven difference between male and female brains is that male brains are larger. Pro-homosexual authors Cohler and Galatzer-Levy go so far as to say, "During the past century, numerous researchers have tried to find anatomic factors differentiating the male and female brain. To date, only one reliable difference has been found — regardless of sexual orientation, men have slightly larger brains than women."[6] Another difference is that, as a general rule, male brains have a higher percentage of "white" matter — tissue composed of nerve fibers which connect the various components of the brain like a networking grid — while women have a higher percentage of "gray" matter — tissue containing neurons which are essential for thinking.[7] Another common difference is that the amygdala is usually larger in males than fe-

---

5 One work says, "In human brains, dimorphisms have so far proven to be small, subtle, few, and of unknown function."Going on to say, "Perhaps the most reliable conclusion we can draw about sexual dimorphisms in human brain structure is that there are so few of them." Mark Bear, Barry W. Connors, Michael A. Paradiso, *Neuroscience: Exploring the Brain*, 3rd ed. (Baltimore: Lippincott, Williams, and Wilkins, 2007), 546, 548.

6 Bertam J. Cohler and Robert M. Galatzer-Levy, *The Course of Gay and Lesbian Lives: Social and Psychoanalytic Perspectives* (Chicago: University of Chicago Press, 2000), 83.

7 Ruben C. Gur, Bruce I. Turetsky, Mie Matsui, Michelle Yan, Warren Bilker, Paul Hughett, and Raquel E. Gur, "Sex Differences in Brain Gray and White Matter in Healthy Young Adults: Correlations With Cognitive Performance," *The Journal of Neuroscience* 19.10 (May 15, 1999): 4,065.

males.[8] Other claims about sex-related brain differences abound, but the ones mentioned here give a sufficient idea of the types that are generally accepted.

Many believe some of the proposed structural differences between male and female brains account for gender-specific abilities. It is widely held that girls are better at empathizing (the ability to respond to someone with an appropriate emotion), while boys are better at systemizing (the ability to understand how non-human systems work by analyzing them).[9] Gender-specific differences are also central to burgeoning research on issues like autism in males and depression in females. Concerning sexual attraction, visual stimuli appear to play a significantly greater role in male sexual desire and behavior.[10]

In 1989, Allen and Gorski of UCLA made a new discovery relevant to gender differences in humans and identified four cell groups of interest in the preoptic area of the hypothalamus. Allen coined a new name for these cell groups: the "Interstitial Nuclei of the Anterior Hypothalamus" (INAH 1-4). Allen and Gorski said the INAH 2 was twice as large in men as in women and that INAH 3 was 2.8 times as large in men as in women.[11] These very specific findings regarding INAH 3 soon became the focus of later studies concerning brain structure, homosexuality, and born-this-way arguments.

In recent decades, the conclusion was reached that human brains are somewhat sexually dimorphic, meaning the brains of males and females exist in two somewhat distinct forms. But the similarities between male and female brains far outweigh the differences. Men and women share the same structures and the various components serve the same functions in both genders. Men and women share equal intelligence. Many sex-specific differences have often been exaggerated by purveyors of pop psychology and the popular media. Differences in particular structures which have been identified are often differences in volume or shape. Nonetheless, as research on gender differences moved forward, some scientists began to speculate that homosexuals may have brain differences which separate them from heterosexuals. The claims and counter-claims regarding findings in this area have often been controversial with significant implications in political arguments for homosexual rights.

---

8   Stephan Hamann, "Sex Differences in the Responses of the Human Amygdala," *The Neuroscientist* 11.4 (2005): 289.

9   Simon Baron-Cohen, Rebecca C. Knickmeyer, Matthew K. Belmonte, "Sex Differences in the Brain: Implications for Explaining Autism," *Science* 310 (November 4, 2005): 820.

10   Hamann, "Sex Differences in the Responses of the Human Amygdala," 288.

11   Laura S. Allen, M. Hines, J. E. Shryne, and R. A. Gorski, "Two Sexually Dimorphic Cell Groups in the Human Brain," *Journal of Neuroscience* 9.2 (February 1989): 497–506. This study compared the brains of the cadavers of twenty-two adult men and women.

We will now review particular born-this-way arguments regarding the corpus callosum, the hypothalamus, the anterior commissure, and brain asymmetry.

THE CORPUS CALLOSUM

One of the most popular subjects of research concerning gender-specific brain differences is the corpus callosum, a thick bundle of nerves that connects the left and right brain. For a number of years, some researchers asserted a significant difference between the thickness of the corpus callosum in males and females, typically claiming that the corpus callosum was thicker in females. Some born-this-way advocates suggested similar trait may differentiate heterosexuals from homosexuals.

In 2005, researchers from Japan claimed to find important differences in the corpus callosum of transgender males. Similar to others, they claimed the corpus callosum was measurably different between males and females. But they then went further and measured the corpus callosum in research subjects with gender identity disorder (GID). These researchers claimed people with GID were more likely to have a corpus callosum more similar to the gender with which they self-identified than the gender with which they were born. In other words, males who identified as females were more likely to have a corpus callosum size similar to females. Likewise, females who identified as males were more likely to have a corpus callosum size similar to males. The researchers went so far as to conclude that their data "can be utilized for diagnosis of GID as an objective and quantitative criteria."[12]

While these claims about GID and the size of the corpus callosum are provocative, they are ultimately unconvincing because an emerging consensus is that purported sex-specific differences in corpus callosum size are ill founded. One group of researchers notes "sex differences in any proportion [of the corpus callosum] measure[d] . . . must be interpreted with caution, since any association with sex and age and the ratio's denominator can create a substantial effect."[13] Gorski and his colleagues attempted to find sexual di-

---

12 Y. Yokota, Y. Kawamura, and Y. Kameya, "Callosal Shapes at the Midsagittal Plane: MRI Differences of Normal Males, Normal Females, and GID," *Conference Proceedings of the 2005 IEEE Engineering in Medicine and Biology 27th Annual Conference, Shanghai, China, September 1–4, 2005,* 3 (2005): 3058.

13 The authors also say, "As a result, significant sex differences in ratio measures have often been found to disappear when analysis of covariance is used on the same data." Paul M. Thompson, Katherine L. Narr, Rebecca E. Blanton, and Arthur W. Toga, "Mapping Structural

morphism in the corpus callosum, but found "no conclusive evidence of sexual dimorphism in the area of the corpus callosum or its subdivisions."[14] Danish scientist Mikkel Wallentin went so far as to say "the alleged sex-related corpus callosum size difference is a myth."[15] If it is not true that men and women have sex-specific corpus callosum sizes, then it is also not true that someone with GID has a corpus callosum similar to the gender with which they identify because no gender-specific corpus callosum size exists!

The Hypothalamus

Because the hypothalamus connects the nervous system to the endocrine system by producing hormones, it affects the human sex drive. It is a hub of regions high in sex steroid receptors, having a high density of estrogen, androgen, and progesterone receptors.[16] This relationship between the sex-drive and the hypothalamus further explains why it has been the focus of research concerning a biological origin for homosexuality.[17] Two studies have been the focus of interest in particular: Swaab and Hofman on the Suprachiasmatic Nucleus and Simon LeVay on the Interstitial Nucleus of the Anterior Hypothalamus.

Alterations of the Corpus Callosum During Brain Development and Degeneration," in *The Parallel Brain: The Cognitive Neuroscience of the Corpus Callosum,* Eran Zaidel and Marco Lacobni, eds. (Cambridge: Massachusetts Institute of Technology Press, 2003), 98.

14   Laura S. Allen, Mark F. Richey, Yee M. Chai, and Roger A. Gorski, "Sex Differences in the Corpus Callosum of the Living Human Being," *The Journal of Neuroscience* 11.4 (April 1991): 933. Even more amazingly, some people are actually born without a corpus callosum, a condition known as agenesis of the corpus callosum. As an example of contradictory evidence, in 2003 John Allen et al. performed MRI measurements of male and female brains and actually found the volume of males to be greater than females. See John S. Allen, Hanna Damasio, Thomas J. Grabowski, Joel Bruss. and Wei Zhang, "Sexual dimorphism and Asymmetries in the Gray–White Composition of the Human Cerebrum," *NeuroImage* 18.4 (April 2003): 880–94. For a recent study re-asserting the corpus callosum is larger in females, see Babak A. Ardekani, Khadija Figarsky, and John J. Sidtis, "Sexual Dimorphism in the Human Corpus Callosum: An MRI Study Using the OASIS Brain Database," *Cerebral Cortex* 23.10 (2013): 2514–20.

15   Mikkel Wallentin, "Putative sex differences in verbal abilities and language cortex: A critical review," *Brain and Language* 108 (2009): 178.

16   Jay N. Giedd et al., "Review: Magnetic Resonance Imaging of Male/Female Differences in Human Adolescent Brain Anatomy," 5.

17   The degree to which the hypothalamus does or does not affect sexual orientation is still debated. Cohler and Galatzer-Levy, authors favorable to homosexual rights, go so far as to say "there is little evidence that the hypothalamus plays any role in human sexual orientation." Cohler and Galatzer-Levy, *The Course of Gay and Lesbian Lives,* 82.

SWAAB AND HOFMAN—
THE HYPOTHALAMUS AND THE SUPRACHIASMATIC NUCLEUS

One of the most influential scientists in the area of homosexuality and brain research has been Dutch neurobiologist Dick F. Swaab. From 1978–2005, he served as the director of the Netherlands Institute for Brain Research. Swaab has published many articles and is widely quoted in literature concerning born-this-way arguments and brain structure. Swaab's most frequently cited study was published in 1990 in the journal *Brain Research*. Cowritten with Michael Hofman, the article was titled "An Enlarged Suprachiasmatic Nucleus in Homosexual Men." The Suprachiasmatic Nucleus (SCN) is a small collection of brain cells in the hypothalamus which governs the body's circadian rhythm, the mental and behavioral changes that follow a 24-hour cycle, responding primarily to light and darkness.[18] Since the circadian rhythm affects mood, sleep, hormones, and body temperature, it is thought perhaps to be connected to sexual desire in some way.

Swaab and Hofman studied the SCN in thirty-four cadavers. Of these thirty-four cadavers, eighteen were a reference group of males who died of various causes, ten were homosexual men who died of AIDS, and six were heterosexuals who died of AIDS (two males, four females). Swaab and Hofman claimed to observe a larger SCN in the cadavers of homosexual men than those in the heterosexual reference group: "The SCN volume in homosexual males was 1.73 times larger than male subjects from the reference group . . . and contained 2.09 times as many cells."[19] They went on to say that this size difference means that homosexuals have a more elongated SCN than heterosexuals. Furthermore, they suggested this enlargement of the SCN might be a cause of homosexuality: "An association was found . . . between sexual orientation in men and SCN size, from which the functional implications are momentarily not clear."[20]

Just as males and females have innate brain differences, Swaab and Hofman were now suggesting homosexuals also have a unique brain structure which caused their sexual orientation. But Swaab and Hofman concluded their research by saying their work "does not support the global hypothesis that ho-

---

18   "Circadian Rhythms Fact Sheet," National Institute of General Medical Sciences, last updated November, 2012, accessed June 3, 2015, http://www.nigms.nih.gov/Education/Pages/Factsheet_CircadianRhythms.aspx.

19   D. F. Swaab and Michael A. Hofman, "An Enlarged Suprachiasmatic Nucleus in Homosexual Men," *Brain Research* 537 (1990): 145.

20   Ibid., 146.

mosexual men have a female brain."[21] In 1995, they were more explicit and argued homosexual men are a "third sex" who have a hypothalamus that is "neither similar to that in females, nor to that in male heterosexuals."[22] So while they are arguing homosexuals have a unique brain structure, they were not arguing that gay men have a "female brain."

While the purported differences found by Swaab and Hofman were at first greeted with fanfare, their research on the SCN was plagued by several problems. First, in the years since their article was published, their findings about the SCN have not been replicated.[23] Byne and Parsons critique the SCN claims and go so far as to say few studies like Swaab and Hofman's have proved to be replicable in the past, adding that "in humans the size of the SCN does not vary with sex."[24]

Second, Swaab's study was very small consisting of only thirty-four cadavers and of these only ten were homosexuals. Third, the reference group identified as heterosexuals may not serve as a reliable comparison, since, as Swaab and Hofman state themselves, "Sexual preference of the subjects of the reference group was generally not known."[25] In other words, the researchers *assumed* the members of the reference group were heterosexuals or arbitrarily assigned them the designation. In either case, if the reference group is not confirmed, all the data comes into question.

Finally, while the hypothalamus in general is associated with sexual desire, the specific connection between the SCN and sexual desire has been strongly questioned.[26] The SCN clearly governs our circadian rhythms, but its connection to sex is speculative. If further research challenges the SCN's association with sex, then it is difficult to see how it can be associated with same-sex desire. Taken as a whole, born-this-way arguments based on purported differences in the SCN are hardly convincing.

---

21   Swaab and Hofman, "An Enlarged Suprachiasmatic Nucleus in Homosexual Men," 146.

22   D. F. Swaab and M. A. Hofman, "Sexual Differentiation of the Human Hypothalamus in Relation to Gender and Sexual Orientation," *Trends in Neuroscience* 18.6 (January 1, 1995); 269.

23   Simon LeVay, *Gay, Straight, and The Reason Why: The Science of Sexual Orientation* (New York: Oxford University Press, 2010), 200.

24   William Byne and Bruce Parsons, "Human Sexual Orientation: Biological Theories Reappraised," *Archives of General Psychiatry* 50 (March 1993): 235.

25   Swaab and Hofman, "An Enlarged Suprachiasmatic Nucleus in Homosexual Males," 141.

26   Simon LeVay, *Gay, Straight, and the Reason Why*, 200.

Simon LeVay: Interstitial Nuclei
of the Anterior Hypothalamus

One of the most widely cited studies in born-this-way arguments was published in August 1991 in *Science* by Simon LeVay, a neuroscientist who worked for the prestigious Salk Institute for Biological Studies from 1984–1993. A homosexual himself, LeVay was the co-founder of The Institute of Gay and Lesbian Education located in West Hollywood, CA, and served as the Institute's chairman of the board of directors from 1992–1996.[27] Building on the earlier findings that the INAH 2 and 3 are larger in males than in females, LeVay also focused on the INAH 1–4 to see if there were any corresponding differences based on sexual preference. Studying 41 cadavers, LeVay identified 19 of the subjects as homosexual men[28] (all of whom died of complications from AIDS), 16 as heterosexual men (6 of whom died of AIDS related illnesses), and 6 as heterosexual women (1 of whom died of AIDS). LeVay could not replicate the finding that the INAH 2 is larger in males than in females. But he did find that the INAH 3 is larger in males than females. Furthermore, he claimed the INAH 3 cell group was more than twice as large in heterosexual men as in homosexual men. LeVay's claims were profound not only because he claimed to replicate the finding that a certain amount of sexual dimorphism existed at INAH 3, but he was claiming that homosexual men have an INAH 3 closer in size to women than to heterosexual men.[29] While LeVay did assert that further interpretation of the results of his study must be considered speculative, he concluded by saying that it is more likely "the size of the INAH 3 is established early in life and later influences sexual behavior than that the reverse is true."[30] Hence, LeVay was saying the size of the INAH 3 — smaller in homosexual males — affects sexual orientation and was rejecting the idea that sexual behavior in adulthood changed the size of the INAH 3.

---

27   Simon LeVay, "My Resume." Accessed January 4, 2013, http://www.simonlevay.com/my-resume.

28   This number includes one man who self-identified as bisexual, but was placed in the category of "homosexual."

29   Van Wyk and Geist noted that the one subject listed as "bisexual" had an INAH 3 that resembled heterosexual men rather than the other homosexual men. Paul H. Van Wyk and Chrisann S. Geist, "Biology of Bisexuality: Critique and Observations," *Journal of Homosexuality* 28.3–4 (1995): 359. Van Wyk and Geist apparently base their comments on LeVay's "Figure 2" in his article. See Simon LeVay, "A Difference in Hypothalamic Structure Between Heterosexual and Homosexual Men," *Science* 253 (August 30, 1991): 1036.

30   Simon LeVay, "A Difference in Hypothalamic Structure between Heterosexual and Homosexual Men," 1036.

LeVay's research was greeted with quite a bit of fanfare, but it is also plagued by some significant problems. First and primarily, there were homosexual men in LeVay's study who had an INAH 3 similar in size to the majority of heterosexuals and there were heterosexual men who had an INAH 3 similar in size to most homosexuals. This means the size of the INAH 3 was not a perfect predictor of the subject's sexuality. Based on LeVay's own data, a particular INAH 3 size is neither necessary nor sufficient for a homosexual identity.

Second, it is important to emphasize that researchers are still uncertain what, if any, relation the INAH 3 has to sexual function. While one can speculate that the INAH 3 has some connection with sex, no one really knows what the area does.[31] Thus, LeVay's assumption that the INAH 3 is necessarily associated with sexual attraction has not yet been proven. Furthermore, much like Swaab and Hofman's research, LeVay's sample was very small, consisting of only 41 subjects. It is imprudent to make global assumptions about same-sex attraction based on a study consisting of such a small number.

Another problem with LeVay's research is related to the manner in which he classified his research subjects as either heterosexual or homosexual. LeVay's definitions for each were very imprecise, nor was there any way of verifying sexual orientation since the subjects being studied were dead.[32] Writing in *Technology Review,* Paul Billings and Jonathan Beckwith commented on LeVay's study, emphasizing that LeVay's "research design and subject sample did not allow others to determine whether it was sexual behavior, drug use, or disease history that was correlated with the observed differences among the subjects' brains."[33]

Another challenge to LeVay's research is that the INAH 3 is a part of the brain no bigger than a pinpoint.[34] Thus, accurate measurement is formidable. In order to study brain cells, the tissues themselves must be preserved and cut into sections thin enough to be translucent. Measuring the volume of something as small as the INAH 3 is therefore difficult, but not impossible.[35]

---

31   Rebecca Jordan-Young and Raffaella I. Rumiati, "Hardwired for Sexism? Approaches to Sex/Gender in Neuroscience," *Neuroethics* 5.3 (December 2012): 307.

32   Jeffrey Satinover, *Homosexuality and the Politics of Truth* (Grand Rapids: Baker, 1996), 78–79.

33   Paul Billings and Jonathan Beckwith, "Born Gay?" *Technology Review* 96.5 (July 1993): 60.

34   Michael R. Kauth, *True Nature: A Theory of Sexual Attraction* (New York: Kluwer Academic / Plenum Publishers, 2000), 126.

35   Swaab and Hofman evaluated LeVay's approach of measuring the volume of the hypothalamic structures and said: "Volume is susceptible to various pre- and post-mortem fac-

But volume measurement is affected by other external factors, such as the process of death itself. Taken as a whole, these variables may have affected LeVay's findings.

LeVay also claims the INAH 3 in humans is comparable to the SDN-POA of rats, an assertion rejected by many scientists. In research on male rats, variations in the size of the SDN-POA has been correlated with the amount of male-typical behavior shown by the rodents, thus LeVay suggests variations in INAH 3 size in humans may influence a homosexual orientation. But the problem with LeVay's line of thinking is the disputed connection between the INAH 3 and the SDN-POA of rats. Michael Kauth, who is himself an advocate for homosexual rights, flatly rejects LeVay's premise and says it is "unlikely that the human INAH 3 is functionally similar to the rat SDN-POA. LeVay's premise is faulty, and his conclusions are suspect."[36]

Many Christians have suggested LeVay's data was flawed because of the effect of AIDS on the subjects. Could AIDS have affected the area of the brain LeVay was examining, thus accounting for the differences?[37] Further research indicates that AIDS most likely did not have an influence on LeVay's measurements. William Byne has found "no evidence for an influence of HIV on INAH 3, lending credence to LeVay's (1991) contention that HIV infection did not account for the disparity of INAH 3 volume he observed between homosexual and heterosexual men."[38] An informed response to LeVay's findings will be cautious in suggesting the degree to which AIDS or AIDS medications affected LeVay's findings.

Further investigation has challenged LeVay's conclusions. In 2001, William Byne, director of the Neuroanatomy and Morphometrics Laboratory at the Icahn School of Medicine at Mount Sinai Hospital, led a research team that

---

tors, such as differences in agonal state and fixation time but also to histological procedures and methods, such as section thickness. Therefore, it is essential to include data on total cell numbers of hypothalamic nuclei, since this parameter is not influenced by such factors." D. F. Swaab and M. A. Hofman, "Sexual Differentiation of the Human Hypothalamus in Relation to Gender and Sexual Orientation," *Trends in Neurosciences* 18.6 (January 1, 1995): 266–67.

36   Kauth, *True Nature*, 127. Kauth is the Lesbian, Gay, Bisexual, and Transgender (LGBT) Program Coordinator, Patient Care Services, at the Veteran's Affairs Central Office.

37   For example, see Stanton L. Jones and Mark A. Yarhouse, *Homosexuality: The Use of Scientific Research in the Church's Moral Debate*, 70.

38   William Byne et al., "The Interstitial Nuclei of the Human Anterior Hypothalamus: An Investigation of Variation with Sex, Sexual Orientation, and HIV status," *Hormones and Behavior* 40 (2001): 91. It is of some interest to note that both Jones and Yarhouse and the Feinbergs cite Byne's criticisms of LeVay's research, but do not mention Byne's conclusion that AIDS did not affect LeVay's data.

measured via autopsy the INAH from 34 men presumed to be heterosexual (10 of whom were HIV positive at death), 34 presumed heterosexual women (9 of whom were HIV positive at death), and 14 homosexual men (all of whom were HIV positive at death). While the Byne study concluded the INAH 3 indeed occupies a larger volume and contains more neurons in heterosexual men than in women,[39] their findings concerning the differences in the INAH 3 between heterosexual and homosexual men were not as dramatic as those claimed by LeVay. In fact, they concluded there was no difference in the number of neurons between heterosexual men and homosexual men, saying, "The primary sexually dimorphic cellular characteristic of INAH 3, neuronal number, did not vary as a function of sexual orientation."[40] There was no difference in the number of neurons in the INAH 3, but the INAH 3 did tend to occupy a smaller volume in homosexual males than in heterosexual males. Basically, the gay men and straight men had the same number of neurons in this region of the brain, but the neurons were packed more densely in gay men.

So what does the Byne study tell us about LeVay's claim that the INAH 3 is different in heterosexual male and homosexual males? First, one of the more robust findings of brain research is that men tend to have a larger INAH 3 than women. However, there is no difference in the number of neurons in the INAH 3 of heterosexual males as compared to homosexual males. The neurons in INAH 3 seem to be more densely packed in homosexual males than in heterosexual males, leading to the finding that the "volume" of the INAH 3 is smaller in gay men than in straight men. Thus, Byne and his co-authors say, "Based on the results of the present study as well as those of LeVay, sexual orientation cannot be reliably predicted on the basis of INAH 3 volume alone."[41] LeVay himself offers a nuanced response to Byne and says, "Byne's findings were in no way a refutation of the findings of my study, but neither were they a clear-cut confirmation."[42] Based on Byne's research, LeVay admits his own claims have not been replicated.

Byne's research also provides some room for reflection on born-this-way arguments regarding prenatal hormones. Byne discusses arguments in favor of both prenatal hormone exposure and postnatal experience on the brain. The researchers acknowledge that "sex difference in the human INAH 3 may depend at least in part on sex differences in developmental exposure to go-

---

39 Ibid., 89.
40 Ibid.
41 Ibid., 91.
42 LeVay, *Gay, Straight, and the Reason Why*, 199.

nadal hormones," but then add that "sex related differences may also emerge later in development as the neurons that survive become part of the functional circuits."[43] Furthermore, since the major expansion of the brain occurs postnatally while the person is in constant interaction with the environment, the elaboration of certain cells "may be influenced by postnatal experience in humans."[44]

The upshot of the research is that these differences between the INAH 3 of heterosexual males and homosexual males are not proof of prenatal, biological determination of sexual orientation. Instead, these differences could be the result of postnatal experience. Jones and Kwee explain the importance of Byne's findings and say, "In other words, if there are brain structure differences between homosexuals and heterosexuals, they could well be the result rather than the cause of sexual behavior and preference."[45] Byne et al. conclude with a cautionary note, saying, "At present, however, nothing is known about the potential importance of either [prenatal] hormone exposure or postnatal experience on neuropil [a dense network of interwoven nerve fibers] development in INAH 3."[46] Thus at the very least, serious questions remain concerning connection between the INAH 3 and the purported influence of prenatal hormones for hardwiring one's sexual orientation.

In 2008, Dick Swaab and Alicia Garcia-Falgueras of Netherlands Institute for Brain Research claimed the INAH 3 of male-to-female transsexual men was smaller than in non-transsexual men. In a triumphant note, the authors end with a discussion of the "transsexual hypothalamus" and say, "Our data reveal a sex-atypical INAH 3 volume and neuron number in transsexual male-to-female people to be in the female range, while the values of a female-to-male subject were in the male range."[47]

However, a careful review of their research indicates the data is not as definitive as is claimed. Much like LeVay's findings, significant overlap existed in the INAH 3 volume, number of neurons, and neuron density between males, females, and male-to-female transsexuals. In other words, having a particular INAH 3 size did not *guarantee* one had a transsexual identity. In this way, the Swaab and Garcia-Falgueras' research demonstrates, much like LeVay's data,

---

43 Byne et al., "The Interstitial Nuclei of the Human Anterior Hypothalamus," 91.

44 Ibid.

45 Stanton L. Jones and Alex W. Kwee, "Scientific Research, Homosexuality, and the Church's Moral Debate: An Update," *Journal of Psychology and Christianity* 24.4 (2005): 307.

46 Byne et al., "The Interstitial Nuclei of the Human Anterior Hypothalamus," 91.

47 Alicia Garcia-Galgueras and Dick F. Swaab, "A Sex Difference in the Hypothalamic Uncinate Nucleus: Relationship to Gender Identity," 3145.

that a particular INAH 3 size is neither necessary nor sufficient for predicting a transsexual identity.[48]

Born-this-way arguments based on the INAH 3 are not persuasive. LeVay's premise that the SDN-POA in the rat and the INAH 3 are related is speculative and flatly rejected by many researchers. His sample was small and the sexual histories of the subjects studied was incomplete. Even in LeVay's own data, a particular INAH 3 size was neither necessary nor sufficient to predict sexual orientation. Byne's research indicates there is no difference in the number of neurons between heterosexual and homosexual males at the INAH 3, though they are more densely packed in homosexuals. Furthermore, LeVay's claims were restricted to males and have no bearing on arguments related to homosexual females. Though LeVay's claims are often repeated, these weaknesses leave born-this-way arguments based on the INAH 3 unconvincing.

ALLEN AND GORSKI AND THE ANTERIOR COMMISSURE (1992)

In 1992 Laura Allen and Roger Gorski published an article in the *Proceedings of the National Academy of Sciences* in which they claimed the anterior commissure (AC) of the brain is larger in homosexual men than in either heterosexual men or women. The AC is a bundle of nerve fibers connecting the two temporal lobes, and is quite a bit smaller than the corpus callosum. In this study, a postmortem comparison was made between the AC of 30 homosexual males, 30 heterosexual males, and 30 heterosexual females. The researchers reported there was a significant difference in the area of the AC between the three groups: the AC of homosexual men was 18.0% larger than that of heterosexual women and 34% greater than that of heterosexual men. Furthermore, the AC of heterosexual women was 13.4% larger than heterosexual men.[49] Allen and Gorski concluded by noting the differences in AC size were intriguing since the AC is not known to be related to sexual reproduction. They then say when

---

48   LeVay cites the Swaab/Garcia-Falgueras research in favor of his own findings. See *Gay, Straight, and the Reason Why*, 199–200. Joe Hebert comments on the Swaab/Garcia-Falgueras research and says, "They show considerable overlap between males, females, and [male to female transsexuals]. So, either the precision of their methods is not very high, or there is an indistinct relation between INAH 3 and gender identity." Joe Hebert, "Who Do We Think We Are? The Brain and Gender Identity," *Brain* 131 (November 2, 2008): 3115.

49   Laura S. Allen and Roger A. Gorski, "Sexual Orientation and the Size of the Anterior Commissure in the Human Brain," *Proceedings of the National Academy of Sciences* 89.15 (1992): 7200. We should acknowledge that this study on the AC appears well constructed.

their findings are combined with other claims about the sexual differences in the hypothalamus, the result "clearly argues against the notion that a single brain structure causes or results from homosexual orientation. Rather, this correlation supports the hypothesis that factors operating early in development differentiate sexually dimorphic structures and functions of the brain in a *global* fashion."[50] Allen and Gorski are thus claiming their research on the AC demonstrates heterosexuals and homosexuals have brains that are different in multiple ways, not in just one structure.

Though this Allen and Gorski study is still quoted as evidence for a biological aspect of homosexuality, there are several reasons it should be taken with caution. First, in the over 20 years since it was published, the findings have not been replicated. In fact, a 2002 study examined the cross-sectional area of the AC in postmortem material from 120 individuals, and found no variation in the size of the AC with age, HIV status, sex, or sexual orientation.[51] Second, when one examines the graph in which Allen and Gorski plotted the average size of the AC in the three groups, it becomes clear that there is significant overlap in the size of the AC of many of the subjects that they studied. In other words, several homosexual men, heterosexual men, and heterosexual women had ACs very similar in size. Not *every* homosexual subject had an AC that was 34% larger than *every* heterosexual male: the data reflects the average of all the subjects studied, and thus shows a *trend* and not an absolute reality in every case. A particular AC size was neither necessary nor sufficient to cause homosexuality. Thus, even their own data did not prove causation, but did show a possible correlation between sexual orientation and the size of the AC.

Savic and Lindström and Brain Asymmetry (2008)

Ivanka Savic and Per Lindström are both associated with the Department of Clinical Neuroscience at the Karolinska Institute in Stockholm, Sweden. In 2008, they investigated the degree of brain asymmetry in homosexuals compared to heterosexuals. Brain asymmetry refers to the size differences in all humans between the two hemispheres of the brain. Savic and Lindström compared the asymmetry of the brains of 25 heterosexual men, 25 heterosexual

---

50   Laura S. Allen and Roger A. Gorski, "Sexual Orientation and the Size of the Anterior Commissure in the Human Brain," 7202. Italics in original.

51   Mitchell S. Lasco et al., "A Lack of Dimorphism of Sex or Sexual Orientation in the Human Anterior Commissure," *Brain Research* 936 (May 17, 2002): 95–98.

women, 20 homosexual men and 20 homosexual women. Using both MRI and PET imaging to evaluate their sample, they made several important claims.

First, they asserted that in heterosexual men the right hemisphere of the brain is slightly larger than the left while in heterosexual women two hemispheres were about equal in size. Second, they claimed the brains of homosexual men looked more like heterosexual women with both hemispheres being equal in size and the brains of homosexual women looked more like heterosexual men with the right hemisphere being slightly larger. Third, Savic and Lindström examined the amygdalae, the two almond-shaped structures in the brain that are closely connected to our emotions, such as fear and anger. They claimed to find that heterosexual men and women have somewhat different connections between the amygdalae and the rest of the brain. Then, homosexual men in their study showed connections between the amygdalae and the rest of the brain more similar to heterosexual females and homosexual females had connections more similar to heterosexual males.[52]

Savic's and Lindström's findings were greeted with acclaim by leading pro-homosexual researcher Qazi Rahman of the University of London, who commented, "As far as I'm concerned there is no argument any more — if you are gay, you are born gay."[53]

One reason some born-this-way advocates find this research on brain asymmetry and the amygdala so compelling is that the study examined areas of the brain outside of those normally connected with sexual desire. Some claim the fact these areas are not directly associated with sex means they are less likely to have been affected by someone's sexual behavior. In other words, differences found here may indicate innate differences. Savic and Lindström believe their findings support the prenatal hormone theory and suggest the differences they observed could be caused by the "interplay between pre- and postnatal testosterone and estrogen, the androgen and estrogen receptors" and other related factors.[54]

One observation concerning Savic and Lindström's research is that there was overlap between the groups they measured. Some homosexual males and heterosexual males shared a similar brain asymmetry or amygdale connec-

52   Ivanka Savic and Per Lindstrom, "PET and MRI Show Differences in Cerebral Asymmetry and Functional Connectivity Between Homo- and Heterosexual Subjects," *Proceedings of the National Academy of Sciences* 105.27 (June 16, 2008): 9403–408.

53   BBC News, "Scans See Brain Differences," June 16, 2008, accessed January 25, 2013, https://news.bbc.co.uk/2/hi/health/7456588.stm.

54   Ivanka Savic and Per Lindstrom, "PET and MRI Show Differences in Cerebral Asymmetry and Functional Connectivity Between Homo- and Heterosexual Subjects," 9407.

tions. A particular brain pattern was neither necessary nor sufficient to predict with absolute certainty a person's sexual identity. What their data shows is a correlation between certain patterns of brain organization, but they have not proven a definite pattern causing homosexuality.

Savic and Lindström were somewhat restrained concerning the broader implications of their study and acknowledged that their findings need to be confirmed by additional research.[55] Indeed, while their research may be replicated, other claims about the sex-based brain differences were also greeted with initial enthusiasm only later to be found less compelling. Furthermore, their somewhat hasty dismissal of environmental explanations for the differences in brain asymmetry may yet be challenged by further investigation. As of this writing (2016), their work has not been replicated.

Summary: "Born This Way" and the Brain

It is a misleading over-simplification of data on brain research to claim homosexual behavior is caused by being born with a brain similar to the opposite sex. Born-this-way arguments often engage in crude simplicities, combining pop psychology and a shallow comprehension of brain research to conclude everyone who participates in same-sex acts must do so because of an innate hard-wiring in their brain. The line of reasoning is as follows: (1) brains of males and females are sexually dimorphic; (2) in a similar way, brains of homosexuals are also sexually dimorphic; (3) since our society says it is wrong to discriminate against someone because of their innate gender differences, it is also wrong to discriminate against homosexuals because they also have scientifically proven innate differences in sexual orientation.

There are several problems with this line of thinking, but I will mention three. First and most importantly, no pattern of brain structure has yet been discovered which is both necessary and sufficient for someone to self-identify as homosexual. To date, no particular measurement of any part of the brain has been found which can predict a person's sexual orientation with complete accuracy. In the studies reviewed here, one finds correlation, not causation: While a higher percentage of homosexuals may have a certain brain-related trait, there are also

---

55 They said, "These observations motivate more extensive investigations of larger study groups and prompt for a better understanding of the neuro-biology of homosexuality." Ivanka Savic and Per Lindstrom, "PET and MRI Show Differences in Cerebral Asymmetry and Functional Connectivity Between Homo- and Heterosexual Subjects," 9407.

heterosexuals with the same trait. Thus, to date, a causal relationship has not been proven between any particular brain structure and homosexuality.

This leads to the second criticism, which is that differences between male and female brains have sometimes been exaggerated to maximize the persuasive power of the "gay brain" argument. Over-stated assertions about male/female brain differences abound on the Internet, popular media, and even the from pulpit. Males and females, both homosexual and heterosexual, have the same structures and components in their brains. Differences which have been identified are usually differences in volume or shape. Attempts to find sexual dimorphism in human brains as clear as that found in animals has produced limited results and the differences in humans do not seem to be as pronounced.

The third problem with the way brain studies have been used relates to brain plasticity. As we saw in chapter 4, brain plasticity is the remarkable manner in which the human brain can form new neural pathways, strengthen existing neural pathways by repetitive use, or bypass damaged pathways. This is important for moral debates because these pathways can be strengthened, discarded, or by-passed based on volitional choices. In other words, some, but not all, of the differences in human brains may be the result of our response to the environment in which we live and the choices we make.

What are Christians to make of the purported sex-related differences in brains and the way they are leveraged in born-this-way arguments? Christians affirm the goodness of the two genders God created (Gen. 1:26–28) and celebrate God-ordained differences between the genders. The observable differences between the bodies of the two genders are central to Paul's critique of homosexuality in Romans 1:18–32. In Romans 1:26–27, Paul emphasizes that homosexuality in both its male and female expressions exchanges the "natural" use of the body for an "unnatural" use. Based on creation references in Romans 1, it is clear that Paul means even pagans without Scriptural revelation should be able to examine the genitalia and realize men and women have sexually complementary bodies. The human body itself teaches that homosexuality is wrong.

Do these gender differences extend to the brain? Some scientific findings are obviously more robust than others, but differences between male and female brains do exist. The degree to which these differences affect temperament or personality are highly debatable. The Bible places far more focus on males and females embracing appropriate expressions of their gender along with corresponding roles in marriage (Gen. 2:18; Eph. 5:21–33) than on gender-specific psychological traits. In our rush to affirm gender differences, Christians have been guilty of too quickly embracing many purported sex-differences in the brain as "proof" of God's design for gender roles only to find later studies refute the claims. We should evaluate the claims carefully and closely, embracing those that are replicated and stand the test of time.

Is it possible that some differences in the brain influence someone's same-sex attraction? Since Christians believe the Fall has infected all of creation with the effects of sin, it is at least possible that some patterns of brain organization can make one more susceptible to homosexual temptation. Yet, a predisposition to a particular sin does not mean one is hopelessly predetermined to participate in the sin. Again, in the research to date, some heterosexuals had brain structures similar to homosexuals but were not homosexuals. Likewise, in some of the research there were homosexuals who had brain structures which resembled the majority of heterosexuals. While causation has not been proven, data does seem to point to a higher incidence of homosexuality being related to some findings.

That said, there are numerous limitations associated with the major born-this-way arguments related to the brain. These weaknesses are enough that even the most secular person should refrain from dogmatically asserting a "gay brain" exists. At the same time, enough has been found that Christians should refrain from dogmatically asserting that differences in the brain have no influence whatsoever on sexual temptation.

As was noted at the beginning of this chapter, one may encounter a person struggling with issues of sexual temptation or gender identity who claims to have a "female brain in a male body" or a "male brain in a female body." Despite such claims, science has only found minor differences between the brains of homosexuals and heterosexuals and none of these differences are necessary for one to claim a homosexual identity as an adult. Claims about the differences in homosexual and heterosexual brains emerged from research in the 1970s and 1980s insisting male and female brains were quite different. While subsequent research does indicate certain sex-typical patterns for male and female brains, the differences are sometimes overstated. One area of interest is the INAH 3, but LeVay's findings have neither been replicated nor completely refuted. However, the size of the INAH 3 was not an absolute predictor of sexual orientation, leaving the evidence inconclusive. Likewise, Savic and Lindstrom's findings are not an absolute predictor of sexual orientation.

Born-this-way arguments are not limited to claims of a particular brain structure, but also include our very genetic code. In the next chapter, we will move deeper and explore the relationship between homosexuality, genetics, and twin studies.

CHAPTER 7

Homosexuality and Twin Studies

IN 1989, HOMOSEXUAL ACTIVISTS MARSHALL KIRK (1957–2005) and Hunter Madsen published *After the Ball: How America Will Conquer Its Fear and Hatred of Gays in the 90's*. Throughout the book they use the tactical device of referring to critics of homosexual behavior as "bigots" while at the same time portraying gays as victims of circumstance and oppression, not as aggressive challengers.[1] Kirk and Madsen argue that making gays appear as victims of circumstance means convincing heterosexuals that homosexuality is an innate characteristic:

> First, the public should be persuaded that gays are *victims of circumstance*, that they no more chose their sexual orientation than they did, say, their height, skin color, talents, or limitations. (We argue that, for all practical purposes, gays should be considered to have been *born gay*–even though sexual orientation, for most humans, seems to be the product of a complex interaction between innate predispositions and environmental factors during childhood and early adolescence.)[2]

In an amazing admission, these authors state homosexuality is the result of a complex set of factors, but urge fellow homosexuals to claim to be "born this way" because it is an advantageous public relations stance.

One common way researchers have tried to prove homosexuals are "born this way" is via twin research. If homosexuality does have a genetic component, then research focusing on the degree to which twins do or do not share a homosexual orientation should be quite informative. Put most simply, a twin

---

1   Marshall Kirk and Hunter Madsen, *After the Ball: How American Will Conquer Its Fear and Hatred of Gays in the 90s* (New York: Doubleday, 1989), 183.

2   Ibid., 184. Italics in original.

study is a genetic study performed to determine the heritability of specific traits. Since identical twins (also known as "monozygotic twins") share the same DNA, the assumption is that any major differences between the twins must be the result of other non-genetic factors. A survey of twin research related to homosexuality reveals Kirk and Madsen were right to acknowledge a host of factors contribute to homosexuality, and not just genetics. To demonstrate this, we will begin by summarizing research of Franz Kallmann, move to Bailey and Pillard's research based in the United States, and then conclude by examining twin-research based on the Australian twin registry.

Franz J. Kallmann (1952)

Franz J. Kallmann was a German-American psychiatrist and one of the first to study the relationship between genetics and mental illness. In 1952, Kallmann reported on the incidence of male homosexuality in 45 non-identical twin pairs and 40 identical twin pairs. To be included in his research, a twin pair had to have at least one brother who was a homosexual. Among the 45 non-identical twin pairs, Kallmann concluded having a homosexual brother only moderately increased the occurrence of homosexuality in the co-twin. However, for identical twins, Kallmann claimed a near 100% concordance for homosexuality and asserted the twin brothers "are fully *concordant* as to the overt practice" of homosexuality and "even tend to be *very similar* in both the part taken in their individual sex activities and the visible extent of feminized appearance and behavior displayed by some of them."[3] Thus, Kallmann was claiming a very strong (almost inevitable) genetic link for homosexual behavior. Despite the wildly impressive statistics from Kallmann indicating homosexual males are "born this way," further research has proved his data was quite flawed.

Bailey and Pillard (1991, 1993)

Michael Bailey, a psychologist and professor at Northwestern University, and Richard Pillard, a professor of psychiatry at Boston University, researched the concordance rate for homosexuality among male twins. In 1991, they

---

3   Franz J. Kallmann, "Twin and Sibship Study of Overt Male Homosexuality," *The American Journal of Human Genetics* 4.2 (June 1952): 143. Italics in original.

published their findings in the *Archives of General Psychiatry* and asserted genetic factors are "important in determining individual differences in sexual orientation."[4] The claim to find a genetic link to homosexuality was greeted with great applause in popular media and Bailey and Pillard have been often-quoted since as evidence in favor of born-this-way arguments for homosexuality.

Bailey and Pillard searched for people within the homosexual community who had a twin. To develop their sample base, they recruited participants via advertisements in gay-friendly magazines and publications, specifically asking for male homosexuals who had a male co-twin or an adopted brother. Adding the adoptive brothers to the research is helpful since they share no DNA with their brothers, but do share the same home, thus giving some insight into the way in which environment shapes sexual identity.

Eventually, Bailey and Pillared collected 161 interviews of homosexual males, 115 of whom had a male twin and 46 with adoptive brothers. Bailey and Pillard's most striking claim was a 52% (29/56) probandwise concordance rate for homosexuality or bisexuality among the identical co-twins.[5] Among homosexual males with a non-identical twin brother, they found a 22% (12/54) probandwise concordance rate for homosexuality. They also found that non-twin biological brothers in the sample had a 9.2% (13/142) concordance rate for homosexuality compared to an 11% (6/57) concordance rate for non-twin adoptive brothers.[6]

Bailey and Pillard initiated a follow-on study of homosexual women with a female co-twin or adoptive sisters. Publishing their findings in 1993 in the *Archives of General Psychiatry*, they again claimed to find a strong genetic component for homosexuality. As in their male study, prospective participants were recruited from advertisements in gay-friendly publications, eventually gathering data from 147 interviews, 115 of whom were homosexual females with a female twin and 32 with adoptive sisters. They reported a concordance

---

4   J. Michael Bailey and Richard C. Pillard, "A Genetic Study of Male Sexual Orientation," *Archives of General Psychiatry* 48.12 (December 1991): 1093.

5   As is common in twin studies, Bailey and Pillard use *probandwise concordance rates* and not *pairwise concordance rates*. In genetic research and twin studies, a *proband* denotes a particular person with a specific genetic trait serving as the starting point for the genetic study of a family. Furthermore, the *pairwise* rate only counts a concordant pair once, but the *probandwise* rate counts such pairs twice. This distinction is important to remember and brings some clarification to Bailey and Pillard's claims.

6   J. Michael Bailey and Richard C. Pillard, "A Genetic Study of Male Sexual Orientation," 1092–93.

rate of 48% (34/71) for identical twins, 16% (6/17) for non-identical twins, 6% (2/35) for adoptive sisters, and 15% (10/73) for non-twin biological sisters.[7] Bailey and Pillard summarized the importance of both of these studies and said, "The most important similarity is that both male and female sexual orientation appeared to be influenced by genetic factors."[8]

Understanding the concept of "probandwise concordance rate" is important for understanding Bailey and Pillard's findings. When the average person hears a concordance rate of 52% (29/56) among identical male homosexual twins, the assumption is Bailey and Pillard found 56 separate twin pairs with at least one homosexual twin, and 29 of these pairs had two homosexuals. Actually, Bailey and Pillard had a total of 41 pairs of identical twins and from this group they found 14 matched groups in which both brothers were homosexual (13 twin pairs and one triplet trio — 29 total individuals). Among the 41 identical twin pairs, they also identified 27 individuals whose co-twin was not homosexual. In the formula below, notice carefully that both of the individuals in a twin set (or the triplets) are counted in the numerator. The formula used to develop the concordance rate can be presented as follows:

$$\frac{13 \text{ pairs or } 26 \text{ homosexual individuals} + 1 \text{ matched triplet set or } 3 \text{ individuals} = 29}{29 \text{ matches} + 27 \text{ failures to match} = 56}$$

The probandwise concordance rate is widely used in genetic research a useful tool, at the same time, it is important to clarify exactly what Bailey and Pillard *did and did not* claim. They *did not* claim to find 56 identical twin pairs with at least one homosexual twin brother. What they did claim was to find 41 identical twin pairs with at last one homosexual brother and 29 pairs where both brothers were homosexual.[9]

---

7   J. Michael Bailey, Richard C. Pillard, Michael C. Neale and Yvonne Agyei, "Heritable Factors Influence Sexual Orientation in Women," *Archives of General Psychiatry* 50 (1993): 219, 221.

8   J. Michael Bailey et al., "Heritable Factors Influence Sexual Orientation in Women," 223.

9   I am extremely thankful for Stanton L. Jones' work in clarifying the exact claims of Bailey and Pillard. This paragraph owes a particular debt to Jones. See Stanton Jones, "Homosexuality: The Use of Scientific Research in the Church's Moral Debate," (Paper delivered to the Council of Christian Colleges and Universities, November 16, 2004).

BAILEY, DUNNE, AND MARTIN:
THE AUSTRALIAN TWIN REGISTRY (2000)

The method in which Bailey and Pillard's sample was obtained by seeking respondents from gay-friendly publications poses another problem. It is not hard
to imagine that homosexuals with a twin who was also a homosexual would
be more motivated to respond to such advertisements and participate in the
study, thus skewing the sample. Bailey and Pillard acknowledged this problem
and in 1993 they stated, "Future studies of sexual orientation that avoid this
bias, for example through the use of twin registries, are clearly desirable."[10]

In 2000, Bailey was able to do just such research and published findings
using a large population-based sample of twins recruited from the Australian National Health and Medical Research Council Twin Registry, ultimately
gathering data from 4,901 participants. Using a much larger and more representative sample provided strikingly lower percentages of concordance rates
for homosexuality among twins. Among identical twins, the Australian data
revealed that if a male was homosexual, there was a 20% concordance rate for
homosexuality and among female homosexuals with an identical twin, there
was a 24% concordance rate. Commenting on the much lower concordance
rate in the Australian study, the authors addressed the sample bias in the previous studies and said, "In those studies, twins deciding whether to participate
in a study clearly related to homosexuality probably considered the sexual
orientation of their co-twins before agreeing to participate."[11]

Yet even the lower incidence of homosexuality among twins in the Australian sample needs more clarification. Bailey, Dunne, and Martin used the
Kinsey scale introduced in chapter two to score people's level of homosexuality. The 20% concordance for identical twin males and 24% concordance
for identical twin females was derived from classifying anyone with a Kinsey
score equal or greater than "2." Remember, a Kinsey score of 2 is defined as
"*predominantly* heterosexual, but more than incidentally homosexual." It is not
clear exactly how many of their homosexual co-twins actually scored a Kinsey
"6" — exclusively homosexual.[12]

---

10   Bailey and Pillard, "Heritable Factors Influence Sexual Orientation in Women," 222.

11   J. Michael Bailey, Michael P. Dunne, and Nicholas G. Martin, "Genetic and Environmental Influences on Sexual Orientation and Its Correlates in an Australian Twin Sample,"
Journal of Personality and Social Psychology 78.3 (March 2000): 533.

12   Bailey et al., "Genetic and Environmental Influences on Sexual Orientation and Its
Correlates in an Australian Twin Sample," 530. Another study with a smaller sample claimed
to find a 2/3 concordance rate for homosexuality in monozygotic twins. See F. L. Whitman,

What are we to make of the Australian study? First, the findings indicate a genetic contributing factor to homosexuality may be at work. The concordance rate for homosexuality among identical twins is higher than the average among the general population. As noted in chapter 2, around 2.2% or less of men self-identify as exclusively homosexual, yet 20% of the identical twins of homosexual brothers in the Australian study had a Kinsey score of 2 or higher. Similarly, around 1.1% or less of women self-identify as exclusively homosexual, yet 24% of identical twins of a homosexual sister had a Kinsey score of 2 or higher. The higher than average occurrence of homosexuality in twins points to a genetic contributing factor which may be at work, but it is not determinative.

Yet the findings are far short of 100% concordance rates. Thus, if there is a genetic aspect to homosexual orientation, the evidence points to an *influence* and not causation. Satinover rightly says:

> If "homosexuality is genetic," as activists and their media supporters repeatedly claim, the concordance rate between identical twins–that is, the incidence of the two twins either both being homosexual or both being heterosexual — will be one hundred percent. There would *never* be a *discordant pair*–a pair with one homosexual twin and one heterosexual twin.[13]

The weakness of the genetic causation argument is further demonstrated by close examination of the data. Bailey, Dunne, and Martin claimed that there was a 22% concordance rate between non-identical twin brothers while non-twin biological brothers had a 9.2% concordance rate for homosexuality. Remembering that non-identical twins and their non-twin biological brothers share the same amount of genetic material, one would expect to see a similar concordance rate between the two groups, yet we do not. This led Byne and Parsons to conclude, "If we rely only on the data presented in their [Bailey, Dunne, and Martin's] study, we must at least consider the possibility that the higher concordance rate for homosexuality in [non-identical] twins compared with non-twin biological brothers is due to increased similarity of the trait-relevant environment in the former."[14] In other words, non-identical twins

---

M. Diamond, J. Martin, "Homosexual Orientation in Twins: A Report of 61 pairs and three Triplet Sets," *Archives of Sexual Behavior* 22 (1993): 187–206.

13   Satinover, *Homosexuality and the Politics of Truth*, 83.

14   William Byne and Bruce Parsons, "Human Sexual Orientation: The Biologic Theories Reappraised," *Archives of General Psychiatry* 50.3 (March 1993): 229.

are more likely to be raised in a similar environment than non-twin biological brothers. The much higher incidence of homosexuality among non-identical twins when compared to non-twin biological brothers may point to unidentified environmental factors at work which contribute to the higher rate of homosexuality.

The significance of the Australian twin study should not be underestimated. The suspected sample bias of the previous studies was proven to be true. Furthermore, the genetic correlation towards homosexuality is much weaker than initially suggested.[15] In 2010, the results were published of a study focusing on homosexuality among twins in Sweden. The Swedish study found concordance rates for homosexuality very similar to the Australian research, reaffirming the lower concordance rates.[16]

SUMMARY OF TWIN STUDIES

Twin research relating to homosexuality reveals some intriguing data. If one member of a twin-pair is homosexual, there is a higher incidence of homosexuality among the twin siblings. However, initial research claiming astoundingly high concordance rates was distorted by various problems and yielded unreliable results.[17] Beginning with Kallmann in 1952, twin studies related to homosexuality were plagued by sample bias, which skewed data in a particular direction. Further research using more representative samples reveals a much lower incidence of homosexuality among twin pairs. In the vast majority of cases where an identical twin is homosexual, his or her co-twin is heterosexual. This strongly argues against a crude born-this-way mentality

---

15   The findings of another twin study based on data gathered from the United States was also published in 2000 which produced results similar to the earlier Bailey and Pillard studies, but the sample was smaller than the Australian one with strong evidence of sample bias similar to Bailey and Pillard. See Kenneth S. Kendler, Laura M. Thornton, Stephen E. Gilman, Ronald C. Kessler, "Sexual Orientation in a U.S. National Sample of Twin and Nontwin Sibling Pairs," *American Journal of Psychiatry* 157.11 (November 2000): 1843–46.

16   Niklas Langström, Qazi Rahman, Eva Carlström, and Paul Lichtenstein, "Genetic and Environmental Effects on Same-sex Sexual Behavior: A Population Study of Twins in Sweden," *Archives of Sexual Behavior* 39.1 (February 2010): 75–80.

17   To demonstrate the conflicting nature of earlier research on twins and homosexuality, consider that in a sample drawn from the Minnesota Twin Registry, Hershberger claimed to have found significant genetic effects for females, but simultaneously claimed no significant genetic effects for males! Scott L. Hersberger, "A Twin Registry Study of Male and Female Sexual Orientation," *The Journal of Sex Research* 34.2 (1997): 212–22.

and instead points to the complex factors Kirk and Madsen readily admitted in *After the Ball*.

Precise understanding of what twin studies have shown is very important when interacting with born-this-way arguments. For example, pro-homosexual authors Glenn Wilson and Qazi Rahman offer an exaggerated summary of the Australian twin study in their book *Born Gay: The Psychobiology of Sex Orientation*. Summarizing the research findings, they claim the Australian study found concordance rates "around 30 percent for both males and females."[18] What Wilson and Rahman do not tell their readers is their "30%" claim is derived from considering anyone with a Kinsey score of "1" as homosexual. Remember, Kinsey 1 is defined as predominantly heterosexual and only incidentally homosexual. In this way, Wilson and Rahman use an extremely broad definition of "homosexual" to substantiate their claims *without* alerting their audience that they are doing so.

While it is at least possible to attribute the higher incidence of homosexuality among homosexual co-twins to environmental forces alone, it seems more likely that a genetic contributing factor seems to exist at a low level of influence. However, it is more important to emphasize the more obvious finding of twin studies: homosexuality *is not* a trait similar to hair color, skin color, or eye color. If it were so, the concordance rate would be 100% and every homosexual twin's sibling would also be homosexual. But clearly the concordance rates are much lower, showing many factors greatly affect the sexual orientation one embraces. Twin studies demonstrate a correlation for a higher incidence of homosexuality when one twin brother is homosexual, but they do not prove causation or that someone is "born this way." As we will see in the next chapter, twin studies also point us to other genetic research focusing on the human genome itself.

---

18   Glenn Wilson and Qazi Rahman, *Born Gay: The Psychobiology of Sex Orientation* (London: Peter Owen Publishers, 2008), 48.

CHAPTER 8

Homosexuality and DNA Research

EQUALITY ROCKS WAS A CONCERT held on April 29, 2000 at Washington, DC's RFK stadium and was a major event in the Millennium March on Washington, a three-day celebration promoting gay rights. One of the many artists to perform at the concert was country music superstar Garth Brooks who sang his popular song *We Shall Be Free*. In the song, Brooks strongly rebukes racism, indifference towards poverty, and generally affirms potential human goodness. The relevance of the song to the Equality Rocks concert is found when Brooks asserts in *We Shall Be Free* that, "When we're free to love anyone we choose, when this world's big enough for all different views. . . . We shall be free."[1] Much like Lady Gaga in her song *Born This Way*, Brooks joins the idea of racial equality and homosexual equality: homosexuality is assumed to be an innate characteristic just like a person's race.

Is homosexuality an innate trait like our skin color? Does our DNA itself code for same-sex attraction in the same way it codes for the color of our eyes? Attempts have been made in recent decades to discover a gene or genes which code for same-sex attraction. While twin studies attempted to trace the heritability of homosexuality via family histories, examining DNA itself is an effort to find a location on the human genome which codes for homosexuality. In what follows, we will see that while there have been some intriguing discoveries regarding DNA and homosexuality, as of yet no evidence confirms a simplistic born-this-way argument. To prove this assertion, we will begin by summarizing some key distinctions within behavioral genetics. Then, various studies by Dean Hamer, Brian Mustanski, and Sanders and Bailey will be summarized. Next, the burgeoning field of epigenetics and its possible importance

---

1   Garth Brooks and Stephanie Davis, "We Shall Be Free," accessed April 23, 2014, http://www.azlyrics.com/lyrics/garthbrooks/weshallbefree.html.

for homosexuality will be addressed. Finally, we will offer some Biblical and theological critiques of genetic behavioralism.

KEY DISTINCTIONS IN BEHAVIORAL GENETICS

What does it mean to say a particular trait is "inherited" or, more specifically, that one "inherits" homosexuality? Though the popular media touts the concept that homosexuality is "genetic" or "inherited," the somewhat straightforward proposition that there is some gene ("x") for homosexuality could have one of many meanings:

1. That everyone possessing gene "x" will definitely be homosexual.
2. That only those possessing gene "x" could possibly be homosexual.
3. A combination of (1) and (2) such that homosexuality will be apparent if and only if the person has gene "x."
4. That there seems to be some sort of statistical correlation between having gene "x" and being homosexual.
5. There is some sort of statistical correlation between particular regions of DNA containing many chromosomes and homosexuality. [2]

The preponderance of data to date supports something like proposition 5: there is possibly some correlation between certain regions of the human genome and homosexual behavior. In contrast, the cultural mindset asserts something very similar to proposition 1 even though *no gay gene has been found.*

Much of the misunderstanding about a purported "gay gene" emerges from confusion about the vital distinction between a trait being "inherited" and a trait's "heritability." To say a trait is "inherited" means it has no connection with choice, that it is completely predetermined, and (except in unusual circumstances) it cannot be prevented. For example, having five toes on each foot is an inherited trait. Some traits are directly related to one specific gene. For example, whether you have a straight hairline or a widow's peak is determined by one gene. Yet most traits are not the simple result of just one gene. Instead, they are the result of the interactions between several genes.

To say that a trait is "heritable" is not the same thing as saying the trait is "inherited." "Heritability" is a term used to describe the complex interaction

---

2   This list of possibilities is modified from Ozan Onay's discussion of criminality and genetics in "The True Ramifications of Genetic Criminality Research for Free Will in the Criminal Justice System," *Genomics, Society, and Policy* 2.1 (2006): 81. Option 5 is added by me.

between genes and environment which results in many traits we express. For example, someone may have a genetic predisposition to be taller than normal. However, if a child with this genetic trait is raised in a war-torn country in which his diet lacks essential nutrients, he will not grow as tall as he would have under better conditions. Both his genetics and his environment contribute to the final height he reaches in adulthood. Usually, heritable traits are those which demonstrate a lot of variation within the population as a whole. For example, someone who is two inches shorter than average is still within the normal deviation for height in a particular community. In contrast, a child born with three toes would be considered abnormal.

One definition for heritability is extent to which individual genetic differences contribute to observed behavior. The degree to which a trait is heritable is typically measured on a scale of 0.0 (genes make no contribution to individual differences) to 1.0 (genes are completely responsible for individual differences). Furthermore, it is important to know that when scientists discuss a trait's heritability, they are talking about the degree to which a trait varies within the population as a whole, and not an individual person. For example, if someone says depression has a heritability of .40, they are claiming that, on average, about 40% of the individual differences that we observe in depression may in some way be attributable to genetic individual difference. It does not mean that 40% of any specific individual's depression is due to his or her genes and the other 60% is due to his or her environment. For human behavior, almost all estimates of heritability are in the moderate range of .30 to .60. [3] Keeping the concepts of inherited and heritable distinct from each other is important to understanding born-this-way arguments and genetics.

DEAN HAMER AND COLLEAGUES (1993 AND 1995)

The first study claiming to discover a specific DNA link to homosexuality was published in the July 16, 1993 edition of *Science* and asserted a region on the X chromosome in males was associated with homosexuality. The primary author was Dean Hamer, an American geneticist who worked as a researcher for the Na-

---

3　The information summarized here about inherited versus heritability is a composite from "Heritability: Introduction," accessed June 10, 2015, http://psych.colorado.edu/~carey/hgss/hgssapplets/heritability/heritability.intro.html; Razib Khan, "Genetic versus heritable Trait," *Discover*, August 30, 2007, accessed June 9, 2015, http://blogs.discovermagazine.com/gnxp/2007/08/genetic-vs-heritable-trait/#.VXh-IUa-Pwc; John S. Feinberg and Paul D. Feinberg, *Ethics for a Brave New World*, 2nd ed. (Wheaton, IL: Crossway, 2010), 366–67.

tional Institutes of Health for thirty-five years where he was director of the Gene Structure and Regulation section at the National Cancer Institute. Hamer and his colleagues claimed to find "a statistically significant correlation between the inheritance of genetic markers on chromosomal region Xq28 and sexual orientation in a selected group of homosexual males."[4] In the years following this article's publication it has been widely cited as evidence of a "gene" for homosexuality and is a popular component of born-this-way arguments. When the average person mentions that scientists have found a "gay gene," they usually have "Xq28" in mind.[5]

Hamer and his colleagues gathered their data by investigating 114 families of homosexual men. Seventy-six of the families were recruited from two Washington, DC area sources: An HIV outpatient center operated by the National Institutes of Health Clinical Center in Washington, DC and local pro-homosexual organizations in the Washington, DC area. The other 38 families were recruited via advertisements in pro-homosexual publications. Preliminary research into the family histories of homosexual men in their sample indicated increased rates of homosexual orientation in the maternal uncles (the mothers' brothers) and male cousins through maternal aunts (the mothers' sisters). Thus, Hamer and his team were curious to know if any genetic markers consistent with male homosexuality were common in homosexual sons via the X chromosome inherited from their mothers. They suspected that in some cases there might be a gene or genes inherited from mothers that predisposed their sons to homosexuality.

From their original sample of 114 families, the researchers selected a subgroup of 40 families in which there were two gay brothers and no indication of paternal transmission of homosexuality. From this select population, Hamer claimed 33 out of 40 pairs of homosexual brothers had co-inherited genetic information from their mothers in a region on the X chromosome called Xq28. Hamer concluded, "We have now produced evidence that one form of male homosexuality is preferentially transmitted through the maternal side and is genetically linked to chromosomal region Xq28."[6]

---

4   Dean Hamer, Stella Hu, Victoria L. Magnuson, Nan Hu, and Angela M. L. Pattatucci, "A Linkage Between DNA Markers on the X Chromosome and Male Sexual Orientation," *Science* 261 (July 16, 1993): 321.

5   The issue of *Science* immediately following publication of Hamer's research included an article critical of Hamer's methods and conclusions. N. Risch, E. Squires-Wheeler, and J. B. K. Bronya, "Male Sexual Orientation and Genetic Evidence," *Science* 262 (December 1993): 2063–65.

6   Dean Hamer et al., "A Linkage Between DNA Markers on the X Chromosome and Male Sexual Orientation," 325.

In 1995, Hamer's team expanded their research to include lesbians as well. They did not discover any link between Xq28 and female homosexuality. But they did claim to replicate some of the findings regarding males and Xq28, but at a much lower level of statistical significance. The 1995 study was also interesting because it documented some non-homosexual men who shared the Xq28 marker with a homosexual brother. In other words, both brothers shared the marker at Xq28, but only one of them was homosexual. The authors thus concluded, "Even within the selected population that was studied, the Xq28 region was neither necessary nor sufficient for a homosexual orientation."[7] Finally, it is important to remember that Hamer himself is not claiming that the Xq28 findings explain all forms of homosexuality, but is specifically related to cases related to maternal heritability.

Understanding what Hamer claimed can be confusing. First, Xq28 is *not* a gene, but it is a section of the X chromosome which contains many genes and is well-known among geneticists for its gene density. While the Xq28 region covers approximately 5% of the chromosome, it contains almost 13% of the X chromosomal genes. The gene density of this area is seen in the fact over 40 different diseases have been traced to abnormalities in the Xq28 region.[8] Hamer and his colleagues were *not* claiming to have identified a specific "gay" gene, but they were asserting such a gene or genes may exist in the Xq28 region.[9]

Furthermore, not all of the men in Hamer's study shared the exact genetic sequence. When the average person reads the popular reports regarding Xq28, they assume all 66 men from the 33 pairs of gay brothers had exactly the same DNA sequence at chromosome Xq28. This is not what Hamer claimed. As was noted in *The Hastings Center Report*, "In fact, all [Hamer] showed was that each member of the thirty-three concordant pairs shared his Xq28 region with his brother but not with any of the other sixty-four men. No single specific Xq28 sequence was common to all sixty-six men."[10] The sequence of genetic

---

7 Stella Hu et al., "Linkage Between Sexual Orientation and Chromosome Xq28 in males but not in females," *Nature Genetics* 11 (1995): 253.

8 Anja Kolb-Kokocinski et al., "The Systematic Functional Characteristic of Xq28 Genes Prioritizes Candidate Disease Genes," *BMC Genomics* 7.29 (February 17, 2006): 1–2.

9 In 1993, Hamer said, "Rather, it appears that Xq28 contains a gene that contributes to homosexual orientation in males." Hamer et al., "A Linkage Between DNA Markers on the X Chromosome and Male Sexual Orientation," 325.

10 Udo Schüklenk, Edward Stein, Jacinta Kerin, and William Byne, "The Ethics of Genetic Research on Sexual Orientation," *Hastings Center Report* 27.4 (July–August, 1997): 7.

information at Xq28 was different among each of the 33 pairs of brothers. What was common was the *location* of the sequences.

In the years following Hamer's research, several attempts to replicate his findings were unsuccessful. An unpublished 1998 study did not find significant Xq28 linkage for homosexuality in 54 U.S. pairs of homosexual brothers.[11] In 1999, Bailey et al. reported no definitive linkage between Xq28 and male homosexuality.[12] Also in 1999, Canadian researchers failed to replicate Hamer's findings, asserting that homosexual brothers are no more likely than their heterosexual brother to have the marker at Xq28.[13]

As was noted by Hamer and his colleagues in 1995, their findings did not prove that a chromosomal pattern at Xq28 is either necessary or sufficient to cause homosexuality. Evangelical authors Jones and Yarhouse comment on this and say:

> If [Xq28] was necessary to the homosexual condition, then [Hamer et al.] would not have found the 7 out of 40 homosexual brother pairs who did not share this characteristic (these 7 brothers did not have the chromosomal pattern but were gay anyway). If it was sufficient to cause homosexuality, then they would not have found, in their second study, non-homosexual brothers who shared the genetic characteristic but not the sexual orientation. Having the genetic marker does not mean you are a homosexual (not sufficient), and not having the genetic marker does not mean you are a homosexual (not necessary).[14]

In spite of weaknesses in Hamer's research, the idea of a "gay gene" has taken on a life of its own and is now commonly accepted by many people as proof homosexuals are "born this way."

---

11   A. R. Sanders et al., "Genetic Linkage Study of Male Homosexual Orientation. Poster Presentation at the 151st Annual Meeting of the American Psychiatric Association. Toronto, Ontario, Canada, 1998; Cited in Khytam Dawood, Michael Bailey, and Nicholas G. Martin, "Genetic and Environmental Influences on Sexual Orientation," in *Handbook of Behavioral Genetics*, Yong-Kyu Kim, ed. (New York: Springer Science Media, 2009), 273.

12   J. M. Bailey et al., "A Family History Study of Male Sexual Orientation Using Three Independent Samples," *Behavior Genetics* 29.2 (1999): 79–86.

13   George Rice, Carol Anderson, Neil Risch and George Ebers, "Male Homosexuality: Absence of Linkage to Microsatellite Markers at Xq28," *Science* 284 (April 23, 1999): 665–67.

14   Jones and Yarhouse, *Homosexuality: The Use of Scientific Research in the Church's Moral Debate*, 81.

Brian Mustanski et al. (2005)

A 2005 study led by Brian Mustanski of Northwestern University's Feinberg School of Medicine also failed to replicate Hamer's findings concerning Xq28. The sample for this study was drawn from 73 families previously studied in Hamer's 1993 and 1995 reports along with 73 new families which had never been researched. When all the families were taken together, it resulted in a sample of 456 individuals from 146 unrelated families, of which 137 families had 2 gay brothers and 9 families had 3 gay brothers. Instead of focusing only on the Xq28 region, this study was a genome wide scan, meaning all 46 chromosomes were examined. Studying the entire sample of 146 families, no statistical significance associated with chromosome Xq28 was discovered, thus Hamer's earlier findings were not confirmed.

The 2005 study did report three new regions of genetic interest concerning male homosexuality on chromosomes 7, 8, and 10. But a careful reading of the report shows a weak linkage between male homosexuality and these chromosomes. The researchers' strongest finding was on chromosome 7 at 7q36. However, Mustanski and colleagues admitted that the connection they found falls just short of "criteria for genomewide significance."[15] They went on to say that certain regions on chromosomes 8 and 10 "approached criteria for suggestive linkage."[16] Their report shows that none of the new data met professionally accepted criteria for statistical significance. Simon LeVay summarizes this study and says, "The statistical power of these findings was low, however, and the findings should be thought of as pointers for future research rather than as actual identifications of regions containing 'gay genes.'"[17]

Sanders and Bailey (2014): Hamer's Research Confirmed?

In 2014, Alan Sanders, associate professor of psychiatry at Northwestern University, and Michael Bailey, also of Northwestern and who was discussed previously in relation to twin studies, published research which claims to have replicated Hamer's findings about the Xq28 region in addition to an area of interest at chromosome 8 previously identified by Mustanski. In the largest

---

15   Brian S. Mustanski et al., "A Genomewide Scan of Male Sexual Orientation," *Human Genetics* 116 (2005): 276.

16   Ibid.

17   LeVay, *Gay, Straight, and the Reason Why*, 172.

study to date on the topic, Sanders and Bailey examined the genetics of 908 individuals from 384 different families, with special emphasis on 409 pairs of homosexual brothers in their sample. The researchers concluded they had found significant linkage in the central region of chromosome 8q12 and Xq28 and said, "In context with the previous linkage scans, it seems likely that genes contributing to variation in male sexual orientation reside in these regions."[18] The authors also added, "While our study results provide further evidence for early (prenatal) biological influences on variation in male sexual orientation, we also emphasize that genetic contributions are far from determinant but instead represent a part of the trait's multifactorial causation, both genetic and environmental."[19]

While the new research from Sanders and Bailey is intriguing, it must be stressed that in their own data only 8q12 met the standard criteria for statistical significance. In genetics, an LOD score ("logarithm of the odds") is a standard way of measuring data. Typically, a score of 3 or higher is deemed to indicate significant linkage. In Sanders and Bailey's research, 8q12 had an LOD score of 4.08 while Xq28 had an LOD score of 2.99. Sanders himself admits data from Xq28 does not clear the threshold for significance.[20] Why then do they emphasize they have found something at Xq28? Because some of their other data (which also failed to reach the threshold for statistical significance) clustered in regions neighboring Xq28. Other researchers also question the strength of these new findings. Neil Risch, a statistical geneticist at the University of California, San Francisco believes the Sanders and Bailey data are statistically too weak to demonstrate any genetic link. [21] Another way of stating the data is to say that not all or even the majority of the men in the study shared something significant at either Xq28 or 8q12. In other words, genetic information at either of these chromosomes is not necessary to cause homosexuality.[22]

---

18   A. R. Sanders et al., "Genome-Wide Scan Demonstrates Significant Linkage for Male Sexual Orientation," *Psychological Medicine* 45 (2015): 1384.

19   Ibid., 1386.

20   Kelly Servick, "Study of Gay Brothers May Confirm X Chromosome Link to Homosexuality," *Science*, November 17, 2014, accessed March 2, 2015, http://news.sciencemag.org/biology/2014/11/study-gay-brothers-may-confirm-x-chromosome-link-homosexuality.

21   "A Large Study of Gay Brothers Adds to Evidence That Genes Influence Men's Chances of Being Homosexual, But the Results Aren't Strong Enough to Prove It," *The Associated Press*, November 17, 2014, accessed May 5, 2015, http://www.nydailynews.com/life-style/health/study-suggests-genes-influence-men-chances-gay-article-1.2013597.

22   This can be clearly seen by examining the plot diagrams on page 1385 of the Sanders/Bailey study. Sanders et al., "Genome Wide Scan," 1385.

Another limitation in the Sanders/Bailey research is their use of older methods which have been surpassed by newer and more precise techniques. Sanders and Bailey performed a genetic linkage study using an approach similar to Hamer in 1993. In genetics, a linkage study only identifies wide regions of a chromosome containing many genes. In contrast, the preferred method now is called a "genome wide association study," a technique which can often identify a specific gene responsible for a particular trait.[23] Sanders and Bailey indicated they wanted to do a linkage study in order to replicate Hamer's findings. They have indicated they will do a genome wide association study in the future. But their current data was derived from an older and less precise technique.

Bailey insists the new findings about Xq28 and 8q12 support a born-this-way argument and yet sounds contradictory when he says, "Sexual orientation has nothing to do with choice. . . . We found evidence for two sets [of genes] that affect whether a man is gay or straight. But it is not completely determinative; there are certainly other environmental factors involved."[24] Bailey sounds triumphant when he says sexual orientation "has nothing to do with choice," but this assertion seems confusing when compared to his follow-on statement that the genes in question "are not completely determinative." Perhaps part of the confusion is caused by Bailey's use of the term "environment." For born-this-way arguments, environmental influences include not only a person's family and culture, but the prenatal environment of the womb.

But Sanders and Bailey's own comments in their published research contradicts the idea they have found a particular gene or genes which cause a person to be born a homosexual. In their conclusion, they address concerns related to a hypothetical scenario where a parent with a strong animosity towards homosexuality might have a genetic test performed on a pre-born infant to determine if it would be homosexual. The fear among some born-

---

23   Kelly Servick, "Study of Gay Brothers May Confirm X Chromosome Link to Homosexuality."

24   Ian Sample, "Male Sexual Orientation Influenced by Genes, Study Shows," *The Guardian*, February 14, 2014, accessed April 23, 2014, http://www.theguardian.com/science/2014/feb/14/genes-influence-male-sexual-orientation-study. Simon LeVay apparently finds the new research convincing. In 2011, he said "Unfortunately, Hamer's report has not been robustly confirmed." Simon LeVay, *Gay, Straight, and the Reason Why: The Science of Sexual Orientation* (New York: Oxford University Press, 2011), 171. However, he comments on the new research and says, "This study knocks another nail into the coffin of the 'chosen lifestyle' theory of homosexuality." Andy Coghlan, "Largest Study of Gay Brothers Homes in on 'Gay Genes,'" *New Scientist*, November 17, 2014, accessed May 5, 2015, http://www.newscientist.com/article/dn26572-largest-study-of-gay-brothers-homes-in-on-gay-genes.html#.VVKNn_lViko.

this-way activists is that if such a test existed, then homosexual children would be aborted. But Sanders and Bailey say this fear is unwarranted because "the small magnitude of effects suggested herein are inconsistent with a test that those motivated to influence their children's sexual orientation would find useful."[25] They then conclude by saying, "While our study results provide further evidence for early (prenatal) biological influences on variation in male sexual orientation, we also emphasize that genetic contributions are far from determinant but instead represent a part of the trait's multifactorial causation, both genetic and environmental."[26] So the authors of the new study admit the purported influences they find are of a small magnitude and are not determinant. With these statements in mind, Bailey's claim that "sexual orientation has nothing to do with choice" seems perplexing, overstated, and inconsistent with his own research.

Sanders and Bailey's research is actually touching on the *heritability* of homosexuality as opposed to it being an *inherited* trait. Sanders himself commented, "When people say there's a gay gene, it's an oversimplification. There's more than one gene, and genetics is not the whole story. Whatever gene contributes to sexual orientation, you can think of it as much as contributing to heterosexuality as much as you can think of it contributing to homosexuality. It contributes to a variation in the trait."[27] Sanders has suggested 30–40% of the variation of the trait of male homosexuality can be connected with genetics.[28] As we saw earlier, virtually all human behavior falls into the range of 30–60% for heritability.

Bailey's claim that sexual orientation has "nothing to do with choice" is a statement reflecting his own personal worldview and not a necessary inference from his findings. Bailey is actually stating a version of biological determinism in which people are automatons driven on to their destiny by irresistible biological urges. Bailey seems willing to admit that environment plays a role in development of one's orientation, but is unwilling or unable to admit that our choices in response to our environment affect our own sexual desires and cravings. Ian Sample of *The Guardian* is favorable to homosexual rights, but even

---

25   Sanders et al., Genome-Wide Scan Demonstrates Significant Linkage for Male Sexual Orientation," 1386.

26   Ibid.

27   Ian Sample, "Male Sexual Orientation Influenced by Genes, Study Shows."

28   Alan Sanders, Interview, accessed April 24, 2014, https://www.youtube.com/watch?v=WANgHtb-NT8#t=29. The webpage home for the Sanders/Bailey study can be found at http://www.gaybros.com/index.html.

he sounded a more restrained note and said, "The gene or genes in the Xq28 region that influence sexual orientation have a limited and variable impact."[29]

To summarize, Sanders and Bailey found one area of interest at Chromosome 8q12 which reached the accepted criteria for statistical significance. They also claimed their data for Xq28 came very close to being statistically significant. However, there were homosexuals in their sample who did not share the markers at either region. Thus, a specific genetic link to either 8q12 or Xq28 is not necessary for homosexuality. By their own admission, the effects for specific areas of DNA are of a small magnitude and do not mean someone with a specific genetic pattern will inevitably become homosexual.

HOMOSEXUALITY AND EPIGENETICS

Epigenetics (a word with a rough literal meaning of "on genes") refers to all modifications to genes other than changes in the DNA sequence itself.[30] DNA is wrapped around proteins called histones and both DNA and the histones are covered with chemical "tags." These histones and chemical tags (or "epimarks") are part of each person's *epigenetics* and constitute an extra layer of information attached to our genes' backbones that regulates their expression.[31] As science has discovered more and more about genetic traits, we have learned that these epigenetic structures govern which genes in the DNA of any given cell will be active. These epigenetic structures can be thought of as switches and knobs which turns things "on or off" or "up and down." Basically, epigenetics-regulating genome activity helps explain odd things like identical twins who have different hair color.

In 2012, a team of researchers associated with the National Institute for Mathematical and Biological Synthesis and led by William Rice of the University of California, Santa Barbara suggested epigenetics may explain the heritability of some forms of homosexuality. To understand their claims, it is important to review just a bit about the prenatal development of males and females, some of which we examined earlier in the chapter on prenatal hormones. As children grow in the mother's womb, certain sex hormones

---

29   Ibid.

30   Joanna Downer, "Backgrounder: Epigenetics and Imprinted Genes," accessed April 24, 2014, http://www.hopkinsmedicine.org/press/2002/november/epigenetics.htm.

31   "Study Finds Epigenetics, Not Genetics, Underlies Homosexuality," National Institute for Mathematical and Biological Synthesis, December 11, 2012, accessed April 24, 2014, http://www.nimbios.org/press/FS_homosexuality.

are produced in quantity at a specific time to help their tiny bodies grow in a gender-specific direction. Testosterone is especially important in this process. Both boys and girls produce testosterone, but boys produce more testosterone than girls in particular between weeks 11–17 of development.[32] Girls have mechanisms that usually protect them from producing too much testosterone while boys have mechanisms that prevent them from producing too little. This allows both boys and girls to develop gender typical traits.

How are prenatal hormones, epigenetics, and homosexuality purportedly linked? Normally, epigenetic marks are not transferred from parent to child, but are erased as the new life forms its own. But Rice et al. suggest there are times when certain epigenetic marks are not erased. When this happens, there are occasions when a young fetus inherits epigenetic marks that are not consistent with the baby's gender. They then hypothesize these sexually-antagonistic (opposed to the child's gender) epigenetic marks "influence androgen signaling in the part of the brain controlling sexual orientation, but not the genitalia nor the brain region(s) controlling gender identity."[33] In other words, the epigenetics cause a child to process the wrong sex hormones or sex hormones in the wrong amounts into the brain. Thus, they hypothesize this causes the child to experience same-sex attraction as he or she matures.

As we consider this hypothesis, it is important to remember some important points of clarification. First, epigenetics is a somewhat new sub-discipline within genetics, so the exact mechanisms of epigenetic function are still being unraveled at a broad level, much less in the specific case of homosexuality. Second, the work by Rice and his team is a specific type of academic research called "meta-analysis, a quantitative, formal study design used to assess systematically previous research studies in order to derive conclusions about a particular body of research.[34] Such work is also called a *review* article, meaning it is an article that synthesizes other research already in print and suggests possible implications. Meta-analysis is often the first step in defining avenues for future research by summarizing what has been done, what conclusions have been reached, and providing suggestions for future research. The important thing for Christians to remember is that as of right now the epigenetic theory

---

32   William R. Rice, Urban Friberg, and Sergey Gavrilets, "Homosexuality as a Consequence of Epigenetically Canalized Sexual Development," *The Quarterly Review of Biology* 87.4 (December 2012): 346.

33   William R. Rice, Urban Friberg, and Sergey Gavrilets, "Homosexuality as a Consequence of Epigenetically Canalized Sexual Development," 358.

34   This definition is from A. B. Haidich, "Meta-Analysis in Medical Research," *Hippokratia* 14 (2010): 29.

has not been proven, but certain researchers suggest it is plausible. Essentially, Rice et al. are saying to other researchers, "Hey, you might look over here."

While William Rice and others are suggesting epigenetics affect a child's sexual orientation *prior* to birth, epigenetic research may also pose challenges to born-this-way arguments. Each person's epigenetics are flexible and react to signals from the outside such as diet or stress. There is indication that lifestyle choices (such as smoking or gluttony) influence which genes are expressed ("turned on" or "turned off") by epigenetic structures. The degree to which sexual behavior affects the epigenetic signals within a person are speculative at present, but it is at least plausible that participation in homosexual behavior may alter one's epigenetics.

Summary

Science has not discovered a gene which causes homosexuality. What some researchers have claimed to discover are regions of the human genome which may contain genes which influence the manner in which male homosexual orientation develops: the Xq28 and 8q12 regions. No region of DNA has been identified or suggested as coding for female homosexuality. Suggestions of an epigenetic contribution to homosexuality have not been substantiated as of yet, though the theory has intrigued many. When we think of a genetic trait, we tend to think of the studies by Gregor Mendel (1822–1884), the famous Augustinian friar whose research on pea plants in the 1800s was the foundation for the science of genetics. No gene or group of genes has been found which codes for homosexuality in the way Mendel described variations in pea plants. There is no gay gene *in the Mendelian sense of the word*.

Scientists accepting the idea that genetics influence sexual orientation debate the way homosexuality is passed from one generation to the next. Some suggest homosexuality is a case of *overdominance*, a genetic circumstance when a heterozygote (two different alleles or "Aa") produces a fitness advantage for humans while a homozygote (two identical alleles or "AA" or "aa") is less fit.[35] Other researchers suggest that a homosexual gene may be a case of a *sexually antagonistic trait*, meaning the allele for homosexuality may be passed via women as a recessive trait that improves the fitness of females without

---

35 The Sickle Cell allele is an example of overdominance. Individuals who are heterozygous (Aa) for the Sickle Cell allele are more resistant to malaria and less likely to contract Sickle Cell Anemia.

providing any benefit for males.[36] Some even suggest male homosexuality remains in a population in order to improve female fecundity.[37] But these explanations are speculative, limited to male homosexuality, and not directly related to female homosexuality.

Christians must be aware of the manner in which activists misrepresent data concerning genetic linkage to homosexuality. In their summary of research on twin data and homosexuality, pro-homosexual authors Wilson and Rahman begin by saying, "Clearly, genetic factors are involved in the origins of sexual orientation."[38] Christians can concur at this point, since no one denies a genetic influence on any number of behaviors. But Wilson and Rahman then immediately follow this statement with the completely false assertion, "Now that we know that 'gay genes' really do exist, how do we go about finding them?"[39] This second statement is a non-sequitor — an unwarranted conclusion. Wilson and Rahman wrongly move from discussing "influence" to claiming causation ("gay genes exist").

Genetic research indicates environment plays a critical role in the formation of a person's sexual identity, a point even granted by Dean Hamer. In 1994, Hamer commented on the relationship between genes and one's environment and said, "Genes might have a somewhat different effect on someone in Salt Lake City than if that person were growing up in New York City."[40] In an amazing admission, Hamer here states that the culture in which one is raised — socially conservative Salt Lake as opposed to socially liberal New York — has an effect on the degree to which genetics influence a person's final behavior. Instead of simply being "born this way," a complex interchange of

---

36 *See* Sergey Gavrilets and William R. Rice, "Genetic Models of Homosexuality: Generating Testable Predictions," *Proceedings of the Royal Society of Britain* 273 (December 22, 2006): 3031–38.

37 See Andrea Camperio Ciani, Paolo Cermelli, and Giovanni Zanzotto, "Sexually Antagonistic Selection in Human Male Homosexuality," *PloS ONE* 3.6 (June 2008): 2,282. Barry Kuhle and Sarah Radtke have argued female homosexuality is an adaptive form of sexual fluidity in women, claiming the ability to have same-sex intimate relationships among primitive women may have allowed for a shared parenting load. Barry X. Kuhle and Sarah Radtke, "Born Both Ways: Alloparenting Hypothesis for Sexual Fluidity in Women," *Evolutionary Psychology* 11.2 (April 2013): 304–23.

38 Glenn Wilson and Qazi Rahman, *Born Gay: The Psychobiology of Sex Orientation* (London: Peter Owen Publishers, 2008), 49.

39 Ibid., 50.

40 Quoted in Charles Mann, "Behavior Genetics In Transition," *Science* 264 (June 17, 1994): 1,687.

genetics, culture, family dynamics, and personal choice all join together to influence the sexual lifestyle and ethics which each of us embrace.

Great caution must be exercised when discussing the behavioral genetics. In the past, claims concerning various genetically "caused" behaviors have been celebrated with much fanfare only to have others be unable to replicate the findings. Behaviors as different as criminality and obesity have been blamed on genetics, with the popular press often overstating the degree to which any genetic sequence actually *causes* a behavior. These missteps should not dissuade Christians from research into the human genome. Genetic research offers great hope for diagnosis and treatment of many of the most frightening diseases. For example, we now know adenosine deaminase deficiency — a disease which severely compromises the immune system — is caused by mutations in the ADA gene, a diagnosis which has led to successful gene therapy for afflicted persons. But the predictive power of behavioral genetics is not the same; it is quite limited.

What if some future study proves incontrovertibly that a specific gene or cluster of genes acts in such a way that every person with these markers is born with a homosexual orientation? Does this mean we must then surrender Scriptural teaching concerning the sinful nature of homosexual acts? No, we should not. One of the major flaws in born-this-way arguments is that advocates seem to want to affirm the basic idea of Genesis 1:26–28 (humans are made in the image of God), while rejecting the equally important fact of Genesis 3 (all humans have been negatively affected by a historic, space-time Fall). As a result, every human being is born with a natural tendency to rebel against God and to sin. It is not inconsistent with Christian anthropology to suggest the effects of sin reach even to the level of how our genetic code influences the way we respond to certain stimuli and our desires are distorted. John and Paul Feinberg rightly say, "Would genes and biology make it impossible to resist the temptation for same-sex sexual acts? No more so than genes and biology make it impossible for heterosexuals disposed toward sexual promiscuity to refrain from that behavior and remain faithful to their spouse."[41] With Paul, we agree that creation itself waits to "be set free from the bondage of corruption into the glorious freedom of God's children" (Rom. 8:21). This includes our genetic code itself which suffers from effects of the Fall.

---

41 John Feinberg and Paul Feinberg, *Ethics for a Brave New World*, 2nd ed. (Wheaton, IL: Crossway, 2010), 383.

CHAPTER 9

Homosexuality and Other Factors

GAY, STRAIGHT, AND THE REASON WHY is an oft-cited book written by Simon LeVay, noted earlier for his research on INAH 3 and homosexuality. A practicing homosexual himself, the British-born neuroscientist surveys a potpourri of arguments often used in favor of a born-this-way moral stance. Moving quickly through multiple claims, LeVay surveys many factors considered to be closely connected to a predisposition for homosexuality, including biology, genetics, brain structure, the role of sex hormones, body symmetry, handedness, visuospatial abilities, and many other ideas mentioned only in passing. The cumulative effect of reading such a book is to feel overwhelmed and many Christians assume the case is settled — homosexuals are indeed born this way, and we must adjust.

But the case is not as clear or intimidating as argued by LeVay. Closer investigation reveals some of the claims are conflicting and in fact LeVay is strongly arguing for his own theory related to the INAH 3 as opposed to other theories purportedly explaining the origin of homosexuality. Many advocates of born-this-way arguments engage in similar tactics, hurling a barrage of claims at the unprepared, hoping at least one or two the ideas will "stick." In what follows, we will quickly survey various claims commonly used in born-this-way arguments, many of which are often used in concert with other data we have already addressed. We will begin with born-this-way arguments associated with homosexual acts in animals, then we will summarize the fraternal birth order effect, finger-length ratios, childhood gender nonconformity, and various other common assertions.

HOMOSEXUALITY IS COMMON IN NATURE

One often repeated argument in favor of homosexuality is the relatively common nature of same-sex acts among animals.[1] The most exhaustive survey

---

1   Yale University professors Clennan S. Ford and Frank A. Beach made one of the earliest

of such behavior is *Biological Exuberance,* a 1999 book by Bruce Bagemihl, a biologist and researcher who has served on the faculty of the University of British Columbia. Bagemihl claims homosexual behavior "occurs in more than 450 different kinds of animals worldwide, and is found in every major geographic region and every major animal group."[2] At many places in Bagemihl's work, one sees his thinly veiled arguments in favor of same-sex marriage based on animal behavior. For example, he stresses that same-sex pairs of birds can be great parents and care for their young: "In a detailed study of parental behavior by female pairs of Ring-billed Gulls, scientists found no significant differences in quality of care provided by homosexual as opposed to heterosexual parents. They concluded that there was not anything that male Ring-billed Gull parents provided that two females could not offer equally well."[3] Furthermore, he argues same-sex animal pairs adopt and successfully raise children, noting "two female Northern Elephant Seals occasionally adopt and coparent [sic] an orphaned pup, while male Hooded Warblers and Black-headed Gulls may adopt eggs or entire nests that have been abandoned by females, and pairs of male Cheetahs occasionally look after lost cubs."[4]

Bagemihl also argues that transvestitism and sex-change are common in the animal kingdom. Concerning transvestite behavior among animals, he says "some female African swallowtail butterflies, for example, resemble males in their wing coloration and patterning, while in some species of squid, males imitate female arm postures during aggressive encounters."[5] Bagemihl also gushes with praise for transsexual invertebrates: "Transsexuality or sex change is a routine aspect of many animals' lives, especially in invertebrates: shrimp, oysters, and sow bugs, for example, all undergo complete reversals of their sex at some stage in their lives."[6] Bagemihl is arguing current moral concerns about transsexuality are unwarranted since the practice is common among animals.

In response, I suggest four criticisms of Bagemihl's work. First, from a Christian theistic moral stance, we insist that humans are not animals, there-

---

and most influential forms of this argument. See Clennan S. Ford and Frank A. Beach, *Patterns of Sexual Behavior* (New York: Harper & Brothers, 1951).

2   Bruce Bagemihl, *Biological Exuberance: Animal Homosexuality and Natural Diversity* (New York: St. Martin's Press, 1999), 12.

3   M. R. Conover, "Parental Care by Male-Female and Female-Female Pairs of Ring-Billed Gulls," *Colonial Waterbirds* 12 (1989): 148; cited in *Biological Exuberance,* 25n12.

4   *Biological Exuberance,* 24.

5   Ibid., 38.

6   Ibid., 39. Sow bugs are crustaceans which live their entire life on land.

fore the behavior of animals is not a morally significant source for determining appropriate human behavior. The actions of animals are not determinative for human morality. Using Bagemihl's logic, one could just as well observe that animals sometimes devour their young, thus infanticide is acceptable! Next, Bagemihl wrongly superimposes controversial and debated human categories on the animals. He applies categories derived from our modern culture wars to animals as if the animals support current attempts at radical re-ordering of marriage and family. Third, while it is not uncommon for animals to engage in same-sex behavior, it is far more rare for animals to engage only in homosexual acts and reject all opportunities for heterosexual acts. In this way, animals do not serve Bagemihl's goal of justifying exclusive homosexual attraction. Finally, I suspect Bagemihl's argument gains some force since fewer people in our industrial society are actually raised around animals and are thus caught off guard by the "gay animals" argument. People with extensive experience around animals have long known of animals of the same sex which mount each other and imitate mating. In fact, hundreds of previous generations of humans have observed such behavior, but it is only now that we are told humans should imitate it. In this way, the born-this-way argument carries a strong overtone of evolutionary abandonment: sex is not a gift from God to be celebrated, but a crude act shared by all animals, and humans are *just another animal.*

FRATERNAL BIRTH ORDER EFFECT

The "Fraternal Birth Order Effect" refers to the claim that males with multiple older brothers are more likely to be homosexual. In other words, the Fraternal Birth Order Effect asserts homosexual males tend to born later in the families than their heterosexual brothers. This idea is most closely associated with an article published by Ray Blanchard and Anthony Bogaert in 1996 in *The American Journal of Psychiatry*, where the authors claimed each additional older brother increases the odds of homosexuality by 33%.[7] According to the theory, around one out of every seven homosexual men can attribute their

---

7 Ray Blanchard and Anthony F. Bogaert, "Homosexuality in Men and Number of Older Brothers," *The American Journal of Psychiatry* 153:1 (January 1996): 27–31. The authors were building on the work of C. T. Gualtieri and R. E. Hicks, "The Immunoreactive Theory of Selective Male Affliction," *Behavior and Brain Sciences* 8.3 (1985): 427–77.

same-sex attraction to the fraternal birth order effect. [8] Furthermore, the birth order effect only applies if the younger brother is right-handed.[9]

Blanchard and Bogaert suggest the connection between birth order and homosexuality may be caused by a maternal immune reaction. To understand their claim, one must first understand the term "antigen." An antigen is something capable of producing an immune response. Blanchard and Bogaert's argument is that in some cases the pregnant mother's immune system may react negatively to specific antigens in the male fetus called "H-Y antigens." If the mother becomes pregnant again, the theory suggests the mother's body immunologically attacks subsequent male fetuses with more intensity. As the mother's body "attacks" a subsequent male baby in utero, H-Y antibodies from the mother possibly cross the placental barrier and enter the brain of the baby boy, somehow diverting his sexual orientation from a male-typical pathway, so that the individual will later be attracted to men instead of women.[10] Basically, Blanchard and Bogaert claim the mother's body reacts negatively to the presence of a baby boy and affects his development, leading to a less-masculinized brain. The effects of the mother's immunological attack becomes more pronounced with each additional pregnancy in which the mother carries a male.

Blanchard and Bogaert's research is plagued by sample problems. For example, they clearly state that homosexuals were recruited for their research at homosexual community organizations and at the 1994 Toronto Lesbian and Gay Pride Day parade.[11] Jones and Kwee suggest this negatively affects the sample because later born gay men were perhaps more apt to be "out and proud."[12] But at the same time, Jones and Kwee add, "Despite various methodological problems with the fraternal birth order research, we concede that the

---

8   James M. Cantor, Ray Blanchard, Andrew D. Paterson, and Anthony F. Bogaert, "How Many Gay Men Owe Their Sexual Orientation to Fraternal Birth Order?" *Archives of Sexual Behavior* 31.1 (February 2002): 63–71.

9   Ray Blanchard et al., "Interaction of Fraternal Birth Order and Handedness in the Development of Male Homosexuality," *Hormones and Behavior* 49.3 (2006): 405–14. See also Ray Blanchard and R. A. Lippa, "The Sex Ratio of Older Siblings in Non-right-handed Homosexual men," *Archives of Sexual Behavior* 37.6 (December 2008): 970–76.

10   Ray Blanchard, "Fraternal Birth Order and the Maternal Immune Hypothesis of Male Homosexuality," *Hormones and Behavior* 40 (2001): 109–10.

11   Ray Blanchard and Anthony F. Bogaert, "Homosexuality in Men and Number of Older Brothers," 28.

12   Jones and Kwee, "Scientific Research, Homosexuality, and the Church's Moral Debate: An Update," 309.

evidence as a whole points to some sort of relationship between the number of older brothers and homosexuality."[13]

There are serious challenges to Blanchard and Bogaert's idea that the mother's body immunologically attacks male babies. Their maternal immunosensitization hypothesis is just that — a hypothesis and has not been proven, and some evidence seems to contradict it. In 1994, a study of 17,283 mother-and-son pairs tested whether enhanced autoimmunity in the mother was associated in the fetus with cerebral palsy, mental retardation, seizures, articulation disorder, reading or arithmetic disability, verbal or performance aptitude deficits and ADHD. Results indicated that immune dysfunction in the mother was not associated with an increased incidence of any neurodevelopmental disorders in the children.[14] The findings from this large study seem to count against the idea the mother's body would shift a boy's brain in a non-typical direction. Other researchers have noted the immune system is not an aggressive, attack and defense mechanism, but rather a complex cell memory system. This led one group of researchers to say, "If the immune system is a memory system, then the mother's immune system is not attacking the male fetus and should not be presented as such."[15]

The fraternal birth order effect is often cited as one of the more robust findings in born-this-way research.[16] But recent research brings the universality of the purported effect into question. In 2006, a survey of the entire population of Denmark found no substantial fraternal birth order effect. This survey used the formal records of those who had entered a homosexual marriage as a measure of same-sex attraction. While not everyone with same-sex attraction will enter into such a marriage, the findings do give reason to use caution when asserting the universal nature of the fraternal birth order effect. Instead of a connection to older brothers, the Danish research found male homosexual

---

13   Ibid., 310.

14   K. A. Flannery and J. Liederman, "A Test of the Immunoreactive theory for the Origin of Neurodevelopmental Disorders in the Offspring of Women with Immune Disorder," *Cortex* 30.4 (December 1994): 635–46.

15   Joseph M. Currin, Linzi Gibson, Randolph D. Hubach, "Multidimensional Assessment of Sexual Orientation and the Fraternal Birth Order Effect," *Psychology of Sexual Orientation and Gender Diversity* 2.2 (June 2015): 119. The authors claimed to find no fraternal birth order effect. Their sample was drawn from online participants.

16   For a summary of some of the more important articles, see Anthony Bogaert and Malvina Skorska, "Sexual Orientation, Fraternal Birth Order, and the Maternal Immune Hypothesis: A Review," *Frontiers in Neuroendocrinology* 32.2 (April 2011): 247–54.

marriage was associated with having older mothers, divorced parents, absent fathers, and being the youngest child.[17]

Beyond male homosexuality, at least three studies have claimed that a fraternal birth order effect is at work to some degree in certain sexual offenders.[18] If this correlation is confirmed, certainly no one would then suggest the sexual offenders are, through no fault of their own, pre-disposed to act in such a way and thus should be excused from moral censure. But the strongest critique of the fraternal birth order effect is the fact that half or more of all homosexual men have zero older brothers.[19]

Finger Length Ratios

Finger length ratios are often cited as evidence that homosexuals are "born this way." Specifically, this claim relates to the ratio of length between the ring (fourth digit) finger and the index (second digit) finger or the "2D:4D ratio." The 2D:4D ratio generally varies according to sex. In males, the ring finger is usually longer than the index finger. In females, the ring finger and the index finger are typically about the same length. Perhaps more than anyone, British researcher John T. Manning has popularized the claim that the observable differences in 2D:4D ratio between males and females is the result of prenatal exposure to hormones.[20]

Some born-this-way arguments claim there is a consistent difference in the 2D:4D ratios of lesbians. Specifically, some researchers have reported

---

17 Morten Frisch and Anders Hviid, "Childhood Family Correlates of Heterosexual and Homosexual Marriages: A National Cohort Study of Two Million Danes," *Archives of Sexual Behavior* 35.5 (October 2006): 533–47.

18 Martin L. Lalumière et al., "Sexual Deviance and Number of Older Brothers Among Sexual Offenders," *Sexual Abuse: A Journal of Research and Treatment* 10.1 (1998): 5–15; K. Côt et al., "Birth order, Birth Interval, and Deviant Sexual Preferences Among Sex Offenders," *Sexual Abuse: Journal of Research and Treatment* 14 (2002): 67–81; S. I. MacCulloch et al., "Birth Order in Sex-Offending and Aggressive Offending Men," *Archives of Sexual Behavior* 33.5 (October 2004): 467–74.

19 Blanchard himself concedes this point and comments, "The maternal immune hypothesis was never intended to account for the sexual orientation of all homosexual men." Ray Blanchard, "Controversies in Sexual Medicine–Male Homosexuality: Nature or Culture?" *Journal of Sexual Medicine* 7.10 (October 2010): 3248.

20 John T. Manning et al., "The Ratio of 2nd to 4th Digit Length: A Predictor of Sperm Numbers and Concentrations of Testosterone, Luteinizing Hormone and Estrogen," *Human Reproduction* 13 (1998): 3000–3004.

that lesbians have finger length ratios more similar to men than to women and suggested this was due to atypical prenatal exposure to androgens.[21] The claim is then made that the same prenatal hormones which affect finger digit ratio patterns in lesbians also affects their brains, causing them to have a same-sex attraction.

Yet, the data concerning the 2D:4D ratio does not necessarily support born-this-way arguments. Beyond homosexuality, Manning also suggests particular finger digit ratios can be correlated to a higher number of sexual partners among heterosexual men,[22] particular forms of aggression in women,[23] and running speed in particular track events.[24] In each case, Manning is arguing the finger digit ratios are indicative of particular levels of exposure to hormones during pregnancy, which result in particular behaviors or abilities. The 2D:4D ratio actually becomes a point of leverage for a view of human nature based on biological determinism: we are highly complex machines programmed prior to birth with certain inclinations. In this way, we see born-this-way arguments actually have a lower view of human freedom and choice than Christian anthropology. For Christians, one is not doomed to homosexual behavior, heterosexual promiscuity, or fits of aggression simply because of one's 2D:4D ratio. Instead, Christians affirm each human is a moral agent responsible for his or her actions.

The weakest part of born-this-way arguments regarding the 2D:4D ratio is that the argument is disputed by the findings of pro-homosexual researchers themselves. Again, central to this particular theory is that if prenatal hormones affect one's sexual orientation, one would expect evidence that lesbians were exposed to too much testosterone while homosexual males would show evidence of too little. Such unusual exposure to prenatal hormones is then suggested as the cause for an atypical 2D:4D ratio in lesbians.

If prenatal hormones affect both the 2D:4D ratio and sexual orientation,

---

21   Bernd Kraemer et al., "Finger Length Ratio (2D:4D) and Dimensions of Sexual Orientation," *Neuropsychobiology* 53.4 (2006): 210–14.

22   Johannes Honekopp et al., "2nd to 4th Digit Ratio (2D:4D) and Number of Sex Partners: Evidence for effects of Prenatal Testosterone in Men," *Psychoneuroendocrinology* 31.1 (January 2006): 30–37.

23   Sarah M. Coyne et al., "Directional asymmetry (right–left differences) in digit ratio (2D:4D) predict indirect aggression in women," *Personality and Individual Differences* 43.4 (2007): 865–72.

24   Robert Trivers, Renato Hopp, and John T. Manning, "A Longitudinal Study of Digit Ratio (2D:4D) and Its Relationships with Adult Running Speed in Jamaicans," *Human Biology* 85.4 (2013): 623–25.

then one would expect lesbian women to have 2D:4D ratios more like men and homosexual men to have 2D:4D ratios more like women. In fact, the data is somewhat ambiguous in this regard. While some studies have claimed that lesbians have a 2D:4D ratio similar to heterosexual men,[25] other studies have found that homosexual men do not have a 2D:4D ratio similar to women. Instead, research indicates homosexual males have a 2D:4D ratio that is *more masculinized* than the average heterosexual male. In other words, if one accepts the premise that prenatal hormones affect the 2D:4D ratio, homosexual men give evidence of exposure to more testosterone, not less. Furthermore, at least three studies have found no difference between the 2D:4D ratios of lesbian and heterosexual women, with two of the studies actually claiming 2D:4D ratios were related to a homosexual orientation for men, but not women — the inverse of what most homosexual activists claim.[26] Findings regarding 2D:4D digit ratios and homosexuality may suggest some possible hormonal factor, but the research is ambiguous and conflicting. It is imprudent to make global assertions about sexual behavior based on such findings.[27]

CHILDHOOD GENDER NONCONFORMITY

Childhood gender nonconformity refers to the degree that a small boy engages in behaviors more typical of girls or that a small girl engages in behaviors more typical of boys. A consistent finding is that childhood gender nonconformity

---

25   For example, T. J. Williams et al., "Finger-length Ratio and Sexual Orientation," *Nature* 404 (March 30, 2000): 455–56.

26   Patricia Hall and Catherine Schaeff, "Sexual Orientation and Fluctuating Asymmetry in Men and Women," *Archives of Sexual Behavior* 37.1 (February 2008): 158–65. While Hall and Schaeff found finger-length ratios were more feminized for homosexual men, they failed to detect any relationship between fluctuating asymmetry levels and 2D:4D finger-length ratios. They concluded elevated levels of developmental stress appear to be linked to shifts in sexual orientation, but the underlying mechanism does not seem to be connected to sex-atypical prenatal hormones; Richard A. Lippa, "Are 2D:4D Finger-length Ratios Related to Sexual Orientation? Yes for Men, No for Women," *Journal of Personality and Social Psychology* 85.1 (July 2003): 179–88; John T. Manning et al., "The Effects of Sex, Ethnicity, and Sexual Orientation on Self-measured Digit Ratio (2D:4D)," *Archives of Sexual Behavior* 36.2 (April 2007): 223–33. Both Lippa and Manning et al. found correlation for 2D:4D ratio in gay men, but not lesbians.

27   In a survey of the major studies on finger digit ratios and homosexuality, Grimbos et al. claim some of the ambiguity in the data is because of ethnic differences among respondents. They conclude the data indicates prenatal hormones affect sexual orientation in women. See Teresa Grimbos et al., "Sexual Orientation and the Second to Fourth Finger Length Ratio: A Meta-analysis in Men and Women," *Behavioral Neuroscience* 124.2 (2010): 278–87.

is strongly correlated with an adult identification as a homosexual. Among the numerous studies in this area, I will mention two here.

Research published in 1981 from the Kinsey Institute drew a sample from the San Francisco Bay area and compared around 1,000 homosexual men and lesbians with 500 heterosexual men and women. They claimed childhood gender nonconformity was a strong predictor of a person's adult sexual orientation. But the authors qualified their findings by saying gender nonconformity "was by no means universal, and conversely, gender nonconformity does not inevitably signal future homosexuality."[28] In 2008, researchers associated with Michael Bailey of Northwestern University reviewed the childhood home videos of homosexual and heterosexual adults. The videos were reviewed by a panel composed of both homosexuals and heterosexuals. The group of reviewers scored the videos of children who grew up to be homosexuals as more gender nonconforming, on average, than children who grew up to be heterosexuals, a pattern which held true for both men and women.[29]

While childhood gender nonconformity is strongly correlated with an adult homosexual identity, many children who engage in such behavior do not grow up to become homosexuals. Thus, childhood gender nonconformity is not necessary to cause homosexuality. Furthermore, the reasons why some children exhibit such behavior are complex and often little understood. The automatic assumption in our culture that these children must have been "born" to act in such a manner is a truncated and inadequate explanation for the origins of the behavior.

Other Various Assertions about Homosexuality

Several other biological or genetic traits among homosexuals are often mentioned in born-this-way arguments. There are frequent claims that handedness — being left-handed versus right-handed — correlates with homosexuality, the assertion being that homosexual men have a higher incidence of being left-handed. Some say that right-handed men with older brothers and left-handed men without older brothers have a higher chance of being homo-

---

28   Alan Paul Bell et al., *Sexual Preference: Its Development In Mena and Women* (Bloomington, IN: Indiana University Press, 1981), 189.

29   Gerulf Rieger et al., "Sexual Orientation and Childhood Gender Nonconformity: Evidence from Home Videos," *Developmental Psychology* 44.1 (January 2008): 46–58.

sexual.[30] In 1998, Dennis McFadden and Edward G. Pasanen claimed the click-evoked otoacoustic emissions [CEOAE]—a particular type of sound produced in the inner ear—are stronger in women than in men, but the CEOAEs of homosexual and bisexual females were found to be intermediate to those of heterosexual females and heterosexual males. McFadden and Pasanen suggested the reason for their findings might be that the auditory systems of homosexual and bisexual females, along with the brain structures responsible for their sexual orientation, have been partially masculinized by prenatal exposure to high levels of androgens.[31] In 2005, researchers associated with the Karolinska Institute in Stockholm claimed homosexual men reacted to male pheromones in a manner similar to heterosexual women.[32] Another study even attempted to find a connection between scalp hair rotation patterns and male homosexuality.[33]

Other claims abound and more will certainly emerge in the near future, but none of the cases mentioned in this chapter are necessary for homosexuality. In other words, there are people with characteristics claimed to be consistent with homosexuality—finger digit ratios, number of older brothers, handedness—who are in fact *not homosexual*. Thus, it is difficult to claim having any of these traits necessarily means a person is born-this-way in reference to homosexuality.

---

30 Ray Blanchard et al., "Interaction of Fraternal Birth Order and Handedness in the Development of Male Homosexuality," *Hormones and Behavior* 49 (2006): 405–14.

31 Dennis McFadden and Edward G. Pasanen, "Comparison of the auditory systems of heterosexuals and homosexuals: Click-evoked otoacoustic emissions," *Proceedings of the National Academy of Sciences* 95.5 (March 3, 1998): 2709–13. For a review critical of McFadden and Pasanen's methodology see Bonnie P. Spanier and Jessica D. Horowitz, "Looking for a Difference: Methodology Is in the Eye of the Beholder," *Gender and the Science of Difference: Cultural Politics of Contemporary Science and Medicine,* Jill A. Fisher, ed. (New Brunswick, NJ: Rutgers University Press, 2011), 43–66. Spanier and Horowitz affirm homosexual rights.

32 Ivanka Savic et al., "Brain Response to Putative Pheromones in Homosexual Men," *Proceedings of the National Academy of Science* 102 (2005): 7356–61.

33 A. J. S. Klar, "Excess of Counterclockwise Scalp Hair-whorl Rotation in Homosexual Men," *Journal of Genetics* 83.3 (December 2004): 251–55.

CHAPTER 10

"I Can't Change, Even If I Wanted To"

BEN HAGGERTY, BETTER KNOWN BY HIS STAGE NAME MACKLEMORE, is a rap music star from Seattle who in 2012 recorded "Same Love," a song affirming same-sex marriage. The tune was released in part to support Washington Referendum 74, a ballot measure in which the Washington voters approved same-sex marriages by a margin of 54% to 46% on November 6, 2012. The cover photo on the single of "Same Love" shows Macklemore's uncle, John Haggerty, and his homosexual partner, Sean. Within the song itself, Haggerty directly attacks the notion that one can change his or her homosexual desires and criticizes Christians who oppose homosexuality, especially "right wing conservatives" who "think it's a decision." In the chorus of "Same Love," Haggerty expresses a core belief of the modern LGBT movement and sings, "And I can't change/ Even if I tried/ Even if I wanted to."[1] In this way, Haggerty is making his own form of the born-this-way argument, insisting homosexuality is hardwired into a person's nature and cannot be changed.

Using a popular musical format, Haggerty asserts two core ideas about homosexuality. First, people who oppose homosexuality are bigoted, uncompassionate religious zealots. Second, a person cannot change his or her sexual desires regardless of how hard he or she tries. The idea a person cannot change his or her sexual desires has become so widely accepted in our culture that anyone who questions the assumption is quickly labeled as a homophobe, a prejudiced fool to be dismissed from any serious discussion.

"I can't change, even if I tried, even if I wanted to!" Is this core assumption of born-this-way arguments true? Mainline mental health professionals now refer to attempts to change person's sexual orientation as Sexual Orientation

---

1 Ben Haggerty, "Same Love," A-Z Lyrics, accessed May 13, 2014, http://www.azlyrics.com/lyrics/macklemore/samelove.html.

Change Efforts (SOCE).[2] In what follows, we will see that some of the evidence is ambiguous concerning the possibility of sexual-orientation change, but the ambiguity does not require us to suspend moral judgment, shrug our shoulders, and concede that no change whatsoever is possible. Instead, we will see that while complete change of sexual orientation is infrequent, movement along a continuum from homosexuality towards heterosexuality occurs more frequently. To explore this complicated debate, we will first summarize the approaches of the American Psychiatric Association, the National Association for Research and Therapy of Homosexuality, Christian ministries to homosexuals, and Sexual Identity Therapy. Then, four major studies regarding the possibility of sexual orientation change will be reviewed. Finally, the various stances and findings will be evaluated through Scripture.

The American Psychiatric Association and SOCE

From the 1940s–1960s, the dominant theory in American psychiatry saw homosexuality as originating in a failure of childhood sexual development associated with conflicts within the triad of father, mother, and child, which is a theory based on Freud's own psychoanalytic model. Viewed from this perspective, homosexuality was treated by mental health professionals as something in need of correction. But with astonishing speed, this consensus was overturned when the American Psychiatric Association (APA) removed homosexuality as a "disease" from the DSM-II in 1973.

Homosexual activists in the early 1970s surely could not have anticipated how rapidly the stance of psychiatry regarding homosexuality would change over the next forty years. In a 2013 Position Statement on Homosexuality, the APA strongly affirmed homosexuality as a valid lifestyle and said:

> The American Psychiatric Association does not believe that same-sex orientation should or needs to be changed, and efforts to do so represent a significant risk of harm by subjecting individuals to forms of treatment which have not been scientifically validated and by undermining self-esteem when sexual orientation fails to change. No credible evidence exists that any mental health intervention can reliably and safely change

---

2   Such efforts are also called Sexual Conversion Therapy or Sexual Reorientation Therapy.

sexual orientation; nor, from a mental health perspective does sexual orientation need to be changed.[3]

In this statement, the APA squarely rejects SOCE and insists that if a person experiences same-sex attraction, there is no reason to be concerned, but instead one should embrace the desire. Furthermore, change is not possible anyway. The American Psychological Association shares a similar view and in 2009 said that "there is insufficient evidence to support the use of psychological interventions to change sexual orientation."[4]

But how does the majority within the modern mental health profession address requests from those who ask for help in adjusting their sexual orientation? First, since the APA has determined that homosexuality is not a disease, then there is no need for a cure. Thus, the goal is to help the person understand that the request is unnecessary.

Second, and perhaps more importantly from their perspective, most modern psychiatrists contend social or religious prejudice against homosexuals causes people with same-sex attraction undue distress. They claim men and women who experience same-sex attraction *and* who want to change are only seeking transformation in order to fit into society. Thus, the way to solve this problem is not to provide SOCE, but to change society's "homophobic" substrata of beliefs, which cause anxiety for homosexuals. Attempts to help people change their sexual orientation are considered the last vestiges of an antiquated, prejudicial view of homosexuality.[5] The stance of the APA against SOCE has shaped laws banning attempts to help minors change their orientation in California, New Jersey, Washington, DC, and Oregon.

California Senate Bill 1172 was signed into law by Governor Jerry Brown on September 30, 2012. This law prohibits any attempt by a licensed professional healthcare worker to help a person under age 18 change his or her sexual orientation. On August 19, 2013, Governor Chris Christie of New Jersey signed a

---

3 "Position Statement on Homosexuality," American Psychiatric Association, December, 2013, accessed May 13, 2014, http://www.psychiatry.org/advocacy--newsroom/position-statements/position statement on homosexuality. This 2013 statement summarizes the APA positions previously expressed in 12 separate documents.

4 "Appropriate Affirmative Responses to Sexual Orientation Distress and Change Efforts," The American Psychological Association, April 5, 2009, accessed May 13, 2014, http://www.apa.org/about/policy/sexual-orientation.pdf.

5 Douglas C. Haldeman, "Gay Rights, Patient Rights: The Implications of Sexual Orientation Conversion Therapy," *Professional Psychology: Research and Practice* 33.3 (June 2002): 260. Haldeman is an open homosexual and psychologist.

similar bill into law making it illegal in that state to attempt to change a minor's sexual orientation. The New Jersey law was sponsored by chiropractor Tim Eustace, the first openly gay person to be elected to the New Jersey legislature. Christie, himself a Roman Catholic, appealed to a born-this-way argument in favor of homosexuality when he signed the bill and said, "I've always believed that people are born with the predisposition to be homosexual. And so I think if someone is born that way it's very difficult to say then that's a sin. But I understand that my Church says that, but for me personally I don't look at someone who is homosexual as a sinner."[6]

It is difficult to gauge the effects of these laws, but the possible implications are extensive. Any therapist who attempts to help a child overcome same-sex attraction could lose his or her license. Furthermore, for therapists who affirm SOCE and practice in states where therapy is still legal, malpractice insurance may become so cost-prohibitive as to prevent some mental health professionals from even approaching the subject of homosexuality.[7]

The National Association for Research and Therapy of Homosexuality

In the wake of the APA's tremendous shift regarding homosexuality, various therapists continued attempts to help people change their sexual orientation. In some ways, these therapists were a "counter-revolution" to the raucous homosexual activists who disrupted APA meetings prior to 1973. Mental health professionals who adhered to the APA's pre-1973 stance regarding homosexuality eventually founded The National Association for Research and Therapy of Homosexuality (NARTH). Established in 1992 by Joseph Nicolosi, Benjamin Kauffman, and Charles Socarides (1922–2005), NARTH publishes its own professional journal (*The Journal of Human Sexuality*), hosts an annual conference to discuss SOCE, and provides referrals to people searching for help with changing sexual orientation.

While not denying a biological component to homosexuality, NARTH places more emphasis on the psychological aspects of family, peers, and social

---

6   State of New Jersey, Governor Chris Christie, "Gov. Christie Signs Bill Banning Gay Conversion Therapy on Minors," August 19, 2013, Accessed May 14, 2014, http://www.state.nj .us/governor/news/news/552013/approved/20130819a.html.

7   In the landmark 2015 *Obergefell* v. *Hodges* ruling mandating legalized same-sex marriage, Justice Kennedy mentioned that professional psychiatrists recognize homosexuality "as a normal expression of sexuality and immutable." 576 U.S. _____ (2015): 8.

influences as the source of homosexuality. Furthermore, NARTH says people who want to change their sexual orientation should be allowed the opportunity to do so: "We believe that clients have the right to claim a gay identity, or to diminish their homosexuality and to develop their heterosexual potential. The right to seek therapy to change one's sexual adaptation should be considered self-evident and inalienable."[8]

NARTH also opposes same-sex marriage, expresses strong concern about gay advocacy in public schools, and protests the use of the term "homophobe" in reference to a person with principled objection to homosexual behavior. Today, NARTH "remains committed to protecting the rights of clients with unwanted same-sex attractions to pursue change as well as the rights of clinicians to provide such psychological care."[9]

NARTH advocates a form of SOCE known as "reparative therapy." The term "reparative therapy" can be somewhat confusing to Christians, with many assuming the term refers to the psychoanalyst's effort to "repair" a person's misguided sexual desires. Actually, the term "reparative therapy" describes a particular theory about the origin of homosexuality. The term was coined by Elizabeth R. Moberly, a British psychologist and author. Moberly rejects the idea homosexuality is derived from a genetic predisposition. Instead, she asserts homosexuals "suffered some deficit in the relationship of the parent of the same sex."[10] As a result, people seek homosexual relationships to compensate for the flaw in the relationship with the parent of the same sex.

Moberly then argues the drive to restore the relationship with the parent of the same sex is manifested in homosexuality. She claims there is a "*reparative* urge that is involved in the homosexual impulse" and "this impulse is essentially motivated by the need to make good earlier deficits in the parent-child relationship."[11] Hence, reparative therapy refers to a particular theory about the origin of homosexuality in regards to one's relationship with his or her same-gender parent. Therapists who adhere to the theory believe people can change their sexual orientation by addressing these flawed relationships.

---

8   National Association for Research and Therapy of Homosexuality, "NARTH Position Statements: Right to Treatment," accessed June 13, 2014, http://www.narth. com/#!narth-position-statements/c1ae.

9   National Association for Research and Therapy of Homosexuality, "NARTH Statement on Sexual Orientation Change," January 25, 2012, accessed May 14, 2014, http://www.narth. com/#!about1/c1wab.

10   Elizabeth R. Moberly, *Homosexuality: A New Christian Ethic* (Cambridge: James Clarke, 1983), 2.

11   Ibid., 6. Emphasis added.

Among NARTH's founders, Socarides in particular deeply opposed the APA's change of stance regarding homosexuality. Both a practicing psychiatrist and a professor of psychiatry, in 1973 he contributed an article to a symposium on homosexuality in *The American Journal of Psychiatry*, in which he stridently opposed a change in the APA's stance. Socarides, similar to other psychoanalysts, believed the roots of homosexuality are found in early childhood in pre-oedipal conflicts and argued that homosexuals experienced a failure in sexual identity as a child, a failure caused by "a pathological family constellation in which there is a domineering, psychologically crushing mother who will not allow the child to attain autonomy from her and an absent, weak, or rejecting father who is unable to aid the son to overcome the block in maturation."[12] When asked in 1995 about the causes of homosexuality, Socarides said, "Something frightened these people [homosexuals] very early in life. Something went wrong in their childhood, some disturbance in the formation of their sexual identity. I also believe that most homosexuals have been abused as infants, or in their early childhood."[13]

Joseph Nicolosi, a clinical psychologist practicing in Encino, CA, is the most well-known current advocate of reparative therapy. Similar to Moberly, he says homosexual men are trying to fill the unmet need of a father's love through homosexual behavior. Nicolosi says, "In our application, the homosexually oriented person is attempting to 'repair' normal, unmet same-sex affective needs (attention, affection and approval), as well as gender identity deficits . . . through an erotic connection with another man."[14] Nicolosi insists that people don't have to be gay, but can diminish unwanted homosexuality and develop their heterosexual potential.[15]

CHRISTIAN MINISTRIES TO HOMOSEXUALS

NARTH's professional opposition to the APA's change in stance regarding homosexuality was mirrored by different religious groups that have continued

---

12 Charles Socarides, "Homosexuality: Findings Derived from 15 Years of Clinical Research," *The American Journal of Psychiatry* 130.11 (November 1973): 1,212.

13 Charles W. Socarides, *Homosexuality: A Freedom Too Far* (Phoenix: Adam Margrave Books, 1995), 87.

14 Joseph Nicolosi, "The Meaning of Same-Sex Attraction," *Handbook of Therapy for Unwanted Homosexual Attractions: A Guide for Treatment*, Julie H. Hamilton and Philip J. Henry, eds. (Maitland, FL: Xulon Press, 2009), 33.

15 These statements are on the masthead of Nicolosi's webpage. "Thomas Aquinas Psychological Clinic," Joseph Nicolosi, accessed June 13, 2014, http://josephnicolosi.com.

to insist it is possible for people to change from homosexual to heterosexual. In the almost 50 years since the Stonewall Riots, a number of "ex-gay" Christian ministries were started in opposition to the radical gay rights movement.

None was more visible than Exodus, International. Exodus existed from 1976 until 2013 when it voted itself out of existence. Exodus was famous for its campaign in the 1990s proclaiming that, after receiving Jesus Christ as Lord and Savior, many people were changed from homosexual to heterosexual. But when Exodus decided to shut down on June 19, 2013, the group apologized for claiming people can change their sexual orientation.[16]

One couple at the forefront of this campaign was John and Anne Paulk, a husband and wife team who both claimed to have been delivered from homosexuality, fallen in love with each other, and being a happily married couple. Together they published their story in the popular 1999 book *Love Won Out*. The "Love Won Out Theme" was also central to Focus on the Family's efforts to reach out to homosexuals with John Paulk serving as the head of Focus's Homosexuality and Gender Department. But on September 19, 2000, Paulk was caught in a gay bar in Washington, DC where he was apparently trying to pick up other men using an assumed identity. As a result, he was removed from his position at Focus on the Family. John and Anne Paulk subsequently divorced and John now completely repudiates the ex-gay movement. In 2013, he said, "Today, I do not consider myself ex-gay and I no longer support or promote the movement. Please allow me to be clear: I do not believe that reparative therapy changes sexual orientation; in fact, it does great harm to many people."[17]

Anne Paulk still argues for the ability to change one's sexual identity and is now the executive director of Restored Hope Network. Restored Hope was started in July 2012 by various people dissatisfied with the theological direction of Exodus.[18] Restored Hope affirms that Jesus Christ provides dramatic

---

16   Melissa Steffman, "Alan Chambers Apologizes to Gay Community, Exodus International to Shut Down," *Christianity Today*, June 21, 2013, accessed May 14, 2104, http://www.christianitytoday.com/gleanings/2013/june/alan-chambers-apologizes-to-gay-community-exodus.html.

17   Sunnivie Brydum, "John Paulk Formally Announces, Apologizes for Harmful 'Ex-Gay' Movement," *The Advocate*, April 24, 2013, accessed April 18, 2014, http://www.advocate.com/politics/religion/2013/04/24/john-paulk-formally-renounces-apologizes-harmful-ex-gay-movement.

18   Anne Paulk asserts Exodus adopted a defective view of salvation by grace. She said, "It was kind of an error in the thinking of once saved always saved, saying that a person need no longer confess or repent from their sin, particularly confess. . . . So, it removes the cleansing power of 1 John 1:9, which says, 'If we confess our sins, He is faithful and just to forgive us

healing and transformation of sexual desires. But this transformation may look different for each individual, with Restored Hope saying, "For some, this transformation may take shape as a significant reduction of unwanted sexual desires. For others, it may mean the grace to live in obedience in spite of ongoing urges to do what God forbids."[19]

SEXUAL IDENTITY THERAPY

Some evangelical Christians have adopted a more nuanced view concerning what it means for one to say he or she has been changed by Jesus Christ, attempting to find a mediating position between the APA's insistence that SOCE are always bad, NARTH's insistence that homosexuality is always rooted in fractured childhood relationships with parents, and Christian ministries that insist everyone can change. One such mediating approach is called Sexual Identity Therapy, a method developed by Christian psychologists Warren Throckmorton of Grove City College in Pennsylvania and Mark Yarhouse of Regent University.

Throckmorton briefly supported reparative therapy and even received NARTH's "Freud Award" for excellence in research in 2002, but his views on the effectiveness of reparative therapy changed over time. Throckmorton's shift in thought was influenced by a 2004 film he helped produce titled *I Do Exist*, a documentary about the lives of five different people who claimed to have experienced a shift in sexual orientation. But within just a couple of years of the film's release, two of the participants announced they were gay and another claimed to be bisexual. These events along with Throckmorton's own research led him to reject reparative therapy and he is now critical of NARTH.

Out of these experiences, Throckmorton, along with Mark Yarhouse, developed Sexual Identity Therapy (SIT). SIT is designed to help people with strong same-sex attraction achieve a synthesis of sexual identity that promotes well-being and integration with one's worldview.[20] The goal of SIT is not to change a person's sexual orientation, but instead to help people live in a man-

our sins and cleanse us from all unrighteousness." Charlie Butts, "Restoring Hope for Homosexuals," *One News Now*, May 15, 2013, accessed June 16, 2014, http://www.onenewsnow.com/culture/2013/05/15/restoring-hope-for-homosexuals.

19 Restored Hope Network, "Doctrinal Statement," accessed June 16, 2014, http://www.restoredhopenetwork.org/index.php/who-we-are/what-we-believe.

20 Warren Throckmorton and Mark A. Yarhouse, "Sexual Identity Therapy: Practice

ner consistent with their religious faith if their faith says homosexual behavior is sinful. SIT does not believe homosexual desires are a sign of mental illness or a form of punishment from God. Furthermore Throckmorton does not believe he can help someone change from gay to straight, but he also believes a person with a strong same-sex attraction does not necessarily have to embrace the gay lifestyle.[21]

Yarhouse echoes the same ideas and says, "The goal of [SIT] is to assist clients so that they can experience greater congruence, which we see as being able to live and identify themselves in ways that are consistent with their beliefs and values."[22] SIT has received positive affirmation from the American Psychological Association's landmark 2009 report on sexual orientation. Throckmorton's and Yarhouse's work is cited positively several times as a healthy way to help people who both have a strong religious faith and experience same-sex attraction, especially in exploring ways to integrate the two.[23]

CAN ANYONE CHANGE?

Is it possible to change one's sexual orientation? Four different studies from the last few years are the center of most debate: (1) a 2002 project by Ariel Shidlo and Michael Schroeder, (2) Robert Spitzer's survey of people who claimed to experience significant change in orientation, (3) a long-term study of SOCE by Stanton Jones and Mark Yarhouse, and (4) a 2014 study on SOCE among Latter-Day Saints. As noted earlier, the consensus of modern psychology is that such change is not possible and attempts to change are detrimental to a person's emotional health. But actually, the research on SOCE is more ambiguous than either secularists or Christians would prefer.

Framework for Managing Sexual identity Conflicts," 2006, accessed May 16, 2014, http://sitframework.com/wp-content/uploads/2009/07/sexualidentitytherapyframeworkfinal.pdf.

21 Stephanie Simon, "A New Therapy on Faith and Sexual Identity," *The Wall Street Journal,* August 6, 2009, accessed May 16, 2014, http://online.wsj.com/news/articles/SB124950491516608883?mg=reno64-wsj&url=http%3A%2F%2Fonline.wsj.com%2Farticle%2FSB124950491516608883.html.

22 Mark Yarhouse, "Sexual Identity Therapy," accessed May 16, 2014, http://www.sexualidentityinstitute.org/sexual-identity-therapy.

23 APA Task Force on Appropriate Therapeutic Responses to Sexual Orientation, *Report of the Task Force on Appropriate Therapeutic Responses to Sexual Orientation* (Washington, DC: American Psychological Association, 2009), 24.

Shidlo and Schroeder

One study frequently cited as evidence that SOCE is harmful is research published in 2002 by Ariel Shidlo and Michael Schroeder. Both men are openly homosexual psychologists practicing in New York City and are hostile to SOCE.[24] Shidlo and Schroeder initially planned to title their research, "Homophobic Therapies: Documenting the Damage," but then chose the less polemical title "Changing Sexual Orientation: A Consumer's Report."[25] Surveying 202 people who had attempted some form of SOCE, 176 from their sample perceived themselves as having failed SOCE, while the remaining 26 perceived their treatment as successful at some level.[26] But the real goal of this research was to discover harmful effects of SOCE, and Shidlo and Schroeder reported SOCE resulted in depression, suicidal ideation, internalized homophobia, and a host of other deleterious effects.

Shidlo and Schroeder used a convenience sample to gather their data, which dramatically affects their conclusions. A "convenience sample" means they gathered data by soliciting responses from the public, specifically via gay-friendly organizations. To grasp the manner in which their data is swayed by specific recruitment methods, consider the provocative way the National Lesbian and Gay Health Association solicited responses to the Shidlo and Schroeder research, "The NLGHA is conducting a survey of lesbians, gay men, and bisexuals who have been in counseling that tried to change their sexual orientation. They intend to use the results to inform the public about the often harmful effects of such therapies."[27] In other words, the study was intended to discover harm and is thus the self-reflection of people who had a negative experience with SOCE. As such, though Shidlo and Schroeder are often cited in arguments opposing the effectiveness of SOCE, all the study really tells us is why some people had a negative experience; it does not provide us with an unbiased measure of the effectiveness of such efforts.

Robert Spitzer

Robert Spitzer is one of the most influential psychiatrists of the latter half of the twentieth century and is the man who spearheaded the APA's change in

---

24   Their research was supported by two pro-homosexual organizations.

25   Ariel Shidlo and Michael Schroeder, "Changing Sexual Orientation: A Consumer's Report," *Professional Psychology: Research and Practice* 33.3 (2002): 251.

26   Ibid., 253.

27   Ibid., Appendix A, 259.

policy regarding homosexuality in 1973. Because of his prominent position, perhaps no research into SOCE received more criticism than Spitzer's 2001 work in which he interviewed 200 self-selected people (143 males and 57 females) who reported some level of change from a homosexual to a heterosexual orientation in the previous five years. The majority of Spitzer's sample was recruited from ex-gay religious ministries (43%) or from NARTH (23%). Most of the participants were religiously motivated, with 93% saying religion was "extremely" or "very" important in their lives.[28]

Spitzer's research involved talking to his participants over the phone and discussing their own reports of change in sexual attraction. Spitzer found that the vast majority of his research participants had experienced significant change in their own self-perception of their sexual orientation, with a strong shift away from homosexual to heterosexual attraction. Commenting on his research in the years that followed, Spitzer said he was not trying to suggest that gay people should pursue therapy to change, but his goal was to determine whether the claim that no one had ever changed his or her sexual orientation via therapy was true.[29] His investigation indicated that for some people change is possible.

Spitzer's research had methodological problems similar to Shidlo and Schroeder. He used a convenience sample of respondents gathered from organizations favorable to data affirming significant change in sexual orientation. In this way, Spitzer's research actually gives insight into the self-perception of people who claimed to experience change in sexual attraction, but it did not really give insight into the percentage of people who have experienced change in sexual attraction.

Spitzer's findings were controversial because he claimed some very highly motivated people can change their sexual orientation, an assertion contrary to the claims of the majority in the mental health profession. Several writers criticized methodological problems in Spitzer's work, but some accused Spitzer of fomenting homophobia and undercutting the political agenda for gay rights. Criticism continued until 2012 when Spitzer apologized for his claims and said, "I believe I owe the gay community an apology for my study making unproven claims of the efficacy of reparative thera-

---

28   Robert Spitzer, "Can Some Gay Men and Lesbians Change Their Sexual Orientation? 200 Participants Reporting a Change from Homosexual to Heterosexual Orientation," *Archives of Sexual Behavior* 32.5 (October 2003): 406.

29   Gabriel Arana, "My So-Called Ex-Gay Life," *The American Prospect* 23.4 (May 2012): 53.

py."[30] He went on to say he apologizes to any gay person who wasted time and energy on reparative therapy based on his findings. However, Spitzer's change in stance is technically *not* a retraction. Ken Zucker, the editor of the *Archives of Sexual Behavior* commented on Spitzer's desire to "retract" his research and said:

> You can retract data incorrectly analyzed; to do that, you publish an erratum. You can retract an article if the data were falsified — or the journal retracts it if the editor knows of it. As I understand it, he's just saying ten years later that he wants to retract his interpretation of the data. Well, we'd probably have to retract hundreds of scientific papers with regard to re-interpretation, and we don't do that.[31]

Thus, Spitzer actually has not retracted his data as much as he has changed his interpretation of the data. The data itself still stands. What is clear is that his apology was at least partly the result of pressure and professional politics within his own circle of colleagues. The study indeed had some methodological flaws, which limited the relevance of his findings, but Spitzer was essentially harassed until he completely capitulated.

Stanton Jones and Mark Yarhouse

Stanton Jones, professor of psychology and provost at Wheaton College, and the aforementioned Mark Yarhouse undertook a long-term study of people who attempted to change their sexual orientation. Over an almost seven-year period, they tracked the progress of 72 men and 26 women who were seeking to change from a same-sex attraction to a heterosexual attraction and who participated in various Exodus, International, ministries to achieve freedom from homosexuality. Over the course of the study, some participants dropped out, leaving 63 people who completed the entire course of research. Jones and Yarhouse summarized their findings and said, "About one third of the final participants abandoned their attempt to change, with many embracing a homosexual identity. About one-third embraced sexual abstinence rather than a homosexual identity. About one-fourth had moved away from a predomi-

---

30   Robert L. Spitzer, "Spitzer Reassesses His 2003 Study of Reparative Therapy of Homosexuality," *Archives of Sexual Behavior* 41 (2012): 757.

31   Alice Dreger, "How to Ex an 'Ex-Gay' Study," *Psychology Today*, April 11, 2012, accessed June 17, 2014, http://www.psychologytoday.com/blog/fetishes-i-dont-get/201204/how-ex-ex-gay-study.

nantly homosexual orientation and reported having satisfactory heterosexual relationships."[32] It is clear many participants in this study made no significant shift towards heterosexuality and some in fact moved closer to a homosexual identity. Yet, more participants experienced a positive shift toward heterosexual experience than did those who experienced either no shift or a negative shift toward homosexual experience.[33] Thus, the data from this study indicates movement on a continuum from homosexuality to heterosexuality is possible for some people.

Dehlin, Galliher, Bradshaw, Hyde, Crowell, and LDS SOCE

In 2014, a group of researchers published their findings on SOCE among members of The Church of Jesus Christ of Latter-Day Saints (LDS). Recruiting participants from the Internet, the study had a large sample of 1,548 people, largely male and mostly (44.7%) from Utah. Only 28.8% described themselves as active LDS, the rest identifying as inactive LDS, resigned from the LDS church, or removed from membership by the church. Of the 1,548 participants, 1,019 engaged in some form of SOCE. Of those who tried to change their orientation, only one person reported both a heterosexual identity and exclusive attraction to the opposite sex.[34] The authors conclude by saying "most LDS SOCE participants reported little or no sexual orientation change as a result of these efforts and instead reported considerable harm."[35] The method considered most harmful from this research was "personal righteousness," a category that included prayer, fasting, Scrip-

---

32   Stanton L. Jones and Mark A. Yarhouse, "Honest Sex Science," *First Things* 226 (October 2012): 18–19.

33   Stanton L. Jones and Mark A. Yarhouse, "A Longitudinal Study of Attempted Religiously Mediated Sexual Orientation Change," *Journal of Sex and Marital Therapy* 37.5 (October–December 2011): 416.

34   John P. Dehlin, Renee V. Galliher, William S. Bradshaw, Daniel C. Hyde, and Katherine A. Crowell, "Sexual Orientation Change Efforts Among Current or Former LDS Church Members," *Journal of Counseling Psychology* , March 17, 2014, 6, accessed May 16, 2014, http://eds.a.ebscohost.com/eds/detail?vid=3&sid=062950df-c38e-4412-b84c 89961a315187e%40sessionmgr4005&hid=4202&bdata=JkF1dGhUeXBlPWlwLHVybCxjcGlkJmN1c3RpZD1zODM4NTA4MCZzaXRlPWVkcy1saXZl#db=pdh&AN=2014-09735-001.

35   Ibid., 10. The LDS church does not believe attraction to the same sex is necessarily sinful, but engaging in homosexual behavior is sin. The Church of Jesus Christ of Latter Day Saints, "Same-Sex Attraction," accessed May 16, 2014, https://www.lds.org/topics/same-gender-attraction?lang=eng.

ture study, improved relationship with Jesus Christ,[36] and consulting with church leaders.[37]

Some factors limit the effectiveness of the LDS research. All of the researchers forthrightly self-identify as "Lesbian-Gay-Bisexual-Transgendered-Queer [LGBTQ] allies" and have "been active in supporting the LGBTQ community through campus, community, online, and national/international engagement."[38] Furthermore advertisements for the study were placed in over one hundred online and print publications, including the *San Francisco Chronicle, Q-Salt Lake,* and the *Huffington Post,* publications known to be ideologically to the left. The authors state 21% of their sample heard about the study via one of these advertisement sources. Another 5% of the sample was derived from LGBT support organizations. Furthermore, Evergreen International, an LDS ministry focusing on homosexuality and affirming traditional sexual ethics, chose not to advertise for the research, though other LDS ministries to homosexuals did participate.[39] These variables may have pushed the sample in a direction more favorable to a negative stance towards SOCE. Nonetheless, the total number of participants is impressive.

An initial glance at the LDS research indicates it is strong evidence against SOCE. But two factors should be kept in perspective when analyzing these findings. First is a methodological flaw in the way in which participants were asked to score the effectiveness of SOCE. The researchers asked each survey respondent to score the effectiveness of a particular method (e.g., "church counseling") as follows: 1 = highly effective, 2 = moderately effective, 3 = not effective, 4 = moderately harmful, and 5 = severely harmful.[40] Notice that the central scoring possibility –"not effective"—is not neutral. For the scale to be useful, the center score should have been "neither effective nor not effective." As it is, the scale introduces a bias into the scores. The second factor to be kept in mind is that the data did indicate some people experienced a moderate level

---

36 "Jesus Christ" in LDS theology does not refer to the same Jesus Christ of orthodox Christian theology. In LDS theology, Jesus Christ is one of billions of preexistent spirit children of Father and Mother God, who are themselves humans who became gods. In biblical theology, Jesus Christ is the eternal Son of God; there was never a time when the Son did not exist.

37 Dehlin et al., "Sexual Orientation Change Efforts among Current or Former LDS Church Members," 9.

38 Ibid., 3.

39 On January 1, 2014, Evergreen merged under the umbrella of another LDS ministry called Northstar.

40 Dehlin et al., "Sexual Orientation Change Efforts among Current or Former LDS Church Members," 4.

success with SOCE. But overall, the majority did not report a good experience with SOCE.

So What Are Christians to Think about SOCE?

A quick survey of efforts to change sexual orientation can be very discouraging to a sincere Christian. In particular, it can be disheartening to listen to someone's testimony of transformation in sexual orientation only later to learn the person now claims he or she never experienced change in sexual attraction. Homosexual activists delight in trumpeting the manner in which people in different Christian ministries wound up returning to the gay lifestyle and repudiating their previous involvement in ex-gay ministries. The resulting disclosures that the purported change was superficial at best can leave Christians feeling gullible and embarrassed in explaining the events to our friends. These stories of "ex ex-gays" can be disappointing to those of us who believe Jesus Christ dramatically changes lives. So how do we interpret and respond to the data on SOCE, which seems to indicate a complete change in sexual desire is rare?

We must face the current data with honesty, but also with discernment. Movement on a continuum of orientation change is possible for some, but is not as easy or as frequent as many of us as evangelicals would wish. The majority of research clearly indicates an attempt to change sexual orientation is a daunting task and a rare occurrence. But even Shidlo and Schroeder admitted *some* homosexuals, though a small minority, did in fact report a consistent level of change over time in their same-sex attraction and management of homosexual behavior. What seems more common is some people have success managing their own sexual actions, but again, there is no guaranteed therapy that results in a complete change. In this light, pastors and therapists should be cautious in assertions made to people struggling with same-sex attraction. Mark Yarhouse offers a healthy word of correction about the danger of glibly telling someone changing sexual desires is simple: "When church leaders communicate a message or expectation of easy change, it can lead to resentment toward the church."[41]

Next, let us agree that some forms of reparative therapy have been misguided and dehumanizing. For example, nausea-inducing drugs were some-

---

41 Mark A. Yarhouse, *Understanding Sexual Identity: A Resource for Youth Ministry* (Grand Rapids: Zondervan, 2013), 77.

times administered simultaneously with homoerotic stimuli.[42] Certainly Christians are opposed to these sorts of crude attempts to change a person's sexual orientation.

Unfortunately, crude accounts of aversion therapy often serve as a straw man for homosexual activists who then suggest anyone who tries to help someone change his or her sexual orientation is equally misguided and perhaps only a few steps away from torture. To add confusion, some biblically faithful disciplines are described as "aversion therapy" by secularists in an apparent effort to discredit them. For example, if a married man claims to be fighting same-sex attraction, a pastor or Christian counselor may encourage him to focus his thoughts on his wife or particular Scripture addressing his temptation.[43] Some health professionals would label this as aversion therapy to be avoided. But Christians have a deep tradition of teaching disciples to focus thoughts on wholesome ideas and God's word, all in an effort to "take every thought captive to the obedience of Christ" (2 Cor. 10:5). We must not let secularists steal spiritual disciplines from us.

Christians must also exercise discernment in discussions about particular family constellations and their relationship to same-sex attraction. While some cases of homosexuality may be traced to a broken relationship with the parent of the same-sex, this is certainly not true for all homosexuals. There are many incidences where children become homosexual who have with warm and affirming relationships with both parents. In this way, NARTH's approach seems incomplete and truncated. Yet a disrupted relationship with the parent of the same sex can (but does not necessarily) lead to great confusion during sexual maturation. The potential confusion caused by a dysfunctional home is affirmed by homosexual psychiatrist Richard Isay (1934–2012). Isay was strongly critical of SOCE and firmly believed homosexuality is constitutional in nature, yet even he said, "Like all forms of love, [homosexuality] is a longing for a lost attachment. That longing, for gay men, is usually for the father."[44] This is an astonishing admission from one of the leading proponents of normalizing homosexuality. Disrupted and unhealthy family relationships are indeed sometimes a factor in the development of same-sex attraction.

Many mistakes have been made in the ex-gay movement of the last several

---

42   Douglas Haldeman, "Gay Rights, Patient Rights: The Implications of Sexual Orientation Conversion Therapy," 260.

43   I am drawing my example from Shidlo and Schroeder, "Changing Sexual Orientation: A Consumer's Report," 255.

44   Richard Isay, *Being Homosexual: Gay Men and Their Development*, rev. ed. (New York: Vintage Books, 2009), 22.

decades. One of the most serious errors is that evangelicals have been too quick to rush born-again homosexuals into the public spotlight without giving them sufficient time to mature in their faith, grow in basic spiritual disciplines, and learn how to overcome temptation. This reflects a broader problem in evangelical Christianity: people with a powerful testimony of transformation are pushed forward and given a large platform presence without sufficient time for growth. Excessive praise and adulation are difficult for even the most mature Christian to accept without at least some hubris. Premature exposure to the public spotlight has contributed to the destruction of many well-meaning people in the ex-gay movement.

Underneath many of these ex-gay failures is a distinct element of spiritual warfare. First Peter 5:8 warns us that the "devil is prowling around like a roaring lion, looking for anyone he can devour." This is most certainly true with anyone wishing to leave the homosexual lifestyle in contemporary America. Such people are in an unenviable position since the culture will ridicule them, their former circle of friends will mock them, and their new Christian brothers and sisters often don't know how to help.

Finally, we should scrutinize the worldview substrata of everyone, even those affirming the effectiveness of SOCE. Charles Socarides adamantly insisted change in orientation is possible. Yet he believed, like Freud and Kinsey, that sex is merely an evolutionary mechanism central to the continuation of the species and said, "It's obvious that nature designed us this way, generously coating the act of reproduction with the most intense pleasure we can have, to insure the survival of the species and the future evolution of life."[45] Socarides also encouraged some patients to use pornography as a step towards discovering a heterosexual identity,[46] a method clearly unacceptable to Christians.

While Christians should use discernment in evaluating research both for and against SOCE, data to date indicates complete change in sexual attraction is rare, but sometimes possible. What seems clearer is that movement on a continuum away from homosexual desire and behavior is more frequently possible. SOCE will be more difficult in a sex-saturated society that has abandoned Judeo-Christian sexual ethics, is hostile to sexual purity, and uses the force of law to stifle attempts to help people overcome same-sex attraction.

---

45   Socarides, *A Freedom Too Far*, 26.
46   Ibid., 141.

The Gospel, Homosexuality, and the Transformed Life

If Jesus transforms a life when someone is saved, then why do some Christians continue to struggle with same-sex attraction? First Corinthians 6:9–11 provides us some perspective on this question. This passage gives a vice list of ten specific sins that demarcate a person as outside of the kingdom of God. Among these ten vices, two are specifically related to male homosexuality; the fourth vice is translated as "effeminate" and the fifth is translated "homosexuals" by the NASB. Taken together, the words refer to passive and active partners in male homosexual intercourse. Immediately after listing these ten lifestyle sins (including homosexuality), Paul then says in 1 Corinthians 6:11, "Such were some of you; but you were washed, but you were sanctified, but you were justified in the name of the Lord Jesus Christ and in the Spirit of our God." The past tense verb "were" in verse 11 indicates that prior to knowing Christ, Paul's readers had a continuous habituation in the ten vices listed,[47] including the two specific ones associated with homosexuality. The Bible insists it is possible for homosexual behavior to be something in which a person once participated *in the past, but no longer does so.*

How do we reconcile the clear teaching of Scripture that it is possible for someone transformed by God's grace to identify as a person who formerly engaged in homosexual behavior with data that indicates a complete change in sexual desire is rare? First, the Bible focuses on homosexual behavior as opposed to sexual orientation. The modern concept of sexual orientation makes a person's central identity sexual in nature. Thomas Schmidt comments on the idea of sexual orientation and says, "In other words, many people think that *orientation* indicates what a person is — and of course, the argument goes, we must *act* according to who we *are.*"[48] But in contrast, Scripture insists we do not have to act upon deep sexual desires inconsistent with God's design.

Second, 1 Corinthians 6:9–11 also includes sins such as fornication, adultery, and drunkenness. Many people who have been born again previously practiced such things prior to knowing Christ, yet the gospel empowered them to put these evil actions in the past. This does not mean these former fornicators, adulterers, and drunkards are never, ever tempted by such things again, but it does mean they have a new desire to serve God and a new power to say

---

47   Anthony Thiselton, *The First Epistle to the Corinthians: A Commentary on the Greek Text* (Grand Rapids: Eerdmans, 2000), 453.

48   Thomas A. Schmidt, *Straight and Narrow? Compassion and Clarity in the Homosexuality Debate* (Downers Grove, IL: IVP Academic, 1995), 150.

no to what God forbids. Likewise, people who practiced homosexuality prior to faith in Christ should not find it unusual if old temptations raise their head from time to time, but the new birth means we do not have to live the way we once did.

SOCE and Christian Teaching about Temptation

When discussing same-sex attraction, we must remember that *temptation* itself is not sin; *giving in* to temptation is sin. First Corinthians 10:13 has given comfort to Christians struggling with any number of temptations: "No temptation has overtaken you except what is common to humanity. God is faithful, and He will not allow you to be tempted beyond what you are able, but with the temptation He will also provide a way of escape so that you are able to bear it." Temptation is the common human experience, but *God is faithful* and will help us. It is often difficult and exhausting to fight temptation, but we also believe that being a disciple of Jesus Christ means we deny ourselves, take up the cross, and follow Jesus (Mark 8: 34). Denying ourselves for the cause of Christ calls for self-sacrifice, but God's grace gives us strength for each new day.

Every Christian has struggled with temptation or besetting sin, yet there are various ways in which victory has been achieved. We know of alcoholics who were delivered from drunkenness in an instant and no longer desired alcohol; we also know alcoholics who trusted Christ and prayed sincerely but must ask God for new strength each day to overcome the desire to drink. Why should we be surprised that similar things happen with other temptations? Some people will be dramatically delivered from any number of sexual temptations in a moment; others will pray each day for new grace to fight another round in an on-going battle. Both groups deserve Christian compassion.

Helping our brothers and sisters overcome same-sex attraction is an important task for the entire church. In a 2010 review of SOCE in men, Elan Karten and Jay C. Wade discovered that among the most effective methods associated with SOCE with males included nonsexual relationships with other men.[49] These findings are very consistent with Christian discipleship in which a more mature group of Christians shows care and support for a fellow believer. For some men, the church may be the first place where another man has genuinely said "I love you" without a sexual agenda. Likewise, for some

---

49   Elan Y. Karten and Jay C. Wade, "Sexual Orientation Change Efforts in Men: A Client Perspective," *The Journal of Men's Studies* 18.1 (Winter 2010): 84–102.

lesbian women, a local congregation of believers may be the first place they encounter genuine female friendship without expectations of sexual favors.

A central theological idea in question here is repentance. Jesus made it clear that we must "repent and believe the gospel" (Mark 1:15). Repentance means we turn from our sins and turn to Jesus. Repentance also implies we have been doing wrong things and need to change our behavior. While the central claim of the gay rights movement is that the homosexual lifestyle is morally praiseworthy, the Bible is explicitly clear that homosexual behavior is inconsistent with God's design for men and women (Gen. 1:26–28; 2:24–25) and Christian sexual ethics (Rom. 1:18–32; 1 Cor. 6:9–11). Thus, following Christ entails repentance from homosexual behavior.

The most painful step for most people who come to Christ is admitting we are sinners and have been engaged in actions in direct opposition to God's will. Some of these sinful acts feel natural and are pleasurable, but the pleasure associated with an act does not determine its morality. Underlying Haggerty's claim that "I couldn't change even if I wanted to" seems to be the assumption that any desire that we experience for a sustained period of time must be impossible to resist and, therefore, the best course of action is for one to surrender to one's sexual wishes.

Does this then mean that all sustained desires are praiseworthy, should be indulged, and granted sanction by the civil government? Are we morally free to act on every sexual impulse? Or is true freedom actually found in restraint and mastery over our desires? Just because something feels good does not mean it is moral. We may not be able to change the things that tempt us, but we can always change the way we respond to temptation. Our central message should be, "You may have a strong disposition, but you don't have to live this way."

CHAPTER 11

Born-This-Way Arguments and Christian Ethics

IN 2004, UNITED ARTISTS RELEASED *SAVED!*, a film which lampooned Evangelical Christians as hypocritical, shallow, and judgmental. The film was directed by Brian Dannelly, who attended a conservative Christian high school as a teenager and now identifies as a homosexual.[1] The film itself centers on the fictional American Eagle Christian High School with characters Dannelly says are drawn from his own experience in a religious school. The movie is replete with common stereotypes of evangelical Christians: The school's principal, "Pastor Skip," is having an extramarital affair; the most outspoken Christian girl in the movie is hateful and mean; and, of course, unkind attitudes towards homosexuals are ever present. What is perhaps most frustrating about *Saved!* is that the characters with the greatest religious devotion are the most self-centered, while the least religious characters display compassion, empathy, and concern for others. The view of the relationship between Christians and homosexuality presented in *Saved!* predominates in our culture. Born-this-way arguments are offered as intelligent, cogent, compassionate, and compelling. The traditional Christian moral stance that homosexual behavior is sin is viewed as antiquated, unkind, rooted in ignorance, and hopelessly inconsistent with the best science while Christians themselves are portrayed as mean-spirited and cruel.

Several scientific studies were initiated in recent decades to substantiate the born-this-way argument that homosexuals are not just different in their sexual behavior, but are constitutionally different from heterosexuals. Pro-homosexual advocates hope these studies will remove the moral stigma associated with homosexuality by proving it is not really a "choice," but an essential part of one's inborn nature. Their goal is to convince others that if homosex-

---

1 Michael Stipe of the rock group R.E.M., who has self-identified as "queer," also co-produced the movie.

uals are "born this way," then they should not receive moral censure for their sexual lifestyle: Homosexuality should be viewed as an innate characteristic as immutable as one's race. The claim is then made that if it is wrong to discriminate against someone because of race, it is equally wrong to discriminate against someone because he or she is homosexual.

How do we evaluate born-this-way claims in light of Christian Ethics? Now that we have reviewed the significant scientific findings regarding homosexuality, we will summarize a Christian response. First, while research shows *correlation* between certain factors and an increased incidence of homosexuality, no variable has yet been found which *causes* homosexuality. The overriding principle that emerges for a correct interpretation of the data is that *correlation does not equal causation*. Second, we will see that no biological or genetic trait has been discovered which is both necessary and sufficient for homosexuality. Third, we will see that there are some traits which seem predispose some people towards same-sex-attraction, but this does not mean a person is *predetermined* to engage in homosexual behavior. Then, Romans 1:18–32 will provide a perspective for interpreting the relevant data.

CORRELATION, BUT NOT CAUSATION

Some genetic and biological factors *correlate* with a higher incidence of homosexuality among select populations. However, there are no genetic or biological factors that have been shown to *cause* homosexuality. In moral debate, this vital distinction between correlation and causation is usually lost. Correlation refers to the degree that two different variables are related. For example, an extensive body of research finds a strong correlation between smoking cigarettes and an increased risk for lung cancer and other diseases which hasten death.[2] The research we have surveyed has tried to find out how one variable, homosexuality, is dependent on other variables, such as prenatal hormones, brain structure, or genetics. While some of these variables correlate with a higher incidence of same-sex attraction within select populations,[3] no correlation as strong as the one between smoking and lung cancer has been discovered.

We must remember: Correlation does not equal causation. When discuss-

---

2   Researchers typically use the terms no relationship, positive relationship, and negative (inverse) relationship. I've used the terms "strong" and "weak" for simplicity and convenience.

3   These correlations may be due to some other confounding variable as yet not studied.

ing human behavior, to say that one variable *causes* another variable is logically immodest and equally difficult to substantiate. In causation, one event or variable necessarily precedes another event or variable. If the first event does not occur, the second event does not follow. In a cause-effect relationship, the effect is unlikely to have occurred without the previous cause. No research to date proves a relationship like this exists between any biological or genetic factors and homosexual behavior.

A more accurate summary of the data is to say there are biological and genetic variables which are *contributing* factors in the development of homosexuality. Christians readily admit the existence of such contributing factors to homosexuality which are genetic or biological in origin. Every choice we make while living on Earth is affected by biology and genetics. Most temptations have a strong biological component: We are tempted to engage in forbidden pleasure because it initially feels good. We seek pleasure and shun pain, sometimes to destructive ends. Yet, the very constitutional nature of our bodies – both genetic or biological structures – exists under the curse of Genesis 3:8–19. As part of the curse of the Fall, even our genetic and biological makeup has been distorted. In New Testament terms, "we battle the flesh." A "natural desire" to participate in an act does not necessarily mean the act in question is approved by God. Because of sin's deleterious effects, Christians should not be surprised to find some genetic or biological factors which contribute to homosexuality.

No Trait Both Necessary and Sufficient for Homosexuality

No genetic sequence, biological structure, sequence of hormone exposure, personality temperament, or pattern of family history has yet been discovered which is both necessary and sufficient to cause homosexuality.[4] This assertion follows closely on the first (some traits show a correlation with a higher incidence for homosexuality, but none show causation). In studies relevant to born-this-way arguments, there is no particular trait which is common to all homosexuals. When research has identified a characteristic more common to homosexuals, there are also individuals with the same characteristic who are not homosexual. A brief summary of the claims about the purported "gay gene,"

---

4 My thinking here is influenced by Stanton Jones and Mark A. Yarhouse, *Homosexuality: The Use of Scientific Research in the Church's Moral Debate* (Downers Grove, IL: InterVarsity Press, 2000), 81.

brain structures, and prenatal hormones emphasizes the point that no trait has been discovered which is both necessary and sufficient for homosexuality.

No Gay Gene

Contrary to popular opinion, scientific research has not found a gay gene. No region of the human genome has yet been found that conclusively links homosexuality with any specific genetic sequence. Dean Hamer's claim to find a region of interest at Xq28 in homosexual males has not been definitively replicated since he first made the claim in 1993. Several attempts to replicate Hamer's claim failed. The much-publicized research from Sanders and Bailey in 2014 that claims to have replicated Hamer's Xq28 find has limitations, not the least of which is their own data regarding Xq28 fell just short of accepted criteria for statistical significance. Likewise, Sanders and Bailey's findings regarding 8q12 await further verification. But what must be emphasized is that not all of the men in their study shared the relevant genetic information at these two locations. Having a particular genetic sequence at either Xq28 or 8q12 was not necessary for any of the males to be homosexual. To date, no region whatsoever of the human genome has been associated with female homosexuality. The very fact that current research has found *no areas of significance* that indicate a genetic link for female homosexuality surely points out the inherent weakness in the overall gay-gene argument. Claims that a gay gene causes homosexuality are simplistic and imprecise.

Twin studies indicate a genetic contributing factor correlating to a higher occurrence of homosexuality. But even in these studies, the variables in play are neither necessary nor sufficient for homosexuality. Earlier twin studies which claimed a much stronger correspondence for homosexuality among co-twin pairs have now been refuted.[5] As was noted, among homosexuals with an identical twin, in only about 20% of the cases was the co-twin also a homosexual. If homosexuality was a genetically predetermined trait, then the correspondence would be 100%. This fact strongly disfavors the idea that a

---

5 Frustratingly, popular literature on homosexuality repeats the findings of earlier twin studies without citing the later research. For example, Cheryl L. Weill cites the twin research of Bailey from 1991 and 1993, but does not mention the later findings from the Australian twin study which contradict Bailey's earlier research even though Weill is clearly aware the findings exist. See Cheryl L. Weill, *Nature's Choice: What Science Reveals about the Biological Origins of Sexual Orientation* (New York: Routledge, 2009): 65–68.

particular genetic sequence is necessary to cause homosexuality. Twin studies do not prove a gay gene exists, but indicate quite the opposite.

The fraternal birth order effect may show a weak correlation between some forms of male homosexuality and maternal inheritance in certain populations. Explanations of this phenomenon are speculative at present. But many homosexuals have *no older brother*, demonstrating yet again that a particular birth sequence in a family is neither necessary nor sufficient to cause homosexuality. At the same time, other research questions the existence of the fraternal birth order effect in its entirety.

To assume sexual orientation is an inherited trait similar to hair color or eye color is incautious and misguided. As an expression of human behavior, homosexuality is the result of a complex interaction between DNA, environment, and the choices made by a particular person. Seen in this way, a person's DNA is only one factor among many influencing the type of person we become. Reducing homosexuality to an inherited trait like eye color assumes humans are genetic automatons, hard-wired to act according to a predetermined set of coded instructions. No evidence indicates homosexuality is a trait equivalent to hair color or skin pigmentation and assuming so confuses the essential distinction between physical traits and behavior. A lifestyle with as many broad expressions as homosexuality is certainly the result of multiple causes.

We should not overlook the worldview conflicts that are inherent in the debate about homosexuality and genetics. As noted in chapter 9, pro-homosexual researchers will sometimes point out that homosexual behavior is observed in animals. Thus, from a naturalistic Darwinian worldview, homosexuality in humans then is neither good nor evil but simply a naturally occurring variation of sexual behavior. In this way, a strong overtone of genetic determinism drones on in the background of many pro-homosexual arguments. If one agrees that Darwinian naturalism is the correct meta-narrative and that humans are nothing more than chemicals that have learned to self-reflect, then we are truly the sum of our DNA and doomed to whatever behavioral destiny is in the millions of base pairs inside the double helix of our genetic structure, and therefore not responsible for our deeds.

In contrast, Christian ethics begins with the assumption that God exists necessarily, has revealed truth about himself, and is the moral judge of the universe. Humans exist contingently and are held accountable for their actions. Humans are a body-soul unity, and as such we really are morally accountable decision-makers with an ability to move beyond the limitations of genetic or biological predispositions.

Brain Research Does Not Provide Incontrovertible Evidence

There is no conclusive evidence that homosexuals have a substantially different brain structure than heterosexuals. Claims that homosexuals have a brain structure that differs from their gender (males have "female" brains or females have "male" brains) find their origin in overstated assertions about the differences in male and female brains. Two findings in particular seem to have found possible differences between heterosexual and homosexual brain structures. First is LeVay's claim that INAH 3 is smaller in homosexual males than in heterosexual males. Yet Byne stressed that the difference is not in the number of neurons, but in the density of the neurons in the INAH 3 in homosexuals. In LeVay's own data, there were homosexuals who had an INAH 3 similar to the majority of heterosexuals and there were heterosexuals who had an INAH 3 similar to the majority of homosexuals. It is clear a particular INAH 3 size is neither necessary nor sufficient for homosexuality.

Second, Savic and Lindström's findings about patterns of brain asymmetry in homosexuals are intriguing, but await replication by other researchers. Also, there are homosexuals who do not share the brain asymmetry patterns identified by Savic and Lindström. Thus, a specific pattern of brain asymmetry is neither necessary nor sufficient to cause homosexuality.

Prenatal Hormones

Research to date does not prove a particular pattern of exposure to prenatal hormones is necessary to cause homosexuality. As was noted, the basic claim is that homosexuals (males and females) were exposed to hormone levels in the womb atypical for their gender, thus "masculinizing" female brains and "feminizing" male brains. A careful study of children with Disorders of Sexual Development shows this theory lacks verification. Most females with Congenital Adrenal Hyperplasia identify as heterosexual females as adults. Likewise, XY children with the most extreme forms of Androgen Insensitivity Syndrome give every physical appearance (except for lack of secondary hair) of being female and the vast majority identify as heterosexual females as adults, a sexual identity that fits the way their bodies look. Homosexuals do not have the same shared experience of children with DSDs. In short, neither CAH nor AIS prove the born-this-way argument in relation to prenatal hormones. Hormones obviously affect the development of children in the womb, but it is still unclear exactly how prenatal or postnatal hormones affect one's later gender identity. It is possible that some avenues of future research may connect the emerging science of epigenetics with particular patterns of prenatal hormone exposure.

PREDISPOSITION DOES NOT EQUAL PREDETERMINATION

Some individuals may have a predisposition towards homosexual behavior, but this does not mean a person is predetermined from birth to act in a particular way. A *predisposition* means there is a tendency or a stronger than average possibility that a person may engage in certain behaviors. A predisposition is different from saying a behavior is *predetermined* — meaning a person's future choices regarding a particular behavior are unalterable. When most people think of a genetic predisposition to homosexuality, they tend to think of genes like a light switch: the same-sex attraction is either on or off. Human behavior, especially sexual behavior, is far more complex than that. Data to date suggests many contributing factors are relevant in the development of same sex attraction, yet these factors vary from person to person in complicated ways. Hence, some people may be predisposed to experience same-sex attraction given the right triggering events or environmental factors. But a predisposition does not mean a person is therefore unaccountable for the morality of their actions.

An example of the way in which a predisposition must be balanced with moral accountability can be seen in alcoholism. There is evidence of a genetic component for susceptibility for risk of alcoholism in some cases.[6] However, a genetic component which contributes to alcoholism does not *require* the specific behavior of consuming alcohol. In fact, awareness of a genetic predisposition would call for increased vigilance in this area of one's life. Likewise, if a person desires to be a fully devoted follower of Jesus Christ, awareness of one's predispositions in various areas of sexual temptation requires special focus.

Predispositions are related to the doctrine of human sinfulness — the innate human predisposition to rebel against God. One of the tragedies of sin is that while most people know how to begin a particular sin or sinful habit, very rarely do we realize the third- and fourth-order consequences of sin. One of the most painful results of sin is that it is habit-forming. As was noted earlier, the brain can construct neural pathways and these pathways become

---

6 Fred Beauvais, "American Indians and Alcohol," *Alcohol Health and Research World* 22.4 (1998): 253–59.

reinforced and stronger each time we engage in various sins. In this way, we begin to live out the consequences of Jesus' warning, "Everyone who commits sin is a slave of sin" (John 8:34).

Many people give testimony of feeling same sex attraction at a young age, with twelve years old being the average age at which homosexuals report first thinking they were other than heterosexual.[7] The reasons for this are not immediately clear, but genetic or biological contributing factors seem plausible enough that we should show sympathy for those who struggle with this temptation. When some homosexuals claim that they have always struggled with same-sex attraction, even from their youth, I believe they are telling the truth. For many, the desire was not intentionally sought. People are not lying when they describe this as a strong attraction. While not compromising the clear biblical message, we should demonstrate compassionate pastoral care, just as we would to someone struggling with other temptations. Yet, we must reassert continually that a *predisposition* to homosexual temptation does not mean one is *predetermined* to participate in homosexual behavior. Francis Collins, who served as the director for the Human Genome Project, says "sexual orientation is genetically influenced but not hardwired by DNA, and that whatever genes are involved represent predispositions, not predeterminations."[8]

If same-sex attraction is unsought, then what causes it? Answers to this question are speculative. First, we must remember male homosexuality and female homosexuality seem to be significantly different in both their occurrence and etiology with men and women apparently arriving at a homosexual orientation via different paths. In this way, a simplistic "one size fits all" answer will be inadequate. Second, as noted above, some characteristics or traits correlate with a higher incidence of homosexuality. Perhaps in some cases these traits lie latent until nudged in a particular direction by triggering events. Third, the higher incidence of both gender nonconformity and sexual abuse among homosexuals indicates childhood events can influence the manner in which a child's future sexual orientation develops. But we must remember that these events are not common to all homosexuals, indicating their limited explanatory power. Fourth, the age of a person's sexual debut, the gender and age of the person with whom it occurred, and the context in which it occurred have powerful organizing effects on a person's future sexual identity. A fifth factor is the least appreciated in our culture: The manner in

---

7   Eleanor Whiteway and Denis R. Alexander, "Understanding the Causes of Same-Sex Attraction," *Science and Christian Belief* 27.1 (2015): 22.

8   Francis Collins, *The Language of God* (New York: The Free Press, 2006), 260.

which our own volitional choices set us on a particular moral course. The choices we make matter. The way we address unwanted desires can influence the strength and persistence of sexual attraction. The final and most frustrating factor is the "unknown": In some ways it is easier to see what science *has not* proven about the origin of homosexuality than what it has proven. We know science has not found a "gay gene" nor has it found a "gay brain," but for some people the mystery of why they experience same-sex attraction may never be answered.[9]

If a member or attender of a church admits he or she has experienced or currently experiences same-sex attraction, we should not automatically assume the person is a militant gay activist. While many Christians now distance themselves from the term "culture war," I do not and I certainly believe there are activists who want to remove Christians from the public marketplace of ideas. But a church-attender who confesses such a struggle is probably not one of these activists. Much like the movie *Saved!*, the culture tells church attenders who experience unwanted, same-sex attraction to expect to be ostracized and abandoned. Without affirming homosexual behavior, a genuine Christian response walks along with a brother or sister to help them follow God's ways, especially when the culture tells them God's ways are actually wrong and should be rejected.

A godly course of life for people who experience same-sex temptation may look different for each individual, falling broadly into three categories. Some single Christians may choose to live a life of godly celibacy. Virtuous singleness is certainly an option for Christians (1 Cor. 7:34). Others may in fact find love and affection with someone of the opposite sex, be faithful in marriage, but still experience homosexual temptations from time to time without surrendering to them. Finally, some may yet find love in a heterosexual marriage and move beyond feelings of same-sex temptation. Each of these options is consistent with Christian sexual ethics. What we must not compromise is that sex is designed by God to be experienced in heterosexual and monogamous

---

9   I am aware of Bem's "Exotic Becomes Erotic" theory. Bem would take a dim view of my reference to childhood sexual abuse as a contributing factor in some cases saying gay men and lesbians "had typically not participated in any "advanced" sexual activities with person of the same sex until about 3 years after they had become aware of same-sex attraction." Daryl J. Bem, "Exotic Becomes Erotic: A Developmental Theory of Sexual Orientation," *Psychological Review* 103.2 (1996): 321. My point is not that all or even the majority of homosexuals have experienced childhood abuse, but it is *more common* than in heterosexuals. The commonality points to the manner in which childhood experiences can have an organizing effect on one's adult orientation. My observation is narrow and not global.

marriage (Gen. 1:26–28, 2:24–25). This original design for sex serves as the foundation for Paul's critique of homosexuality in Romans 1:18–32.

ROMANS 1:18–32 AND BORN-THIS-WAY ARGUMENTS

Romans 1:18–32 details humanity's rejection of God (1:18–23) and the ensuing consequences of this rejection (1:24–32).[10] In the middle of this argument is the most explicit rejection of homosexual behavior in the Bible (Rom. 1:24–27), explicitly condemning both male and female homosexual acts. From this passage, we can derive at least three biblical starting points for evaluating born-this-way arguments.

First, central to Paul's argument in Romans 1:18–32 is that God has designed sex to be experienced between the male and female genders and that homosexuality is a distortion of God's creation order as described in Genesis 1:26–28. This emphasis on God's design is amplified when Paul says in Romans 1:26–27 that "women exchanged the natural function for that which is unnatural, and in the same way also the men abandoned the natural function of the woman and burned in their desire toward one another." The idea of a "natural use" here infers a degree of mutuality, meaning that males and females have a natural sexual use for each other, a use distorted by homosexual acts.[11] In other words, if one looks at the male and female bodies, the sexual parts complement each other and are designed for the proper expression of sex within biblical parameters (heterosexual, monogamous marriage). Homosexual behavior is a fundamental rejection of God's design and purposes.

Second, Romans 1:18–32 declares homosexual behavior to be idolatrous. Romans 1:18 stresses the idolatrous nature of human sinfulness, saying humanity "exchanged the glory of the incorruptible God for an image in the form of corruptible man and of birds and four-footed animals and crawling creatures." In context, homosexuality serves as an example of how this idolatry is lived out in ethics. Idolatry inverts the creation order and worships things made by God instead of God Himself. When humanity rejects the Creator and worships the creation, "Everything then becomes Libido: life becomes

---

10 Cranfield says, "That in this sub-section Paul has in mind primarily the Gentiles is no doubt true. But it may be doubted whether we shall do justice to his intention, if we assume — as many interpreters seem inclined to do — that these verses refer exclusively to them." C. E. B. Cranfield, *The International Critical Commentary: Romans*, vol. 1, rev. ed. (Edinburgh: T. & T. Clark, 2001), 105.

11 Robert A. J. Gagnon, *The Bible and Homosexual Practice: Texts and Hermeneutics*, 237.

totally erotic.″[12] In this light, born-this-way arguments are a form of idolatry: one's libido becomes the central organizing principle of life with no regard for God's original design.

Third, Romans 1:18–32 gives a sobering warning about the degree to which surrender to temptation can lead to dire consequences. Specifically, three times in Romans 1:24–28 Paul says God "gave them over" to sin: "Therefore God gave them over in the lusts of their hearts to impurity (1:24); "God gave them over to degrading passions" (1:26); "God gave them over to a depraved mind" (1:28). The language is stern and jarring. God actively hands people over to the consequences of sin, and in context homosexuality is the immediate reference. The idea is that God does not merely passively hand people over to the natural consequences of their sin, but he is actively and judicially involved. This means he hands men over in his perfect justice to their own passions and lusts. Born-this-way arguments dangerously overlook the manner in which complete surrender on one's part to sin can lead to being handed over to the idolatrous passions one worships.

With the warnings of Romans 1:18–32 in mind, we must reject the notion of so-called gay-Christians. Much as Lady Gaga appeals to God as the cause of any number of sexual preferences in her song "Born This Way," the gay-Christian movement appeals to vague forms of God's love and justice to substantiate their claim that God created them as homosexuals. Scientific arguments for an innate propensity towards same-sex attraction are leveraged by those seeking to defend a pro-homosexual biblical hermeneutic. A major flaw in this line of reasoning is that it assumes science has proven homosexuality is an innate characteristic similar to hair or skin color. Science has not proven this. While research does indicate a positive correlation between some limited factors and a somewhat higher incidence of same-sex attraction, the scientific evidence does not require us to abandon the historical, biblical stance of the church and adopt a new hermeneutic normalizing all forms of licentious behavior.

Christians do not hyphenate their identity: their identity is found in Christ alone. Ephesians 1:7 says, "We have redemption in Him through His blood, the forgiveness of our trespasses, according to the riches of His grace." Our identity is found only in Christ and His redemption. For many, the hyphen in gay-Christian is being used to purchase a freedom to participate in sins for which Christ died. To be faithful to Scripture, we must insist we are sim-

---

12   Karl Barth, *The Epistle to the Romans*, 6th ed., trans. Edwyn C. Hoskyns (London: Oxford University Press, 1968), 52. Though I cite Barth here, I reject his neo-orthodoxy as a whole.

ply *Christians*: people purchased by his blood. Our primary identity is not found in our sexuality; our primary identity is found in our redemption and relationship with Jesus Christ. When a person insists on calling himself a gay-Christian, he has made an idol of his sexual desires.

CHILDREN BECOME CASUALTIES

Born-this-way arguments are closely tied to sexualizing young children prematurely. One example of an adult imposing his own view of sexuality on children is found in Simon LeVay's 2011 book *Gay, Straight, and the Reason Why*. LeVay addresses several arguments that seem to contradict his theory that homosexuality is innate. Among the data, he reviews some findings indicating gay men and lesbians are far more likely than heterosexuals to have had sexual contact with an older person of their own sex during childhood. In other words, homosexuals have a statistically higher incidence of being molested by a homosexual when they were a child. If such data is accurate, it could mean that being sexually molested as a child affects one's future sexual orientation. Conversely, this data would weaken LeVay's claim that one is born homosexual. In a paragraph devoid of sympathy for abused children, LeVay addresses the claim that homosexual molestation may influence sexual orientation and says:

> For this to be true, however, we would have to assume that children or adolescents were sexually passive targets for molestation by their elders. In reality, it is likely that many of them, especially the adolescents, already felt sexually attracted to same-sex partners. If so, they may have initiated the contacts or responded willingly to the older person's advances. Even if not, the older person may have picked up on the cues that were indicative of the child's future sexual orientation and selected the child on that basis.[13]

LeVay blames young children for being molested. The children may actually have been "attracted to same-sex partners." The children possibly "initiated" the sexual contact with an adult. Even if an adult initiated the contact, the children "responded willingly." This calloused and cruel view of homosexual child molestation demonstrates a man accustomed to same-sex attraction forc-

---

13   Simon LeVay, *Gay, Straight, and the Reason Why: The Science of Sexual Orientation* (New York: Oxford University Press, 2011), 35.

ing his own sexual worldview on innocent boys and girls. Essentially he says, "They really wanted the adult to have sex with them!"

LeVay's opinion is not an isolated one among homosexual authors. Wilson and Rahman make a similar claim in their 2005 book *Born Gay*. After summarizing some research on homosexual sex-play among children, they claim boys who had homosexual play with other boys knew about their purported homosexual orientation prior to these childhood encounters. Wilson and Rahman then say this "strongly suggests that childhood sex play or willing sexual activity with unrelated older males is not a cause, but rather a consequence, of inborn early homosexual feelings."[14] Much like LeVay, these authors suggest some children abused by pedophiles were not actually seduced, but desired the contact because they were "born this way."

Imposing adult sexuality on young children is exactly the vision of Alfred Kinsey. Recall his inability to identify the pain of children being molested by adults. He believed children should be exposed to sexual variations and practices in order to overcome inhibitions to sexual experimentation. Kinsey's vision has arrived and American children suffer. In fact, parents who oppose the sexualization of children are called narrow-minded, while the descendants of the sexual revolution assert their own sexual views. Meanwhile, boys and girls are forced to learn about adult matters at younger and younger ages and innocence is lost.

Worldview War

The worldview war at the heart of scientific research and homosexuality is more intense than most evangelicals realize. Modern psychiatry asserts that sexual orientation cannot be changed. Thus, many mental health professionals believe Christians should not ask people to repent of homosexual behavior. Most Christian ministers may be unaware of how strongly this idea of an "immutable" sexual orientation is embedded within modern mental health doctrine. When someone comes to a pastor and admits homosexual sin, a faithful pastor will encourage confession, repentance, and prayers to God for forgiveness. Furthermore, a pastor will encourage the development of spiritual disciplines such as prayer, Scripture memory, fasting, and accountability partners in order to find victory over sin.

---

14   Glenn Wilson and Qazi Rahman, *Born Gay: The Psychobiology of Sex Orientation* (London: Peter Owen Publishers, 2008), 36.

In contrast, most mental health professionals would consider this type of spiritual counsel counter-productive to the mental health of someone involved in homosexuality. Instead, this type of pastoral care is considered harmful to the well-being of an individual, and in fact they believe this will push the person deeper into conflicted feelings about their sexuality. Modern psychiatry argues the healthiest thing a person can do is accept their own sexual orientation, embrace it in a healthy manner, and celebrate who they are.[15]

The worldview collisions associated with homosexuality are clearly seen in the personal examples of many of the researchers attempting to find genetic or biological causes to homosexuality. As was noted, Kinsey was sexually adventurous. Dean Hamer is in a same-sex marriage to Joe Wilson. The two of them produced *Out in the Silence*, a film with the stated purpose of changing the way rural communities and small towns view homosexuality. Simon LeVay is an open homosexual and avid activist for gay rights. Richard Pillard was the first openly gay psychiatrist in the United States. Brian Mustanski is the director of the Impact GLBT Health and Development program at Northwestern University. Michael Bailey generated controversy in 2011 when he let two sexual "exhibitionists" perform sex acts in front of a college class.[16] The idea that these are coldly analytical scientists with no biases is ludicrous; these are agenda-driven activists with a significant emotional investment into the cause of sexually libertine morals and gay rights.

Conclusion

While there are no variables yet discovered that conclusively cause homosexuality, there are genetic and biological contributing factors to same-sex attraction and homosexual orientation, with some evidence pointing to a low-level correlation between certain variables and an increased incidence of same-sex attraction. This should not surprise us. The Christian worldview asserts that we are body-soul unity and variables in the body can influence

---

15   With this strong animus against the Christian position, it is difficult to believe the current Department of Defense policy — allowing military chaplains to preach within their faith convictions about homosexuality — will be retained for any length of time. To be blunt: in the armed forces, chaplains who tell people to repent of sexual sin will be considered part of the problem and not the solution. More likely, the current policy is a half-step towards prohibiting military chaplains from publicly or privately suggesting homosexuality is sinful.

16   "NU Cancels Human Sexuality Class," CBS 2 Chicago, May 9, 2011, accessed January 31, 2013, http://chicago.cbslocal.com/2011/05/09/nu-cancels-human-sexuality-class.

our susceptibility to temptation in many areas. But we are not just biological automatons, and thus we are not doomed by a genetic predisposition towards participation in any number of sinful behaviors. The Christian worldview also asserts that the entire creation has been damaged by a historical Fall, wherein sin entered the world and distorted everything, including our biological and genetic predispositions. Homosexuality is rooted in multiple factors and future research will probably address different homosexualities as opposed to one form of homosexuality. I suspect future research will demonstrate that homosexuality is a highly complex combination of many factors, including biology, genetics, family of origin, social environment, and human choice. Regardless, a strong inclination towards a particular behavior does not prove that the behavior in question is necessarily good or that we should suspend moral judgment about it. A life of moral virtue requires more than the vacuous excuse, "I was born this way."

Bibliography

Allen, Laura S., M. Hines, J. E. Shryne, and R. A. Gorski. "Two Sexually Dimorphic Cell Groups in the Human Brain." *Journal of Neuroscience* 9.2 (February 1989): 497–506.

The American Psychiatric Association. "Position Statement on Homosexuality." American Psychiatric Association, December, 2013. http://www
.psychiatry.org/advocacy--newsroom/position-statements/position statement on homosexuality.

———. *DSM V/American Psychiatric Association: Diagnostic and Statistical Manual of Mental Disorders.* 5th ed. Arlington, VA: American Psychiatric Association, 2013.

———. "LGBT-Sexual Orientation." No date posted. http://www.psychiatry.org/mental-health/people/lgbt-sexual-orientation.

The American Psychological Association Task Force on Appropriate Therapeutic Responses to Sexual Orientation. *Report of the Task Force on Appropriate Therapeutic Responses to Sexual Orientation.* Washington, DC: American Psychological Association, 2009.

The American Psychological Association. "Appropriate Affirmative Responses to Sexual Orientation Distress and Change Efforts," April 5, 2009. http://www.apa.org/about/policy/sexual-orientation.pdf.

Bagemihl, Bruce. *Biological Exuberance: Animal Homosexuality and Natural Diversity.* New York: St. Martin's Press, 1999.

Bancroft, John. "Alfred C. Kinsey and the Politics of Sex Research." *Annual Review of Sex Research* 1.15 (2004): 1–39.

Barth, Karl Barth, *The Epistle to the Romans.* 6th ed. Trans. Edwyn C. Hoskyns. London: Oxford University Press, 1968.

Baskin, Hillary Copp, Michael DiSandro, Ann Arnhym, Angelique Champeau, Christine Kennedy. "Disorders of Sexual Development," University of California, San Francisco, Pediatric Urology, n.p., date posted March 18,

2013. https://urology.ucsf.edu/sites/urology.ucsf.edu/files/uploaded-files/basic-page/disorders_of_sex_development_0.pdf.

Baron-Cohen, Simon, Rebecca C. Knickmeyer, Matthew K. Belmonte. "Sex Differences in the Brain: Implications for Explaining Autism." *Science* 310 (November 4, 2005): 819–23.

Bayer, Ronald. *Homosexuality and American Psychiatry: The Politics of Diagnosis.* Princeton, NJ: Princeton University Press, 1987.

Bear, Mark, Barry W. Connors, and Michael A. Paradiso. *Neuroscience: Exploring the Brain.* 3rd ed. Baltimore: Lippincott, Williams, and Wilkins, 2007.

Bell, Alan Paul, Martin S. Weinberg, and Sue Kiefer, *Sexual Preference: Its Development In Men and Women.* Bloomington, IN: Indiana University Press, 1981.

Bem, Daryl J. "Exotic Becomes Erotic: A Developmental Theory of Sexual Orientation." *Psychological Review* 103.2 (1996): 320–35.

Bieber, Irving. "Homosexuality – An Adaptive Consequence of Disorder in Psychosexual Development." *American Journal of Psychiatry* 130.11 (November 1973): 1209–11.

Blanchard, Ray. "Controversies in Sexual Medicine — Male Homosexuality: Nature or Culture?" *Journal of Sexual Medicine* 7.10 (October 2010): 3245–53.

Blanchard, Ray, and R. A. Lippa. "The Sex Ratio of Older Siblings in Non-right-handed Homosexual Men." *Archives of Sexual Behavior* 37.6 (December 2008): 970–76.

Blanchard, Ray, J. M. Cantor, Anthony F. Bogaert, S. M. Breedlove, and Lee Ellis. "Interaction of Fraternal Birth Order and Handedness in the Development of Male Homosexuality." *Hormones and Behavior* 49.3 (2006): 405–14.

Blanchard, Ray, and Anthony F. Bogaert. "Homosexuality in Men and Number of Older Brothers." *The American Journal of Psychiatry* 153:1 (January 1996): 27–31.

Bogaert, Anthony, and Malvina Skorska. "Sexual Orientation, Fraternal Birth Order, and the Maternal Immune Hypothesis: A Review." *Frontiers in Neuroendocrinology* 32.2 (April 2011): 247– 54.

Boyse, Kayla, and Talyah Sands. "Congenital Adrenal Hyperplasia." University of Michigan Health System. May, 2011. http://www.med.umich.edu/yourchild/topics/cah.htm.

Brydum, Sunnivie. "John Paulk Formally Announces, Apologizes for Harmful 'Ex-Gay' Movement." *The Advocate*, April 24, 2013. http://www.advocate.com/politics/religion/2013/04/24/john-paulk-formally-renounces-apologizes-harmful-ex-gay-movement

Butts, Charlie. "Restoring Hope for Homosexuals." *One News Now*, May 15, 2013. http://www.onenewsnow.com/culture/2013/05/15/restoring-hope -for-homosexuals.

Bullough, Vern L. *Science in the Bedroom: The History of Sex Research*. New York: HarperCollins / Basic Books, 1994.

Byne, William, and Bruce Parsons. "Human Sexual Orientation: Biological Theories reappraised," *Archives of General Psychiatry* 50 (March 1993): 228–39.

Cantor, James M., Ray Blanchard, Andrew D. Paterson, and Anthony F. Bogaert. "How Many Gay Men Owe Their Sexual Orientation to Fraternal Birth Order?" *Archives of Sexual Behavior* 31.1 (February 2002): 63–71.

Coghlan, Andy. "Largest Study of Gay Brothers Homes in on 'Gay Genes.'" *New Scientist*, November 17, 2014. http://www.newscientist.com/article/ dn26572-largest-study-of-gay-brothers-homes-in-on-gay-genes.html# .VVKNn_lViko.

Cohler, Bertam J., and Robert M. Galatzer-Levy, *The Course of Gay and Lesbian Lives: Social and Psychoanalytic Perspectives*. Chicago: University of Chicago Press, 2000.

The Committee on Nomenclature and Statistics of the American Psychiatric Association. *DSM II / Diagnostic and Statistical Manual of Mental Disorders*, 7th printing. Washington, DC: The American Psychiatric Association, 1974.

The Committee on Nomenclature and Statistics of the American Psychiatric Association. *DSM II / Diagnostic and Statistical Manual of Mental Disorders*. Washington, DC: The American Psychiatric Association, 1968.

The Committee on Nomenclature and Statistics of the American Psychiatric Association. *Diagnostic and Statistical Manual of Mental Disorders*. Washington, DC: American Psychiatric Association Mental Hospital Service, 1952.

Currin, Joseph M., Linzi Gibson, and Randolph D. Hubach. "Multidimensional Assessment of Sexual Orientation and the Fraternal Birth Order Effect." *Psychology of Sexual Orientation and Gender Diversity* 2.2 (June 2015): 113–22.

Côté, K., C. M. Earls, and Martin L. Lalumière. "Birth Order, Birth Interval, and Deviant Sexual Preferences among Sex Offenders." *Sexual Abuse: Journal of Research and Treatment* 14 (2002): 67–81.

Coyne, Sarah M., John T. Manning, Leanne Ringer, and Lisa Bailey. "Directional Asymmetry (Right–Left Differences) in Digit Ratio (2D:4D) Predict Indirect Aggression in Women." *Personality and Individual Differences* 43.4 (2007): 865–72.

Cranfield, C. E. B. *The International Critical Commentary: Romans*. Vol. 1. Rev. ed. Edinburgh: T. & T. Clark, 2001.

Dawood, Khytam, Michael Bailey, and Nicholas G. Martin, "Genetic and Environmental Influences on Sexual Orientation." In *Handbook of Behavioral Genetics*, edited by Yong-Kyu Kim. New York: Springer Science Media, 2009.

Dehlin, John P., Renee V. Galliher, William S. Bradshaw, Daniel C. Hyde, and Katherine A. Crowell. "Sexual Orientation Change Efforts among Current or Former LDS Church Members." *Journal of Counseling Psychology*, 62.2 (April 2015): 95–105.

Délot , Emmanuèle C., and Eric J. Vilain. "Nonsyndromic 46,XX Testicular Disorder of Sex Development." *Gene Reviews*. Last updated May 7, 2015. http://www.ncbi.nlm.nih.gov/books/NBK1416/.

De Mees, Christelle, Jean-François Laes, Julie Bakker, Johan Smitz, Benoît Hennuy, Pascale Van Vooren, Philippe Gabant, Josiane Szpirer, and Claude Szpirer, "Alpha-Fetaprotein Controls Female Fertility and Prenatal Development of the Gonadotrophin-Releasing Hormone Pathway Through an Antiestrogenic Action." *Molecular and Cell Biology* 26.5 (March 2006): 2,012–18.

Douglas, Alfred. *The Two Loves*. In Douglas O. Linder, "The Three Trials of Oscar Wilde." University of Missouri-Kansas City School of Law. http://law2 .umkc.edu/faculty/projects/ftrials/wilde/poemsofdouglas.htm.

Downer, Joanna. "Backgrounder: Epigenetics and Imprinted Genes." http://www. hopkinsmedicine.org/press/2002/november/epigenetics.htm.

Doyle, Christopher. "Transgendered 'Woman' Lies About Therapy Torture." *WND*, March 21, 2013. http://www.wnd.com/2013/03/transgendered -woman-lies-about-therapy-torture/.

Dreger, Alice. "How to Ex an 'Ex-Gay' Study." *Psychology Today*, April 11, 2012. http://www.psychologytoday.com/blog/fetishes-i-dont-get/201204/how -ex-ex-gay-study.

Ellis, Lee, and M. Ashley Ames. "Neurohormonal Functioning and Sexual Orientation: A Theory of Homosexuality-Heterosexuality." *Psychological Bulletin* 101.2 (March 1, 1987): 233–58.

Erickson, Millard. *Christian Theology*, 2nd ed. Grand Rapids: Baker, 1998.

Fausto-Sterling, Anne. *Sexing the Body: Gender Politics and the Construction of Sexuality*. New York: Basic Books, 2000.

Ferreira, Florbela, Joao Martin Martins, Sónia do Vale, Rui Esteves, Garção Nunes and Isabel do Carmo, "Rare and Severe Complications of Congenital Adrenal Hyperplasia Due to 21-Hydroxylase Deficiency: A Case

Report." *Journal of Medical Case Reports* 7.39 (February 6, 2013): 7–39. http://www.jmedicalcasereports.com/content/7/1/39.

Flannery, K. A., and J. Liederman. "A Test of the Immunoreactive Theory for the Origin of Neurodevelopmental Disorders in the Offspring of Women with Immune Disorder." *Cortex* 30.4 (December 1994): 635–46.

Ford, Clennan S., and Frank A. Beach. *Patterns of Sexual Behavior.* New York: Harper & Brothers Publishers and Paul B. Hoeber Medical Books, 1951.

Freud, Sigmund. "Certain Neurotic Mechanisms in Jealousy, Paranoia and Homosexuality." In *Sexuality and the Psychology of Love,* translated by Joan Riviere. New York: Collier Books, 1963.

——. *Leonardo Da Vinci: A Psychosexual Study of an Infantile Reminiscence.* Translated by A. A. Brill. New York: Moffat, Yard, & Co., 1916. The Medical Heritage Library. https://archive.org/details/leonardodavincipoofreu.

——. "Letter to the Mother of a Homosexual." *American Journal of Psychiatry* 107 (1951): 787. Edited by Paul Halsall, Internet History Sourcebooks Project. http://www.fordham.edu/halsall/pwh/freud1.asp.

——. *Moses and Monotheism.* Translated by Katherine Jones. Letchworth, Hertfordshire: Hogarth Press and the Institute of Psychoanalysis, 1939.

——. "The Psychogenesis of a Case of Homosexuality in a Woman." In *Freud on Women: A Reader*, edited by Elizabeth Young-Bruehl. New York: W. W. Norton & Company, 1990.

——. *Three Essays on the Theory of Sexuality.* Translated by James Strachey. New York: HarperCollins, 1975.

Gagnon, Robert A. J. *The Bible and Homosexual Practice: Texts and Hermeneutics.* Nashville: Abingdon Press, 2001.

Galea, Liisa A. M., Kristian A. Uban, Jonathan R. Epp, Susanne Brummelte, Cindy K. Barha, Wendy L. Wilson, Stephanie E. Lieblich, and Jodi L. Pawluski. "Endocrine Regulation Of Cognition and Neuroplasticity: Our Pursuit to Unveil The Complex Interaction Between Hormones, the Brain, and Behavior." *Canadian Journal of Experimental Psychology* 62.4 (December 2008): 247–60.

Garcia-Galgeuras, Alicia, and Dick F. Swaab. "A Sex Difference in the Hypothalamic Uncinate Nucleus: Relationship to Gender Identity." *Brain* 131 (November 2008): 3132–46.

Gates, Gary J. "How Many People Are Lesbian, Gay, Bisexual, and Transgender?," The Williams Institute, April, 2011. http://williamsinstitute.law.ucla.edu/wp-content/uploads/Gates-How-Many-People-LGBT-Apr-2011.pdf.

Gay Liberation Front. *Manifesto.* London, 1971. Revised 1978. Edited by Paul Halsall. Internet History Sourcebooks Project. http://www.fordham.edu/halsall/pwh/glf-london.asp.

Giedd, Jay N., Armin Raznahan, Kathryn L. Mills, and Roshel K. Lenroot. "Review: Magnetic Resonance Imaging of Male/Female Differences in Human Adolescent Brain Anatomy." *Biology of Sex Differences* 3.19 (2012): 1–9. http://www.ncbi.nlm.nih.gov/pmc/articles/PMC3472204/pdf/2042 -6410-3-19.pdf.

Gillies, Glenda E., and Simon McArthur. "Estrogen Actions in the Brain and the Basis for Differential Action in Men and Women." *Pharmacological Reviews* 62.2 (2010): 155–98.

Gorski, Roger, J. H. Gordon, J. E. Shryne, and A. M. Southam. "Evidence for a Morphological Sex Difference Within the Medial Preoptic Area of the Rat." *Brain Research* 148 (1978): 333–46.

Greenough, W. T., C. S. Carter, C. Steerman, and T. J. DeVoogd. "Sex Differences in Dentritic Patterns in Hamster Preoptic Area." *Brain Research* 126.1 (April 22, 1977): 63–72.

Grimbos, Teresa, Kenneth Zucker, Khytam Dawood, Robert P. Burriss, and David A. Puts. "Sexual Orientation and the Second to Fourth Finger Length Ratio: A Meta-analysis in Men and Women." *Behavioral Neuroscience* 124.2 (2010): 278–87.

Gualtieri, C. T., and R. E. Hicks. "The Immunoreactive Theory of Selective Male Affliction." *Behavior and Brain Sciences* 8.3 (1985): 427–77.

Gur, Ruben C., Bruce I. Turetsky, Mie Matsui, Michelle Yan, Warren Bilker, Paul Hughett, and Raquel E. Gur, "Sex Differences in Brain Gray and White Matter in Healthy Young Adults: Correlations with Cognitive Performance." *The Journal of Neuroscience* 19.10 (May 15, 1999): 4065–72.

Haidich, A. B. "Meta-Analysis in Medical Research." *Hippokratia* 14 (December 2010): 29–37.

Haldeman, Douglas C. "Gay Rights, Patient Rights: The Implications of Sexual Orientation Conversion Therapy." *Professional Psychology: Research and Practice* 33.3 (June 2002): 260–64.

Hall, Patricia, and Catherine Schaeff. "Sexual Orientation and Fluctuating Asymmetry in Men and Women." *Archives of Sexual Behavior* 37.1 (February 2008): 158–65.

Hamann, Stephan. "Sex Differences in the Responses of the Human Amygdala," *The Neuroscientist* 11.4 (2005): 288–93.

Hamer, Dean, Stella Hu, Victoria L. Magnuson, Nan Hu, and Angela M. L. Pattatucci. "A Linkage Between DNA Markers on the X Chromosome and Male Sexual Orientation," *Science* 261 (July 16, 1993): 321–27.

Haskell, Josh. "Men Dancing in Drag Angers Some Thanksgiving Day Parade Watchers," *ABC News*, November 29, 2013. http://abcnews.go.com/US/

kinky-boots-performance-yorks-thanksgiving-parade-sparks-outrage/
story?id=21050776.

Honekopp, Johannes, Martin Voracek, and John T. Manning. "2nd to 4th Digit
Ratio (2D:4D) and Number of Sex Partners: Evidence for effects of Prenatal Testosterone in Men." *Psychoneuroendocrinology* 31.1 (January 2006):
30–37.

Hooker, Evelyn. "The Adjustment of the Male Overt Homosexual." *Journal of
Projective Techniques* 21.1 (1957): 18–31.

Hu, Stella, Angela M. L. Pattatucci, Chavis Patterson, Lin Li, David W. Fulker,
Stacey S. Cherny, Leonid Kruglyak, and Dean H. Hamer. "Linkage Be-
tween Sexual Orientation and Chromosome Xq28 in Males but not in
Females." *Nature Genetics* 11 (1995): 248–56.

Hyde, Krista L., Jason Lerch, Andrea Norton, Marie Forgeard, Ellen Winner,
Alan C. Evans, and Gottfried Schlaug. "The Effects of Musical Training
on Structural Brain Development." *Annals of the New York Academy of
Sciences* 1169 (2009): 182–86.

Imperato-McGinley, Julianne, Luis Guerrero, Teofilo Gautier, Ralph E. Peterson.
"Steroid 5 Alpha Reductase Deficiency in Man: An Inherited Form of
Male Pseudohermaphroditism." *Science* 186 (December 27, 1974): 1,213.

Isay, Richard. *Being Homosexual: Gay Men and Their Development.* Revised ed.
New York: Vintage Books, 2009.

Jones, James. H. *Alfred C. Kinsey: A Life.* New York: W. W. Norton & Company,
1997.

Jones, Stanton L., and Mark A. Yarhouse. *Homosexuality: The Use of Scientific
Research in the Church's Moral Debate.* Downers Grove, IL: InterVarsity
Press, 2000.

———. "Honest Sex Science." *First Things* 226 (October 2012): 18–20.

———. "A Longitudinal Study of Attempted Religiously Mediated Sexual Orientation Change." *Journal of Sex and Marital Therapy* 37.5 (October–
December 2011): 404–27.

Kinsey, Alfred Charles, Wardell Pomeroy, and Clyde Martin. *Sexual Behavior in
the Human Male.* Philadelphia: W. B. Saunders Company, 1948.

Kinsey, Alfred Charles, Wardell Pomeroy, Clyde E. Martin, and Paul H. Gebhard. *Sexual Behavior in the Human Female.* Philadelphia: W. B. Saunders
Company, 1953.

Kirby, Andrew. "Freud on Homosexuality," *Psychotherapy Papers.* http://
psychotherapypapers.wordpress.com/2008/11/12/kirby1/.

Kiser, Clyde V. Kiser. "A Statistician Looks at the Report." In *Problems of Sexual
Behavior: Proceedings of a Symposium Held by the American Social Hy-*

giene Association March 30–April 1, 1948, 28–46. New York: American Social Hygiene Association, 1948.

Klar, A. J. S. "Excess of Counterclockwise Scalp Hair-whorl Rotation in Homosexual Men." *Journal of Genetics* 83.3 (December 2004): 251–55.

Kolb, Bryan, and Robbin Gibb. "Brain Plasticity and Behavior in the Developing Brain." *Journal of the Canadian Academy of Child and Adolescent Psychiatry* 20.4 (November 2011): 265–76.

Kolb, Bryan, and Ian Q. Whishaw. "Brain Plasticity and Behavior." *Annual Review of Psychology* 49:1 (February 1998): 43–64.

Kolb-Kokocinski, Anja, Alexander Mehrle, Stephanie Bechtel, Jeremy C. Simpson, Petra

Kioschis, Stefan Wiemann, Ruthe Wellenreuther, and Annemarie Poustka. "The Systematic Functional Characteristic of Xq28 Genes Prioritizes Candidate Disease Genes." *BMC Genomics* 7.29 (February 17, 2006): 1–12.

Kraemer, Bernd, Thomas Noll, Aba Delsignore, Gabriella Milos, Ulrich Schnyder, and Urs Hepp. "Finger Length Ratio (2D:4D) and Dimensions of Sexual Orientation." *Neuropsychobiology* 53.4 (2006): 210–14.

Kuhn, Betsy. *Gay Power! The Stonewall Riots and the Gay Rights Movement, 1969.* Minneapolis: Twenty-First Century Books, 2011.

Lalumière, Martin L., Grant T. Harris, Vernon L. Quinsey, and Marnie E. Rice. "Sexual Deviance and Number of Older Brothers among Sexual Offenders." *Sexual Abuse: A Journal of Research and Treatment* 10.1 (1998): 5–15

Lasco, Mitchell S., T. J. Jordan, M. A. Edgar, C. K. Petito, and W. Byne. "A Lack of Dimorphism of Sex or Sexual Orientation in the Human Anterior Commissure." *Brain Research* 936 (May 17, 2002): 95–98.

Latham, Tyger Latham. "Scientific Homophobia: When It Comes to Homosexuality, We Have Not Always Practiced What We Preach." *Psychology Today*, April 19, 2011. http://www.psychologytoday.com/blog/therapy-matters/201104/scientific-homophobia.

LeVay, Simon. *Gay, Straight, and the Reason Why: The Science of Sexual Orientation.* Oxford: University Press, 2011.

———. "A Difference in Hypothalamic Structure Between Heterosexual and Homosexual Men," *Science* 253 (August 30, 1991): 1034–37.

Lewes, Kenneth. *Psychoanalysis and Male Homosexuality: Twentieth Anniversary Edition.* Lanham, Maryland: Rowman & Littlefield, 2009.

Lippa, Richard A. "Are 2D:4D finger-length ratios related to sexual orientation? Yes for Men, No For Women," *Journal of Personality and Social Psychology* 85.1 (July 2003): 179–188.

Livingood, John, ed. "Final Report of the Task Force on Homosexuality." In

National Institute of Mental Health Task Force on Homosexuality: Final Report and Background Papers. Washington DC, GPO, 1972.

Mann, Charles. "Behavioral Genetics In Transition." *Science* 264: 1,686–89.

Manning, John T., A. J. Churchill, M. Peters, "The Effects of Sex, Ethnicity, and Sexual Orientation on Self-measured Digit Ratio (2D:4D)." *Archives of Sexual Behavior* 36.2 (April 2007): 223 –33.

Manning, John T., D. Scutt, J. Wilson, and D. I. Lewis Jones. "The Ratio of 2nd to 4th Digit Length: A Predictor of Sperm Numbers and Concentrations of Testosterone, Luteinizing Hormone and Estrogen." *Human Reproduction* 13 (1998): 3,000–3,004.

Marmor, Judd. "Homosexuality and Cultural Value Systems." *American Journal of Psychiatry* 130.11 (November 1973): 1,208–209.

Marmor, Judd. "Homosexuality: Mental Illness or Moral Dilemma?" *International Journal of Psychiatry* 10.1 (March 1972): 114–17.

Maslow, Abraham H., and James M. Sakoda. "Volunteer-Error in the Kinsey Study." *Journal of Abnormal Psychology* 47.2 (April 1952): 259–62.

Marx, Karl, and Friedrich Engels. "Private, Property and Communism." Chapter 1A in *The German Ideology.* http://www.marxists.org/archive/marx/works/1845/german-ideology.

McCarthy, Margaret M. "Estradiol and the Developing Brain." *Physiological Review* 88.1 (January 2008): 91–124. http://www.ncbi.nlm.nih.gov/pmc/articles/PMC2754262/pdf/nihms117872.pdf.

McFadden, Dennis, and Edward G. Pasanen. "Comparison of the Auditory Systems of Heterosexuals and Homosexuals: Click-evoked Otoacoustic Emissions." *Proceedings of the National Academy of Sciences* 95.5 (March 3, 1998): 2709 –13

MacCulloch , S. I., N. S. Gray, H. K. Phillips, J. Taylor, and M. J. MacCulloch. "Birth Order in Sex-offending and Aggressive Offending Men." *Archives of Sexual Behavior* 33.5 (October 2004): 467–74

Merke, Deborah P., and Stefan R. Bornstein. "Congenital Adrenal Hyperplasia." *Lancet* 365 (June 18, 2005): 2125–36.

Metropolitan Community Church. Trans-Glossary: Gender. http://www.mccchurch.org/AM/Template.cfm?Section=Transgender2&Template=/CM/HTMLDisplay.cfm&ContentID=1054#Gender.

Mitchell, Gareth. "The Development of Psychoanalytic Understandings of Male Homosexuality: Moving Beyond Pathology." *Psycho-Analytic Psychotherapy in South Africa* 20.1 (2012): 1–32.

Moberly, Elizabeth R. *Homosexuality: A New Christian Ethic.* Cambridge: James Clarke, 1983.

Moller, Aage R. *The Malleable Brain: Benefits and Harms from Plasticity of the Brain*. New York: Nova Biomedical Books, 2009.

Meyer-Bahlburg, Heino F. L., Curtis Dolezal, Susan W. Baker, and Maria I. New, "Sexual Orientation in Women with Classical or Non-classical Congenital Adrenal Hyperplasia as a Function of Degree of Prenatal Androgen Excess." *Archives of Sexual Behavior* 37.1 (2008): 85–99.

Meyer-Bahlburg, Heino F. L. "Gender and Sexuality in Classic Congenital Adrenal Hyperplasia." *Endocrinology and Metabolism Clinics of North America* 30.1 (March 2001): 155–71.

Mustanski, Brian S., Michael G. DuPree, Caroline M. Nievergelt, Sven Bocklandt, Nicholas, J. Schork, and Dean H. Hamer. "A Genomewide Scan of Male Sexual Orientation." *Human Genetics* 116 (2005): 272–78.

National Association for Research and Therapy of Homosexuality. "NARTH Position Statements: Right to Treatment." http://www.narth.com/#!narth -position-statements/c1ae.

———. "NARTH Statement on Sexual Orientation Change." January 25, 2012. http://www.narth.com/#!about1/c1wab.

National Institute of General Medical Sciences. "Circadian Rhythms Fact Sheet." Last updated November 2012. http://www.nigms.nih.gov/Education/ Pages/Factsheet_CircadianRhythms.aspx.

National Institute for Mathematical and Biological Synthesis. "Study Finds Epigenetics, Not Genetics, Underlies Homosexuality." December 11, 2012. http://www.nimbios.org/press/FS_homosexuality.

Nef, Serge, and Luis F. Parada. "Hormones in Male Sexual Development." *Genes and Development* 14 (2000): 3075–86.

Nicolosi, Joseph. "The Meaning of Same-Sex Attraction." *Handbook of Therapy for Unwanted Homosexual Attractions: A Guide for Treatment*. Edited by Julie H. Hamilton and Philip J. Henry. Maitland, FL: Xulon Press, 2009: 27–51.

Nordenskjöld, A., G. Holmdahl, L Frisén, H. Falhammar, H. Filipsson, M. Thorén, P. O. Janson, and K. Hagenfeldt. "Type of Mutation and Surgical Procedure Affect Long-Term Quality of Life for Women with Congenital Adrenal Hyperplasia." *Journal of Clinical Endocrinology and Metabolism* 93.2 (February 2008): 380–86.

Ogilvie, Cara Megan, Naomi S. Crouch, Gill Rumsby, Sarah M. Creightont, Lih-Mei Liao, and Gerard S. Conway. "Congenital Adrenal Hyperplasia in Adults: A Review of Medical, Surgical, and Psychological Issues." *Clinical Endocrinology* 64 (January 2006): 2–11.

Onay, Ozan. "The True Ramifications of Genetic Criminality Research for Free

Will in the Criminal Justice System." *Genomics, Society, and Policy* 2.1 (2006): 80–91.

Perry, Troy. *The Lord Is My Shepherd and He Knows I'm Gay*. Los Angeles: Nash Publishing, 1972.

Raisman, Geoffrey, and Pauline Field. "Sexual Dimorphism in the Neuropil of the Preoptic Area of the Rat and Its Dependence on Neonatal Androgen." *Brain Research* 54 (1973): 1–29.

Raisman, Geoffrey, and Pauline Field. "Sexual Dimorphism in the Preoptic Area of the Rat." *Science* 173 (August 20, 1971): 731–33.

Reisman, Judith A., and Edward W. Eichel. *Kinsey, Sex, and Fraud: The Indoctrination of a People*. Lafayette, LA: Huntington House, 1990.

Restored Hope Network. "Doctrinal Statement." http://www.restoredhopenetwork.org/index.php/who-we-are/what-we-believe.

Rice, William R., Urban Friberg, and Sergey Gavrilets. "Homosexuality as a Consequence of Epigenetically Canalized Sexual Development." *The Quarterly Review of Biology* 87.4 (December 2012): 343–68.

Rieger, Gerulf, Joan A. W. Linsenmeier, Lorenz Gygax, and J. Michael Bailey. "Sexual Orientation and Childhood Gender Nonconformity: Evidence from Home Videos." *Developmental Psychology* 44.1 (January 2008): 46–58.

Roberts, Andrea L., M. Maria Glymour, and Kareston C. Koenen. "Does Maltreatment in Childhood Affect Sexual Orientation in Adulthood?" *Archives of Sexual Behavior* 42.2 (February 2013): 161–71.

Rosariao, Vernon A. Rosario. *Homosexuality and Science: A Guide to the Debates*. Santa Barbara, CA: ABC-CLIO, 2002.

Rouse, W. B., K. R. Boff, P. Sanderson, and David F. Batten. "Plasticity and Causal History in Complex Adaptive Systems: The Case of the Human Brain." *Information Knowledge Systems Management* 10 (2011): 313–33.

Sample, Ian. "Male Sexual Orientation Influenced by Genes, Study Shows." *The Guardian*, February 14, 2014. http://www.theguardian.com/science/2014/feb/14/genes-influence-male-sexual-orientation-study

Sanders, A. R., E. R. Martin, G. W. Beecham, S. Guo, K. Dawood, G. Rieger, J. A. Badner, E. S. Gershon, R. S. Krishnappa, A. B. Kolunddzija, J. Duan, P. V. Gejman, and J. M. Bailey. "Genome-Wide Scan Demonstrates Significant Linkage for Male Sexual Orientation." *Psychological Medicine* 45 (2015): 1379–88.

Savic, Ivanka, and Per Lindstrom. "PET and MRI Show Differences in Cerebral Asymmetry and Functional Connectivity Between Homo- and Heterosexual Subjects." *Proceedings of the National Academy of Sciences* 105.27 (June 16, 2008): 9403–408.

Savic, Ivanka, H. Berglund, and Per Lindstrom. "Brain Response to Putative Pheromones in Homosexual Men." *Proceedings of the National Academy of Science* 102 (2005): 7356–61.

Servick, Kelly. "Study of Gay Brothers May Confirm X Chromosome Link to Homosexuality," *Science,* November 17, 2014. http://news.sciencemag.org/biology/2014/11/study-gay-brothers-may-confirm-x-chromosome-link-homosexuality.

Sheridan, Margaret A., Nathan A. Fox, Charles H. Zeanah, Katie A. McLaughlin, and Charles A. Nelson, III. "Variation in Neural Development as a Result of Exposure to Institutionalization Early in Childhood." *Proceedings of the National Academy of Sciences of the United States of America* 109.32. July 23, 2012. http://www.pnas.org/content/early/2012/07/17/1200041109.full.pdf+html?sid=dbeea634-db89-4bbc-9336-7903edf61fdd.

Shidlo, Ariel, and Michael Schroeder. "Changing Sexual Orientation: A Consumer's Report." *Professional Psychology: Research and Practice* 33.3 (June 2002): 249–59.

Socarides, Charles W. *Homosexuality: A Freedom Too Far*. Phoenix: Adam Margrave Books, 1995.

———. "Homosexuality: Findings Derived from 15 Years of Clinical Research." *The American Journal of Psychiatry* 130.11 (November 1973): 1212–13.

Spanier, Bonnie P., and Jessica D. Horowitz. "Looking for a Difference: Methodology Is in the Eye of the Beholder." *Gender and the Science of Difference: Cultural Politics of Contemporary Science and Medicine*. Edited by Jill A. Fisher. New Brunswick, NJ: Rutgers University Press, 2011, 43–66.

Spitzer, Robert L. "Spitzer Reassesses His 2003 Study of Reparative Therapy of Homosexuality." *Archives of Sexual Behavior* 41 (2012): 757.

———. "Can Some Gay Men and Lesbians Change Their Sexual Orientation? 200 Participants Reporting a Change from Homosexual to Heterosexual Orientation." *Archives of Sexual Behavior* 32.5 (October 2003): 403–17.

State of New Jersey, Governor Chris Christie. "Gov. Christie Signs Bill Banning Gay Conversion Therapy on Minors," August 19, 2013. http://www.state.nj.us/governor/news/news/552013/approved/20130819a.html.

Steffman, Melissa. "Alan Chambers Apologizes to Gay Community, Exodus International to Shut Down," *Christianity Today*, June 21, 2013. http://www.christianitytoday.com/gleanings/2013/june/alan-chambers-apologizes-to-gay-community-exodus.html.

Stein, Rob. "Brain Study Shows Differences Between Gays, Straights." *The Washington Post,* June 23, 2008. http://www.washingtonpost.com/wp-dyn/content/story/2008/06/22/ST2008062202006.html.

Struthers, William M. *Wired for Intimacy: How Pornography Hijacks the Male Brain*. Downers Grove, IL: InterVarsity Press, 2009.

Stufflebeam, Robert. "Neurons, synapses, Action Potentials, and Neurotransmission," Consortium on Cognitive Science Instruction. Posted 2008. http://www.mind.ilstu.edu/curriculum/neurons_intro/neurons_intro.php.

Swaab, D. F., and M. A. Hofman. "Sexual Differentiation of the Human Hypothalamus in Relation to Gender and Sexual Orientation." *Trends in Neurosciences* 18.6 (January 1, 1995): 264–70.

———. "An Enlarged Suprachiasmatic Nucleus in Homosexual Men." *Brain Research* 537 (1990): 141–48.

Swaab, D. F., and E. Fliers. "A Sexually Dimorphic Nucleus in the Human Brain." *Science* 228 #4703 (May 1985): 1112–15.

Tanfer, J. O. Billy, K., W. R. Grady, and D. H. Klepinger. "The Sexual Behavior of Men in the United States." *Family Planning Perspectives* 25.2 (March-April 1993): 52–60.

The Kinsey Institute. "Facts about *Kinsey,* The Film." www.kinseyinstitute.org/about/Movie-facts.html.

Thompson, Paul M., Katherine L. Narr, Rebecca E. Blanton, and Arthur W. Toga. "Mapping Structural Alterations of the Corpus Callosum during Brain Development and Degeneration." In *The Parallel Brain: The Cognitive Neuroscience of the Corpus Callosum,* edited by Eran Zaidel and Marco Lacobni. Cambridge: Massachusetts Institute of Technology Press, 2003.

Throckmorton, Warren, and Mark A. Yarhouse. "Sexual Identity Therapy: Practice Framework for Managing Sexual identity Conflicts." Posted 2006. http://sitframework.com/wp-content/uploads/2009/07/sexualidentity therapyframeworkfinal.pdf.

Tilman, Jr., William M. Tillman, Rodney S. Taylor, and Lauren C. Brewer, eds. *Both-And: A Maston Reader: Selected Readings from the Writings of T. B. Maston*. Dallas: T. B. Maston Foundation For Christian Ethics, 2011.

Trivers, Robert, Renato Hopp, and John T. Manning. "A Longitudinal Study of Digit Ratio (2D:4D) and Its Relationships with Adult Running Speed in Jamaicans." *Human Biology* 85.4 (2013): 623–25.

U.S. Department of Health and Human Services. *Understanding the Effects of Maltreatment on Brain Development*. https://www.childwelfare.gov/pubs/issue_briefs/brain_development/how.cfm.

Vilain, Eric J. "46, XX Testicular Disorder of Sex Development." *Gene Reviews*. Last updated May 26, 2009. http://www.ncbi.nlm.nih.gov/books/NBK1416/.

Wallentin, Mikkel. "Putative Sex Differences in Verbal Abilities and Language Cortex: A Critical Review." *Brain and Language* 108 (2009): 175–83.

Wallis, W. Allen. "Statistics of the Kinsey Report." *Journal of the American Statistical Association* 44 (December 1949): 463–84.

Weill, Cheryl L. *Nature's Choice: What Science Reveals about the Biological Origins of Sexual Orientation*. New York: Routledge, 2009.

Westermarck, Edward. *The Origin and Development of the Moral Ideas*. London: Macmillan and Company, 1917.

Westfall, Bruce. "Kinsey Report." In *Encyclopedia of Biblical and Christian Ethics*. Revised ed., edited by R. K. Harrison. Nashville: Thomas Nelson, 1992.

Whiteway, Eleanor, and Denis R. Alexander. "Understanding the Causes of Same-Sex Attraction."*Science and Christian Belief* 27.1 (2015): 17–40.

The White House, Office the Press Secretary. "Inaugural Address of President Barack Obama." January 21, 2013. http://www.whitehouse.gov/the-press -office/2013/01/21/inaugural-address-president-barack-obama.

Wiker, Benjamin. *Moral Darwinism: How We Became Hedonists*. Downers Grove, IL: InterVarsity Press, 2002.

Williams, T. J., M. E. Pepitone, S. E. Christensen, B. M. Cooke, A. D. Huberman, N. J. Breedlove, T. J. Breedlove, C. I. Jordan, and S. M. Breedlove. "Finger-length Ratio and Sexual Orientation." *Nature* 404 (March 30, 2000): 455–56.

Wilson, Glenn, and Qazi Rahman. *Born Gay: The Psychobiology of Sex Orientation*. London: Peter Owen Publishers, 2005.

Wu, Melody V., Devanand S. Manoli, Eleanor J. Fraser, Jennifer K. Coats, Jessica Tollkuhn, Shin-Ichiro Honda, Nobuhiro Harada, and Nirao M Shah. "Estrogen Masculinizes Neural Pathways and Sex-specific Behaviors." *Cell* 139.1 (October 2, 2009): 61–72.

Yarhouse, Mark. "Sexual Identity Therapy." http://www.sexualidentityinstitute .org/sexual-identity-therapy.

———. *Understanding Sexual Identity: A Resource for Youth Ministry*. Grand Rapids: Zondervan, 2013.

Young, William F., Jr. *The Netter Collection of Medical Illustrations*. Vol. 2, *Endocrine System*. 2nd ed. Philadelphia: Elsevier Saunders, 2011.

Zhu, Yuan-Shan, and Julianne Imperato-McGinley. "Male Sexual Differentiation Disorder and 5 Alpha Reductase-2 Deficiency." *The Global Library of Women's Medicine,* last updated November 2008. http://www.glowm .com/section_view/heading/Male%20Sexual%20Differentiation%20 Disorder%20and%205%CE%B1-Reductase-2%20Deficiency/item/349.

General Index

5-Alpha Reductase Deficiency, 61–63, 63; and born-this-way arguments, 62–63; and "guevedoces" ("penis at 12"), 61

adenosine deaminase deficiency, 107
"Adjustment of the Male Overt Homosexual, The" (Hooker), 34–35
After the Ball: How America Will Conquer Its Fear and Hatred of Gays in the 90's (Kirk and Madsen), 85, 92
alcoholism/alcoholics, 136, 144
Allen, John et al. study (2003) of male and female brains, 71n14
Allen, Laura S., 69: on the AC, 79–80; on the INAH, 69
Allen, Laura et al. study (1989) of the human hypothalamus, 67n4
Allen, Laura et al. study (1991) of the corpus callosum, 70–71
American Psychiatric Association (APA): 2013 Position Statement on Homosexuality, 119–20; and born-this-way arguments, 38–39; Christian evaluation of the APA's change in stance toward homosexuality, 39–40; homosexual activists' perception of as their most hated

enemy, 32; and homosexuality pre-Stonewall, 33–34; and SOCE, 119–21, 125. See also *Diagnostic and Statistical Manual of Mental Disorders* (DSM)
American Psychological Association, on homosexuality, 38n21
Ames, Ashley, prenatal hormone theory of, 51, 54n11
Ames-Ellis hypothesis. *See* prenatal hormone theory
Androgen Insensitivity Syndrome (AIS), 58–61, 143; and born-this-way arguments, 60–61; Complete Androgen Insensitivity Syndrome (CAIS), 58, 59, 60–61, 63; Mild Androgen Insensitivity Syndrome (MAIS), 59; Partial Androgen Insensitivity Syndrome (PAIS), 58–59, 59–60, 61
animals, sexual behavior of, 108–10
Ardekani et al. study (2013) of the corpus callosum, 71n14
Australian National Health and Medical Research Council Twin Registry, 89–91
aversion therapy, 132–33

Scripture Index